Judith Joy Ross

Photographien seit 1982 | Photographs since 1982

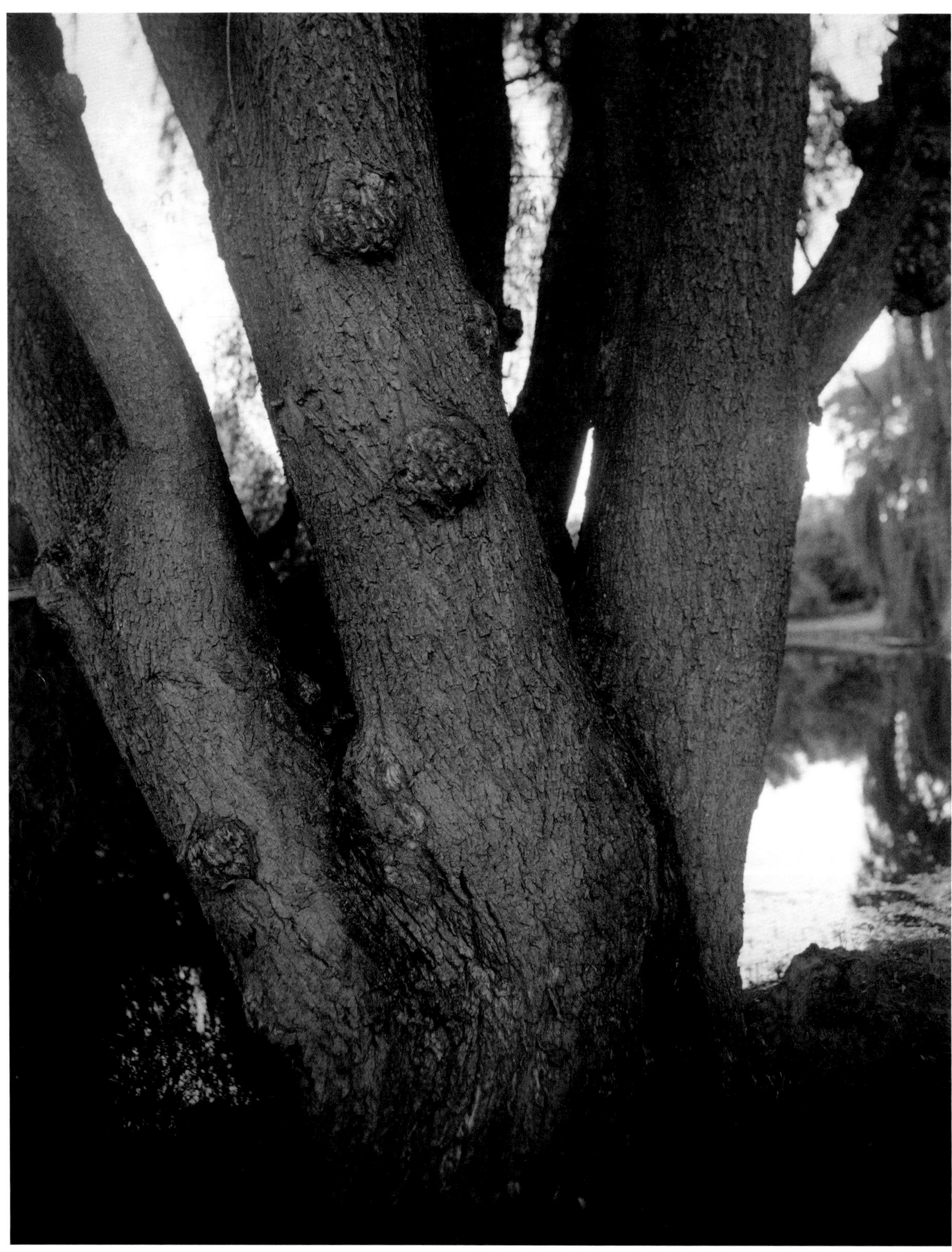

Ohne Titel | Untitled, Dorrance, Pennsylvania, 1985

Judith Joy Ross

Photographien seit 1982 | Photographs since 1982

Herausgegeben von | edited by
Die Photographische Sammlung/SK Stiftung Kultur

Schirmer/Mosel

Diese Publikation erscheint anlässlich der Ausstellung
Judith Joy Ross. Photographien seit 1982
This book is published on the occasion of the exhibition
Judith Joy Ross. Photographs since 1982

Die Photographische Sammlung/SK Stiftung Kultur
Im Mediapark 7
50670 Köln | Cologne
www.photographie-sk-kultur.de
24.9.2011 – 5.2.2012

weitere Stationen | further venues:
Kunstmuseum Kloster Unser Lieben Frauen Magdeburg:
Mai | May – August 2012
Fondation A Stichting Brüssel | Brussels: Herbst | Fall 2012

Herausgeber | Editor:
Die Photographische Sammlung/SK Stiftung Kultur, Köln | Cologne

Ausstellungs- und Katalogkonzeption | Exhibition and catalog concept:
Judith Joy Ross, Gabriele Conrath-Scholl, Claudia Schubert

Die Photographische Sammlung/SK Stiftung Kultur:
Leiterin | Director: Gabriele Conrath-Scholl
Wiss. Mitarbeiterin, Katalogredaktion | Research associate, Catalog editing:
Claudia Schubert
Wiss. Mitarbeiterin, Registrar | Research associate: Rajka Knipper
Assistenz, Verwaltung | Management assistant, Administration: Patricia Edgar
Etatverwaltung | Budgeting administration: Ursula Hollington
Ausstellungstechnik | Exhibition technician: Enrik Hüpeden
Bibliothek | Library: Tanja Löhr-Michels

Lektorat | Editorial Coordination: Daniela Kumor-Böhning, Köln | Cologne;
Dr. Birgit Mayer, Schirmer/Mosel

Dank an:
Sabine Schmidt Galerie, Köln | Cologne; Pace/MacGill Gallery, New York;
Astrid Ullens, Brüssel | Brussels

Publikation | publication:
Übersetzung | Translation: Rebecca van Dyck, Hannover | Hanover
Scans: Thomas Palmer, Newport, Rhode Island
Gestaltung: Klaus E. Göltz, Halle
Druck und Bindung | Printing and binding: Passavia, Passau
Printed in Germany

Cover: *Ohne Titel* | *Untitled*, 1984, aus | from *Portraits at the Vietnam Veterans Memorial, Washington, D.C.,* 1983/1984

ISBN 978-3-8296-0565-6

Eine Schirmer/Mosel-Produktion
www.schirmer-mosel.com

INHALT | CONTENTS

Vorwort | Foreword

Das in über 30 Jahren entstandene Portraitwerk der amerikanischen Photographin Judith Joy Ross überzeugt durch seine künstlerische Bildqualität ebenso wie durch seinen humanitären Ansatz. Die Aufnahmen verdeutlichen die unbedingte Hinwendung zum Menschen, jedem Einzelnen misst die Künstlerin hohe Bedeutung zu. Angelegt in Bildserien, mit einer souveränen und dabei eigenwilligen Handhabe der Großbildtechnik, ist ihr Œuvre von einnehmend ästhetischem Ausdruck. Eine Faszination der Portraits liegt sicher darin, dass sie Konzentration und Ruhe ausstrahlen, ohne Stillstand zu assoziieren. Sie entfalten eine Aura, die die Individualität der Dargestellten wie auch wechselseitig wirkende emotionale Dimensionen zwischen der Photographin und ihrem Gegenüber zum Klingen bringen.

Judith Joy Ross taucht in die Mitte der amerikanischen Gesellschaft ein und nimmt vor allem jene in den Blick, die zwar unauffällig und eher leise daherkommen, aber umso nachhaltiger präsent sind und das alltägliche Leben formen. Sie lässt direkte Begegnungen mit zunächst fremden Mitmenschen zu und nimmt persönlichen Kontakt zu ihnen auf. Die Photographie ist dabei Anlass und Hilfsmittel zugleich. Sie wird zur Vermittlerin der Welt, weist der Künstlerin den Weg und bildet eine wesentliche Konstante in ihrem Leben.

Da Judith Joy Ross das Portraitwerk *Menschen des 20. Jahrhunderts* von August Sander ausgesprochen schätzt, ist es der Photographischen Sammlung/SK Stiftung Kultur, Köln, dem Standort des August Sander Archivs, ein besonderes Anliegen, dem künstlerischen Schaffen der amerikanischen Photographin umfassend nachzugehen. Die Institution besitzt eine Auswahl ihrer Portraits, die bereits verschiedentlich präsentiert wurden. So fand im Jahr 2002 in den Räumlichkeiten der Photographischen Sammlung eine Kabinettausstellung mit Aufnahmen von Ross statt. Des Weiteren waren einige Werke 2004 in *Best of*, der ersten umfangreichen Präsentation des hauseigenen Bestands, vertreten, 2006 wurden Aufnahmen von Ross im Rahmen der Sonderschau der Photographischen Sammlung anlässlich der Art Cologne gezeigt.

Das Kunstmuseum Magdeburg, Projektpartner und zweite

The artistic quality as well as the humanitarian approach of the portraits created by the American photographer Judith Joy Ross over a period of more than thirty years are compelling. The photographs illustrate her unconditional orientation toward people; the artist attributes great importance to each individual. Arranged in series, with a confident and at once unconventional application of the large-format technique, in terms of aesthetics her oeuvre is captivatingly expressive: one of the fascinating aspects of the portraits is certainly the way they radiate concentration and stillness, without, however, evoking standstill. They develop an aura that causes the individuality of those being depicted, as well as the reciprocal emotional dimensions between the photographer and her counterpart, to resound.

Judith Joy Ross plunges into the middle of American society, taking into account in particular those who may appear to be unobtrusive and rather quiet but who are all the more lastingly present and shape everyday life. She allows for direct encounters with people who are initially strangers and approaches them on a personal level. In the process, photography is both motivation and an aid. It communicates the world, shows the artist the way, and constitutes an important constant in her life.

As Judith Joy Ross highly values August Sander's *People in the 20th Century*, for Die Photographische Sammlung/SK Stiftung Kultur, Cologne, the site of the August Sander Archive, it is a special concern to extensively pursue the artistic work of the American photographer. The institution possesses a selection of her portraits, which has already been presented on a variety of occasions. In 2002, a showcase exhibition of her photographs took place on the premises of Die Photographische Sammlung. In addition, in 2004 several of her works were featured in *Best of*, the first comprehensive presentation of the collection's holdings. And in 2006, photographs by Ross were displayed within the scope of a special exhibition by Die Photographische Sammlung at Art Cologne.

For several years now, the Kunstmuseum Magdeburg, project partner and second station of the exhibition, has intensified

Station der Ausstellung, hat seit einigen Jahren den Schwerpunkt Photographie in seinem Ausstellungsprogramm und in seiner Sammlung vertieft. Mit Judith Joy Ross verbinden sich zwei Ausstellungsprojekte in Magdeburg, in denen verschiedene Serien der Künstlerin zu sehen waren: *Second View. Amerikanische Fotografie aus der Sammlung der Niedersächsischen Sparkassenstiftung*, 2007, und *Everyday Ideologies. Standort Alltag*, 2008. Für letzteres gab Judith Joy Ross ein Interview, in dem sie ihre photographische Intention mit den Worten beschrieb: „Ich mache Bilder immer in der Hoffnung, den Augenblick so genau und wahrhaftig wie möglich zu beschreiben. Ich möchte, dass die Betrachter wissen, dass das, was sie auf dem Bild sehen, tatsächlich der Realität entspricht."[1] Ihr Einfühlungsvermögen in unterschiedlichste soziale Kontexte ist in der Tat faszinierend, und so wurden Judith Joy Ross' Portraits weit über die Ausstellung hinaus zu einem gelungenen Beispiel der Balance, derer es bedarf, den Betrachter für gesellschaftlich relevante Situationen zu interessieren, ohne ihn ideologisch zu agitieren. An der Grenze zwischen Alltäglichkeit und Ausnahme, zwischen ungewohnten Zugängen zu Vertrautem und gewohnten Sehweisen auf Unbekanntes beschreitet sie einen Weg, der dem photographischen Abbild ganz eigene, einmalige Bedeutung verleiht.

Dass nun mit der vorliegenden Publikation und der begleitenden Ausstellung ein umfassender Überblick über das Schaffen von Judith Joy Ross gegeben werden kann, verdanken wir zuallererst der Künstlerin selbst, die ihr umfangreiches Bildarchiv bereitwillig geöffnet hat. Zum Vorschein kam – neben den bekannten Portraitreihen – auch zuvor nie gezeigtes Material, das Ross' konsequente künstlerische Haltung zusätzlich verdeutlicht und einmal mehr vor Augen führt, mit welcher Ernsthaftigkeit sie vorgeht. Bei zwei mehrtägigen Arbeitsaufenthalten im Haus der Künstlerin und einem Treffen in Paris haben Gabriele Conrath-Scholl und Claudia Schubert gemeinsam mit Judith Joy Ross die Bildauswahl getroffen. Über einen Zeitraum von zwei Jahren fand ein intensiver Austausch über das Projekt statt, zahlreiche Gespräche wurden geführt, die ein großer Gewinn waren und in den Katalogessay

its focus on photography in its exhibition scheme and its collection. The exhibition of works by Judith Joy Ross combines two projects that included different series by the artist: *Second View: Amerikanische Fotografie aus der Sammlung der Niedersächsischen Sparkassenstiftung*, 2007, and *Everyday Ideologies. Standort Alltag*, 2008. Ross gave an interview for the latter in which she described her photographic intent as follows: "I make pictures always in the hope that I am describing the moment as accurately as truthfully as possible. I want the viewer to believe what they see in the picture to know that this really is the way things are."[1] Her sensitivity to highly diverse social contexts is certainly fascinating, prompting Judith Joy Ross's portraits to become a successful example of balance far beyond the scope of the exhibition—balance the viewer requires to evoke interest in socially relevant situations without it leading to agitation. The photographer treads a path at the boundary between the everyday and the exceptional, between unconventional access to the familiar and habits of viewing the unfamiliar—a path that lends the photographic image its very own, unique meaning.

The fact that this publication and the accompanying exhibition afford a comprehensive overview of the creative work by Judith Joy Ross is first and foremost due to the artist herself, who willingly opened her extensive archive of photographs. What it revealed—besides the well-known series of portraits—was material that has never before been shown in public which casts added light on her consistent artistic stance and once again brings home the wholeheartedness of her approach. During two visits to the artist's home, each of which lasted several days, and a meeting in Paris, Gabriele Conrath-Scholl, Claudia Schubert, and Judith Joy Ross assembled a selection of photographs for the exhibition. Over a period of two years, an intense exchange took place regarding the project; numerous conversations were had that were of great benefit and have been integrated into the catalogue essay. At this point, we would also like to thank the other partners who generously supported and backed the project. The Pace/MacGill Gallery in New York was a particularly reliable and competent partner

eingeflossen sind. Auch den weiteren Partnern, die das Projekt großzügig unterstützt und mitgetragen haben, sei an dieser Stelle gedankt. Die New Yorker Galerie Pace/MacGill war insbesondere in organisatorischen Fragen ein zuverlässiger und kompetenter Ansprechpartner. Die Sabine Schmidt Galerie in Köln hat von Beginn an das Projekt engagiert begleitet. Sabine Schmidt stand uns stets mit Rat und Tat zur Seite.

Lothar Schirmer und das Verlagsteam in München haben die Realisation der Publikation mit gewohntem Know-how betreut; Thomas Palmer, Newport, Rhode Island, hat dazu die hochwertigen Scanarbeiten für den Druck geleistet.

Wir freuen uns, die Ausstellung auch in der Fondation A Stichting in Brüssel zeigen zu können, die mit dieser Ausstellung eröffnet wird.

Last but not least, liebe Judith Joy Ross: der Photographischen Sammlung/SK Stiftung Kultur und dem Kunstmuseum Kloster Unser Lieben Frauen, Magdeburg, war es die allergrößte Freude, das Projekt vorbereiten zu dürfen. Wir sind sehr dankbar dafür.

[1] *Everyday Ideologies. Standort Alltag*, Hrsg.: Annegret Laabs, Uwe Gellner, Nürnberg: Verlag für moderne Kunst, 2010, S. 21.

with respect to organizational issues. The Sabine Schmidt Gallery in Cologne dedicatedly accompanied the project from the outset. Sabine Schmidt was always on hand for help and advice.

Lothar Schirmer and his team in Munich supervised the production of this publication with their vast store of know-how. Thomas Palmer in Newport, Rhode Island, executed the high-quality scans for the printing.

We are also delighted to be presenting the exhibition at the opening of the Fondation A Stichting in Brussels.

Last but not least, dear Judith Joy Ross: it afforded Die Photographische Sammlung/SK Stiftung Kultur, Cologne, and the Kunstmuseum Kloster Unser Lieben Frauen, Magdeburg, the utmost pleasure to be allowed to prepare the project. We are extremely grateful to you.

Gabriele Conrath-Scholl
Die Photographische Sammlung/SK Stiftung Kultur, Cologne

Dr. Annegret Laabs
Kunstmuseum Kloster Unser Lieben Frauen, Magdeburg

[1] *Everyday Ideologies. Standort Alltag*, eds. Annegret Laabs, Uwe Gellner, (Nuremberg: Verlag für moderne Kunst, 2010), p. 20.

Judith Joy Ross – "Taken from Life"[1]

Gabriele Conrath-Scholl, Claudia Schubert

[...] wenn ich wirklich das sehen kann, was vor mir geschieht, ist das für mich eine Gnade. Ohne Kamera bin ich oft zu ängstlich und unnachsichtig in meinem Urteil. Mit der Kamera bekomme ich zu allem einen Zugang und kann mir einen Reim darauf machen.[2] Judith Joy Ross, 2005

When I can really see what is going on in front of me, it is my saving grace. Without a camera, I am often too anxious and unforgiving in my judgment. With a camera, I can come to see and make sense of it all.[2]

Judith Joy Ross, 2005

Lapidar formuliert zeigt Judith Joy Ross Bilder von Menschen – berückend geradlinig, aber genauso einnehmend, voller Realitätssinn und Poesie. Die Portraits entstehen aus einem persönlichen Impuls heraus, motiviert von einem starken Interesse am Gegenüber und vor allem aus Leidenschaft zur Photographie. Immer wieder geben ihr die betrachteten Personen, deren Mienenspiel und Gestik Anlass, über die vielfältigen Lebensprozesse, über Einflüsse und Schicksale nachzudenken und sie tiefergehend zu ergründen. Dabei verliert ihr Blick nie die Konzentration auf den einzelnen Menschen. Das besondere Potential jedes Einzelnen kommt so unmittelbar zur Wirkung, gelegentlich verstärkt durch den Vergleich verschiedener Personen innerhalb eines Bildes oder die Kontextualisierung von Einzelaufnahmen in Werkreihen. Ihre Arbeit spielt sich außerhalb eines Ateliers ab, weitgehend ohne Auftrag, und nur selten kennt Judith Joy Ross die Abgebildeten näher oder nimmt später noch einmal Verbindung zu ihnen auf. Das Geheimnis ihrer Photographien scheint in der intensiv wahrgenommenen Begegnung während der Aufnahme zu liegen. Viele der Portraits könnten auf ein langes vertrauensvolles Verhältnis schließen lassen, jedenfalls spricht aus ihnen eine große Offenheit der Abgebildeten gegenüber der Photographin. Auf die Frage, wie die Menschen reagieren, wenn sie um eine Aufnahme gebeten werden, antwortet Judith Joy Ross, dass sie ihr meist positiv entgegenkommen, sich vielleicht sogar darüber freuen, als etwas Besonderes angesehen zu werden. Letztlich begreift Ross das Photo als eine Art Annäherung und Gemeinschaftsarbeit. Die Kunst liegt darin, dem Motiv im treffenden Moment einen Rahmen zu geben. Weniger sie selbst will mit ihren Aufnahmen Geschichten er-

Succinctly put, Judith Joy Ross presents pictures of people—enchantingly straightforward, yet equally captivating and full of a sense of reality and poetry. Her portraits emerge from a personal impulse, one that is motivated by a strong interest in the people she encounters and above all out of a passion for photography. Time and again, the facial expressions and gestures of those she observes prompt her to think about her subjects' various life processes, their influences, and their destinies and to perceive them with acute sensitivity. In the process, her concentrated, intent gaze at the individual never falters. In her pictures, the unique potential of each individual is immediately apparent, occasionally heightened through the comparison of different people within one image or contextualizing individual photographs in a series. Her work takes place outside of the studio and is for the most part uncommissioned. Only rarely does Judith Joy Ross become better acquainted with her subjects or approach them at a later date. The secret of her photographs seems to lie in the intense experience of the encounter between photographer and subject. Her pictures suggest a long-term, trusting relationship; in any case, the people being depicted exude great openness vis-à-vis the photographer. When asked how people react when she asks if she can take their portrait, Judith Joy Ross says that they are for the most part happy to accommodate her and are perhaps even delighted to be regarded as something special. Ross sees the photo as a way of approaching people and as a kind of collaboration. The art lies in giving the motif a framework at the right moment. She does not see herself as the one telling a story with her pictures; rather, the people she photographs are given an opportunity to tell something about themselves by way of a photo.[3]

zählen, vielmehr sollen die von ihr betrachteten Menschen Gelegenheit erhalten, via Bild etwas von sich zu erzählen.[3]

Das Arbeitskonzept der in über drei Dekaden erarbeiteten rund 20 Werkgruppen erweist sich als ebenso lebendig wie konsequent. Der Zeitraum, den Judith Joy Ross auf die Aufnahmen ihrer Bildreihen verwendet, ist flexibel. Teilweise entstehen sie über Jahre, manchmal aber nur innerhalb weniger Tage, auch korrespondieren sie verschieden stark miteinander. Durchgehend widmet sie sich ausgesuchten Gruppierungen, seien es Kinder und Jugendliche in Schule und Freizeit oder Erwachsene in der Auseinandersetzung mit eigens gesetzten oder beruflichen Aufgaben und Zielen. Die von ihr gewählten Aufnahmesituationen sind vollkommen alltäglich, fern jeden inszenierten oder exotischen Auftritts. Veranschaulicht werden dabei psychologische, gesellschaftliche, kulturelle oder politische Wechselwirkungen, die die Persönlichkeit eines jeden unweigerlich beeinflussen, ihr Grenzen setzen oder Entfaltungsspielräume öffnen und immer wieder – freiwillig oder unfreiwillig – die Übernahme neuer Rollen in unterschiedlichen Lebenssituationen abverlangen. Sind die Betrachtungen von Ross überdies durch ihr persönliches Interesse an Bürgerfragen und -rechten motiviert, untersucht sie nicht allein die äußeren Bedingungen, sondern befragt auch das Gefühlsleben der Menschen als ursächliche Komponente für einen Status quo. Immer wieder ermöglichen es ihre Bildreihen, über die Anschauung des Einzelnen hinaus in das mitschwingende Lebensklima einzutauchen und – zumindest in Ansätzen – ein Psychogramm der amerikanischen Bevölkerung zu entwickeln.

Bereits 1995 hat Susan Kismaric, damals Kuratorin am Museum of Modern Art, New York, das Bildwerk von Judith Joy Ross in einem Buch und einem grundlegenden Essay in vielen Facetten erschlossen.[4] Dieser Publikation war 1993 die Präsentation *New Work: Photographs by Judith Joy Ross* im San Francisco Museum of Modern Art vorausgegangen. Auch in Deutschland setzte in der Folge eine verstärkte Rezeption der Photographien von Judith Joy Ross ein. So zeigte das Sprengel Museum Hannover 1996 die von Thomas Weski kuratierte

The working concept behind the approximately twenty groups of works made in over three decades proves to be as vibrant as it is consistent. The time frame Judith Joy Ross applies to her photographic series varies. Some of them develop over years, and yet others within several days. They also correspond to each other to markedly different degrees. She consistently devotes herself to selected groups of people, be they children and youths at school or during recreational activities, or adults dealing with the tasks and goals they set themselves or which are job-related. The situations she seeks out are utterly everyday, far from any staged or exotic scenes. She sheds light on psychological, social, cultural, or political correlations that inevitably influence the personality and lives of all individuals, set limits on it, or provide an opportunity for development, and time and again—either voluntarily or involuntarily—demand that we adopt new roles to accommodate each situation. Moreover, when Ross's observations are motivated by her personal interest in civil issues and rights, she does not simply examine the external conditions, but inquires deeply into people's emotional states as causal components for the status quo. Her series of photographs consistently describe the resounding atmosphere of people's lives beyond the individual and, to some extent, they provide a psychological profile of the American population.

As early as 1995, Susan Kismaric, at the time curator at the Museum of Modern Art in New York, made Judith Joy Ross's photographs accessible in many of their facets in a book and an extensive essay.[4] This publication was preceded in 1993 by the presentation *New Work: Photographs by Judith Joy Ross* at the San Francisco Museum of Modern Art, which subsequently led to a greater reception of her photographs in Germany as well. In 1996, the Sprengel Museum, Hanover presented the first solo exhibition, curated by Thomas Weski, which comprised a total of fifty portrait photographs. In 2003 and 2008, under the direction of Heinz Liesbrock, the Josef Albers Museum Quadrat in Bottrop devoted solo exhibitions to Ross.

For the first time, the current publication, which accompanies a retrospective presentation of around 150 photographs,

erste Einzelausstellung, die insgesamt 50 Portraitaufnahmen umfasste. 2003 und 2008 widmete das Josef Albers Museum Quadrat in Bottrop unter der Leitung von Heinz Liesbrock der Photographin Einzelausstellungen.

Mit der aktuellen Publikation, die eine Präsentation von ca. 150 Exponaten begleitet, bietet sich nun erstmals die Gelegenheit, das Werk von Judith Joy Ross retrospektiv, im Zusammenspiel annähernd aller Bildreihen vorzustellen, die sie seit 1982, beginnend mit der Serie *Eurana Park*, entwickelt hat. Ausgehend von ihrer Heimatregion in Pennsylvania, USA, hat Ross ein individuelles Gesellschaftspanorama entworfen, das inhaltliche und formale Berührungspunkte zu den Arbeiten des deutschen Photographen August Sander (1876–1964) aufweist. Sein Leitsatz „Sehen, Beobachten, Denken“ kann auch für ihre Arbeit geltend gemacht werden, verweist er doch auf die kulturhistorisch kritische Aussagekraft einer feinfühlig registrierten, ins Bild gebannten Realität. Auch Ross schafft ausgehend vom Individuum und basierend auf sorgfältig zusammengestellten Bildreihen einen „Spiegel der Zeit“[5] – nur, dass Sander seinem Projekt eine weitgreifende, fast wissenschaftliche Systematik zugrunde legte, die er über Jahrzehnte hinweg beibehielt und vervollständigte, während Ross einem persönlichen Arbeitsprogramm folgt, in dem alle von ihr erarbeiteten Sequenzen als Einheiten verstanden werden, die auf verschiedenen Ebenen Aspekte des menschlichen Lebens berühren. Der Komplexität der Wirklichkeit und ihrem schnellen Wandel begegnet sie mit einem inneren Plan, der neben langfristigen Zielen auch weniger strategische, kurze Wege und subjektive Entscheidungsprozesse zulässt. Einer manipulierend eingreifenden Handschrift verweigert sich die Künstlerin ebenso wie ihr historisches Vorbild, beide stellen die authentische Eigenwirkung ihrer Motive in den Mittelpunkt. 1927 schrieb ein Ausstellungskritiker über Sanders Photographien: „Man sieht einfachste Photographie in technischer Vollkommenheit, aber – das ist das Künstlerische [...] – das Wesen und der Charakter des Objekts leb[en] in diesen Bildern, [...] [sind] dem Leben wahrhaft abgelauscht.“[6] Das trifft auch auf die Aufnahmen von Judith Joy Ross zu.

provides an opportunity to introduce close to all of the series in Judith Joy Ross's oeuvre that she has developed since 1982, beginning with *Eurana Park*. Rooted in her native region in Pennsylvania, Ross has created an individual panorama of American society that in terms of content and form bears a similarity to the work of the German photographer August Sander (1876–1964). His guiding principle of "seeing, observing, thinking" can also be applied to Ross's work, as it refers to the historically critical force of expression of a sensitively registered reality captured in an image. Beginning with the individual and based on carefully assembled series of pictures, Ross also creates a "mirror of the time."[5] Sander based his project on far-reaching, almost scientific systematics that he maintained and perfected for decades, while Ross adheres to a personal working program in which all of the sequences she compiles are regarded as units that touch aspects of people's lives on various levels. She faces the complexity of reality and its rapid change with an internal plan that, in addition to long-term goals, allows for less strategic, shorter paths and subjective decision-making. Like her historical paragon, the artist rejects a manipulatingly intervening signature: both of them focus on the authentic self-agency of their motifs. In 1927, an exhibition critic wrote the following about Sander's photographs: "One sees the simplest of photographs in technical perfection, but—and that is the artistic ...—the essence and the character of the object live in these images, ... [have been] veritably culled from life."[6] This also holds true for the photographs by Judith Joy Ross.

Another reference is the American photographer Walker Evans (1903–1975), who introduced the term "documentary style" to an approach characterized by personal restraint and precise observation and in doing so did away with the much-discussed, alleged antagonism between an objective notion of reality and creative artistic skill in the medium of photography.[7] In Bethlehem, the town where she lives, Walker Evans took some of his best-known photographs for the Farm Security Administration in 1935.[8]

These specific surroundings—the streets around the vast steel plant in the center of the town, the humble living circum-

Eine weitere Bezugsgröße ist der amerikanische Photograph Walker Evans (1903–1975), der für jenes durch persönliche Zurückhaltung und genaue Beobachtung gekennzeichnete Vorgehen den Begriff des „dokumentarischen Stils" einführte und damit den viel diskutierten, vermeintlichen Gegensatz zwischen sachlicher Realitätsauffassung und künstlerischem Schaffen für das Medium der Photographie aufhob.[7] Walker Evans hat übrigens in Ross' Wohnort Bethlehem 1935 einige seiner bekanntesten Motive für die Farm Security Administration aufgenommen.[8]

Von der Industrie geprägte Städte wie Bethlehem mit seinen Straßen rund um das große Stahlwerk mitten im Ort und den bescheidenen Lebensbedingungen lassen auch an Lewis Hine (1874–1940) denken. Für Ross spielt er insofern eine wichtige Rolle, als auch in ihrem Schaffen der soziale Blick und Kinder einen zentralen Platz einnehmen. Hine photographierte Kinder, die als Arbeitskräfte im Bergbau, in Fabriken oder in der Landwirtschaft eingesetzt wurden. Seine Bilder haben in den ersten beiden Jahrzehnten des 20. Jahrhunderts maßgeblich dazu beigetragen, dass die Kinderarbeit kritisch ins Licht der Öffentlichkeit gerückt wurde.[9] Auch suchte Lewis Hine seine Motive in den verschiedenen Minen Pennsylvanias, und nicht zuletzt aus diesem regionalen Bezug fühlt sich Judith Joy Ross seinem Werk verbunden.

Als Judith Joy Ross 1982 im Eurana Park, Weatherly, Pennsylvania, zu photographieren begann, hatte sie bereits ihre Ausbildung und eine längere Phase künstlerischer Ideenfindung und Studien durchlaufen. 1946 als Tochter von Edward Stanley Ross und Margaret Ellen Ross geboren, wuchs sie mit ihren beiden Brüdern, Robert und Edward, in Hazleton auf – einem Ort in einer Bergbauregion Pennsylvanias, in dem vorwiegend Anthrazitkohle abgebaut wurde und der sich schon damals im wirtschaftlichen Niedergang befand. Der Vater war Geschäftsführer von mehreren „five-and-dime Stores", die der Familie gehörten, die Mutter gab Klavierunterricht und leitete vor ihrer Heirat einen privaten Kindergarten. Beide Eltern spielten Klavier, und die Brüder hatten als Kinder ausgezeichnete Sopranstimmen. Die Liebe der Eltern zu Musik und

stances of the region—bring Lewis Hine (1874–1940) to mind. He plays an influential role in view of the fact that social aspects as well as children take center stage in her work too. Hine photographed children put to work in the mining industry, in factories, or on farms. These pictures made a substantial contribution to the public scrutiny of child labor in the first two decades of the twentieth century.[9] Hine selected some of his motifs in various mines in Pennsylvania, and Judith Joy Ross feels linked to his work also through this regional connection.

When Judith Joy Ross made portraits in 1982 in Eurana Park, Weatherly, Pennsylvania, she had already pursued an education and experienced an extended phase of artistic ideation and studies. Born in 1946 to Edward Stanley Ross and Margaret Ellen Ross, she grew up with her two brothers, Robert and Edward, in Hazleton, an economically depressed anthracite coal-mining region in Pennsylvania. Her father was the manager of a chain of family five-and-dime stores, her mother was a piano teacher and ran a private kindergarten prior to her marriage. Classical music was ever-present in her parental home—her father also played the piano, and as children her brothers had superb soprano voices. Ross attributes her artistic inclination to the parental love of music and of nature. She and her mother and brothers attended local community concerts that featured major artists such as the American mezzo-soprano Risë Stevens. Her father instilled in his children the joy of seeing through the close observation of the natural world. The popular *Life's Picture History of Western Man*[10], a mass-produced book of reproductions of great paintings and architecture, was a part of the household, and as simple as that may seem, it was an important influence. Even as a child, Judith Joy Ross wanted to become an artist. She often drew and painted, and was encouraged by her mother, who made sure she had art lessons and experiences in the local Art League. She and her mother took bus trips to New York City to museums and exhibitions when she was a teenager and college student.

In 1964, to fulfill a long-held dream to be an artist, Ross became a student at the Moore College of Art in Philadelphia.

Natur haben die künstlerischen Neigungen der Tochter durchaus gefördert. Mit ihrer Mutter und ihren Brüdern besuchte Judith Joy Ross klassische Konzerte von führenden Künstlern wie der amerikanischen Mezzosopranistin Risë Stevens, und der Vater suchte den Kindern die Freude am Sehen durch die genaue Beobachtung der Natur zu vermitteln. Auch gehörte das äußerst populäre Buch *Life's Picture History of Western Man*[10] mit zahlreichen Abbildungen berühmter Gemälde und Bauten zum Haushalt; und so schlicht es seiner Konzeption nach auch war, übte es doch eine große Faszination auf Judith Joy Ross aus. Schon von Kindheit an wollte sie Künstlerin werden und zeichnete und malte viel. Ihre Mutter unterstützte sie dabei und sorgte dafür, dass sie Kunstunterricht erhielt und erste Erfahrungen in der regionalen Kunstszene sammeln konnte. Als Heranwachsende und noch als Studentin fuhr sie zusammen mit ihrer Mutter im Bus nach New York, um dort Museen und Ausstellungen zu besuchen.

1964 erfüllte sich der lang gehegte Traum von Judith Joy Ross, Künstlerin zu werden, und sie ging ans Moore College of Art nach Philadelphia. 1966 stieß sie eher zufällig auf das Angebot einer Photographieklasse. Sie begann, Menschen in den Straßen von Philadelphia und ihrer Heimat zu photographieren, auch von ihrer Familie nahm sie zahlreiche Portraits auf. Das Bildermachen wurde für Ross zu einer Möglichkeit, die Gefühle der sie umgebenden Menschen zu verstehen und wiederzugeben. Die Welt schien sich für sie durch die Photographie zu öffnen und ihren Sinn zu erhalten. 1968 setzte sie das Studium der Photographie am Institute of Design, Illinois Institute of Technology in Chicago fort, wo sie insbesondere die Lehrveranstaltungen von Aaron Siskind und Arthur Siegel besuchte. Zwei Jahre später schloss sie ihr Studium ab, ohne jedoch ihr eigentliches Thema gefunden zu haben.

Rückblickend beurteilt sie ihre Studienzeit als wenig erfolgreich und für ihre künstlerische Entwicklung als eher irritierend. Zu sehr habe sie sich von ästhetischen Vorstellungen anderer beeinflussen lassen. Ihre Vorliebe für die Photographie war allerdings ungebrochen, und mit den beiden Europa-Reisen 1976 und 1979 nach Italien und Frankreich sollte sich für

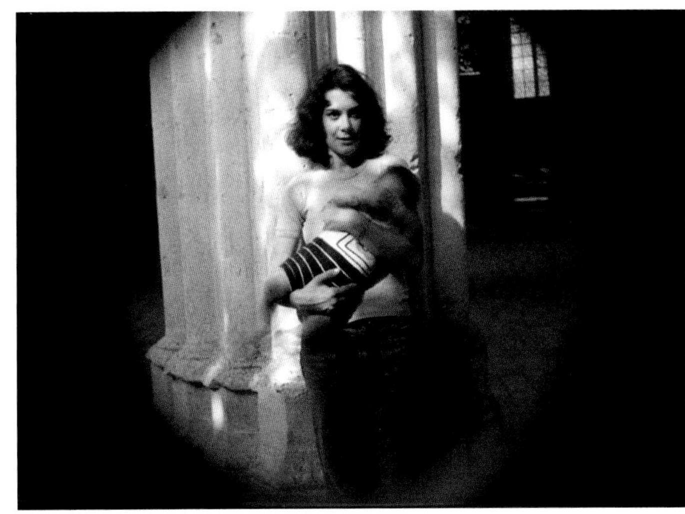

1 Frankreich | France, 1979

By chance she took a photography class in 1966. She began photographing strangers on the street in Philadelphia and at home, and she extensively photographed her family; taking pictures became a way to understand and to express the emotional life of those around her. The world seemed to open up—photographs made sense of the world. In 1968 she began graduate studies in photography at the Institute of Design at the Illinois Institute of Technology in Chicago, where she attended classes taught by Aaron Siskind and Arthur Siegel. She graduated two years later, without having found her ultimate subject.

Looking back on her time in graduate school as not exactly successful and of little benefit to her artistic development—she feels she was too easily influenced by the aesthetic concepts of others. However, her passion for photography continued, and her trips to Italy and France in 1976 and 1979 would ultimately prove to be fertile ground for the development of her own approach to the medium. Crucial in this respect were less theoretical considerations than the experience of direct reality and those everyday aspects of life that exercise a special charm when discovered away from home, such as the displays of fruit and vegetables in an open-air market. She first took photographs with a five-by-seven-inch camera used at the turn of the century, outfitted with a sharp wide-angle lens. Later, in 1977, she used a shutterless daguerreotype lens on a new Deardorff five-by-seven-inch camera, which created a circle within the five-by-seven-inch film plane, as the historic lens was not designed for the sheet film size of her camera (ill. 1). Paris, Pisa, Venice, and Florence afforded her exceptional experimen-

sie schließlich ein eigener Zugang zum Medium eröffnen. Ausschlaggebend waren hier weniger theoretische Überlegungen als vielmehr das Erlebnis der unmittelbaren Wirklichkeit und jene alltäglichen Momente wie die ausladenden Obst- und Gemüsestände auf den Wochenmärkten, die, in der Fremde entdeckt, einen besonderen Reiz ausübten. Sie photographierte damals mit einer gebrauchten 5x7 inch-Kamera, wie sie zur Jahrhundertwende verwendet wurde, ausgestattet mit einem präzise zeichnenden Weitwinkelobjektiv. Ende 1977 wechselte sie zu einer neuen Deardorff 5x7 inch-Kamera, die mit einem Daguerreotypie-Objektiv ohne Verschluss ausgestattet war. Es erzeugte ein zirkulares Bild auf 5x7 inch-Planfilm, denn die historische Linse war nicht für die Größe der Kamera ausgerichtet (Abb. 1). Paris, Pisa, Venedig und Florenz boten ein besonderes Experimentierfeld, und sie genoss es, mit der Kamera die Straßen mit ihren Geschäften und die stadttypischen Sehenswürdigkeiten zu erforschen (Abb. 2). Judith Joy Ross fühlte sich dabei wie Eugène Atget auf seinen photographischen Streifzügen durch das Paris der Jahrhundertwende. Bald stellte sie zudem fest, dass inszenatorische Anweisungen oder nachträgliche Bildmanipulationen keine Verbesserung bedeuteten. Bei einer in Paris aufgenommenen Photographie etwa, die ihren Bruder Edward mit Mme. DuPont – die er damals betreute – zeigt, hatte sie eine schroff ins Bild ragende Glühbirne zunächst als so störend empfunden, dass sie diese im Negativ wegretuschierte. Rückblickend bereute sie die Retusche, denn die vermeintliche Korrektur nahm dem Bild jene authentische, ungeschönte Qualität, die sie heute, sozusagen wie ein spezielles Gewürz, als unverzichtbar empfindet (Abb. 3).[11]

Die Bildreihe *Eurana Park* ist das erste Konvolut, das Judith Joy Ross unter den Vorzeichen eines künstlerischen Konzepts erarbeitet hat. Zugleich ist es die Serie, die erstmals in größerem Umfang in einem Museum gezeigt wurde: 1984/85 stellte das Allentown Art Museum eine Auswahl von 24 Aufnahmen aus.[12] Als Judith Joy Ross mit den Photographien im Eurana Park begann, befand sie sich in einer schwierigen Lebensphase. 1981 war ihr Vater verstorben, mit dem sie ein vertrauensvolles Verhältnis verbunden hatte. In der Zeit der Trauer kreisten

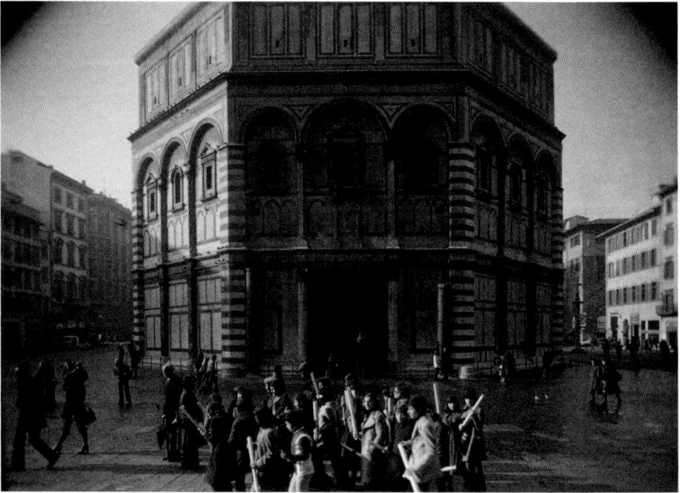

2 Florenz, Baptisterium | Florence, Baptistery San Giovanni, 1976

tal ground, and she enjoyed using the camera to explore the streets with their shops and their typical places of interest (ill. 2). Ross wanted to feel like Eugène Atget on his photographic journeys through turn-of-the-century Paris. She occasionally manipulated her images or directed her subjects but soon realized that it made no improvement. For example, in one photograph made in Paris, which features her brother Edward in a room with an elderly woman he cared for, Madame DuPont, Ross thought a light bulb that protruded into the picture was so disturbing that she deleted it on the negative. In retrospect, she regrets having done this. This alleged correction robbed the image of that authentic, unadorned quality she now, like a special spice, so to speak, finds indispensable (ill. 3).[11]

The *Eurana Park* series is the first body of work that Judith Joy Ross compiled based on an artistic concept. It was also the first series to be presented within a larger scope at a museum: in 1984/85, the Allentown Art Museum exhibited a selection of twenty-four photographs.[12] When Ross began taking photographs in Eurana Park, she was experiencing a difficult phase in her life. Her father, with whom she had a trusting relationship, died in 1981. Throughout her period of grief, her thoughts revolved around the question of what really makes life worth living, and this led her back to one of the places where she had spent part of her childhood and she and her brothers liked to play: Eurana Park in Weatherly.[13] When she sought out the park around thirty years later, it seemed as though little had changed. Children still played at the pool or among the tall trees; explored, virtually undisturbed by adults, the grounds; or played to their heart's delight in nature. Judith Joy Ross was enthralled by the children's abandon and their

ihre Gedanken um die Frage, was das Leben tatsächlich lebenswert macht, und das führte sie an die Orte ihrer Kindheit zurück. Auch der Eurana Park[13] in Weatherly gehörte dazu, in dem sie und ihre Brüder gerne gespielt hatten. Als sie den Park rund 30 Jahre später aufsuchte, schien sich nur wenig verändert zu haben. Noch immer spielten die Kinder am Pool oder zwischen den hoch gewachsenen Bäumen, erkundeten, von Erwachsenen beinahe ungestört, das Gelände oder tobten sich nach Lust und Laune in der Natur aus. Judith Joy Ross war fasziniert von der Unbekümmertheit und frischen Ausstrahlung der Kinder, allein deren selbstverständliche Präsenz schien die Frage nach dem Sinn des Lebens zu beantworten.

Eines der ersten Portraits – laut Ross die erste ihr überhaupt geglückte Aufnahme – zeigt drei Mädchen in Badeanzügen, die mit ihrem Eis beschäftigt vor der Photographin stehen geblieben sind (Tafel S. 41). Zunächst glaubt man an einen Schnappschuss, doch die von Judith Joy Ross verwendete Kameratechnik spricht eindeutig dagegen. 1981 hatte sie sich eine Großbildkamera für Negative im Format von 8x10 inch zugelegt, die wie eine 5x7 inch-Kamera nur mit einem Stativ und umfangreichem Equipment zu bedienen ist. Unbemerktes oder spontanes Photographieren ist damit nicht möglich. Drei quirlige Kinder mit dieser Kamera aufzunehmen, verlangt sogar ein außergewöhnliches Reaktionsvermögen, will man den angetroffenen Moment festhalten. Ein technisch schnelles Vorgehen hinsichtlich Bildeinstellung, Fokussierung und Einschub der Planfilmkassette sowie eine intuitiv sichere Vorausschau auf das Bildergebnis sind notwendige Bedingungen. Hinzu kommt, dass verschiedene Faktoren, die nur bedingt steuerbar sind, günstig zusammenfallen müssen. So spricht Ross bei solchen Motiven nicht selten von einem Wunder – einem „miracle". Auf den kurzen Appell „Bleibt so!" hatten sich die Kinder sofort auf den Aufnahmeprozess eingelassen und über mehrere Sekunden eine natürlich wirkende Haltung eingenommen. Bewusst hatte die Photographin das Objektiv auf Augenhöhe der Kinder gebracht, um deren Körper in richtiger, unverzerrter Perspektive zu erfassen und um sich selbst und später auch den Betrachter auf die Ebene der

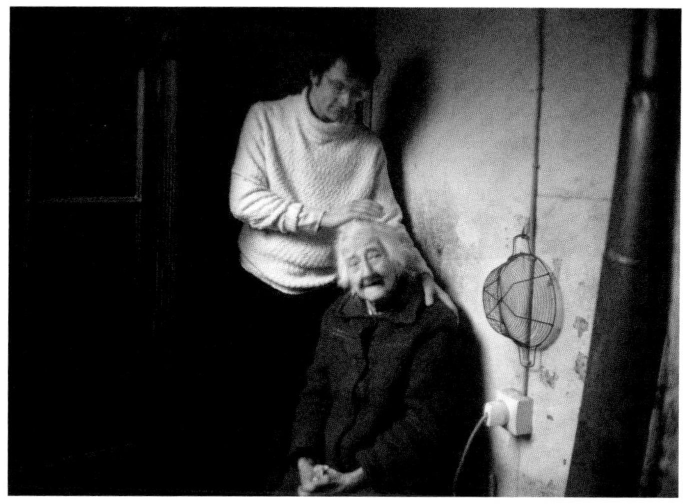

3 Paris, 1976

fresh radiance; their presence alone seemed to answer her question about the meaning of life.

One of the first portraits, according to Ross the first successful picture she ever made, describes three girls in bathing suits, busy eating their popsicles and standing still in front of the photographer (plate p. 41). One initially thinks it is a snapshot, but the camera technique used by Ross clearly tells a different story. In 1981, she had bought a larger-format camera for eight-by-ten-inch negatives that, like the five-by-seven, can only be operated with a tripod and bulky equipment. Taking photographs unnoticed or spontaneously with it is not possible. Capturing three lively children with this camera demands an extraordinary capacity of reaction if one wants to record the moment on film. The necessary conditions are a technically rapid approach with respect to framing the subject, focusing, and inserting the sheet film holder, as well as an intuitively confident mental preview of a possible image. In addition, various factors that are only controllable to a certain extent have to coincide favorably. Ross thus often speaks of a miracle in reference to such motifs. Told to "Hold still!" the children immediately engaged in the photography process and assumed natural poses lasting several seconds. Ross consciously brought the lens to the children's eye level in order to "draw" their bodies in the proper perspective and to enable the photographer and the viewer of the resultant picture to experience the children at their level. She also succeeded in integrating the light and the surroundings into the image in order to support the motif. One even sees the complete profile of the popsicle one of the girls is holding that is shaped like the Pacman game-console figure popular at the time. Against a dark back-

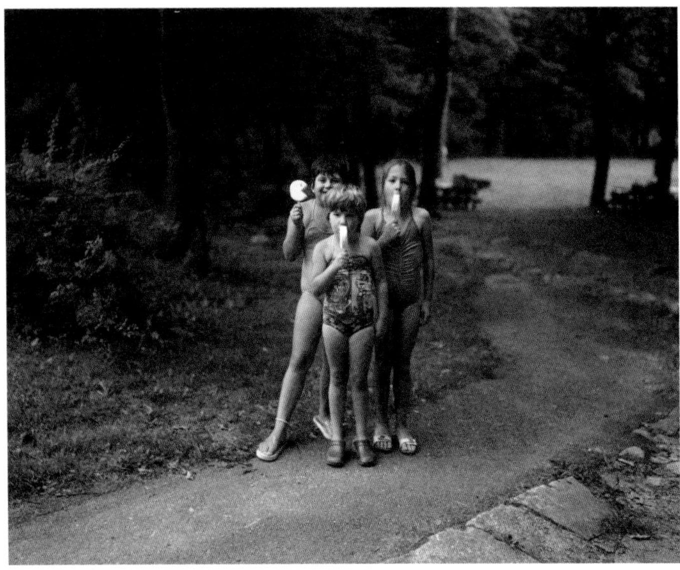

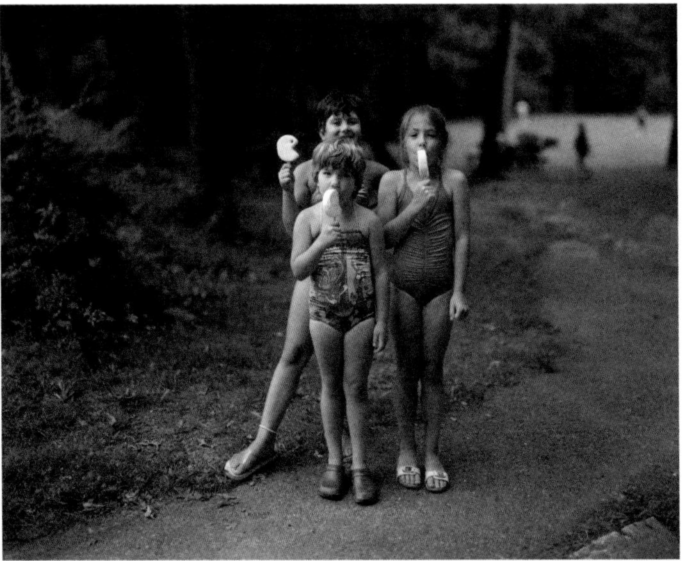

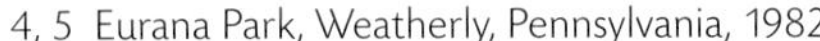

4, 5 Eurana Park, Weatherly, Pennsylvania, 1982

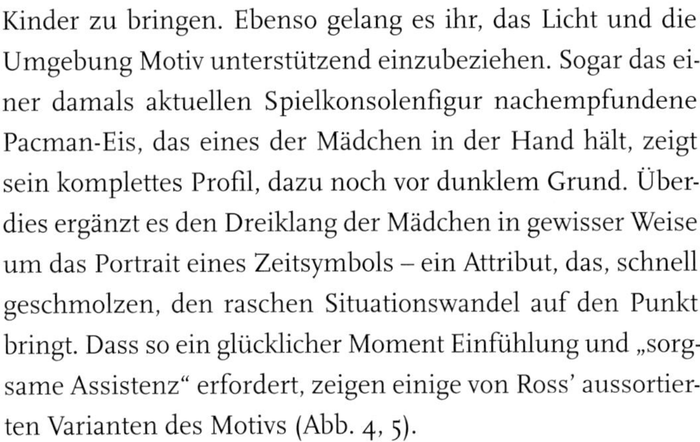

Kinder zu bringen. Ebenso gelang es ihr, das Licht und die Umgebung Motiv unterstützend einzubeziehen. Sogar das einer damals aktuellen Spielkonsolenfigur nachempfundene Pacman-Eis, das eines der Mädchen in der Hand hält, zeigt sein komplettes Profil, dazu noch vor dunklem Grund. Überdies ergänzt es den Dreiklang der Mädchen in gewisser Weise um das Portrait eines Zeitsymbols – ein Attribut, das, schnell geschmolzen, den raschen Situationswandel auf den Punkt bringt. Dass so ein glücklicher Moment Einfühlung und „sorgsame Assistenz“ erfordert, zeigen einige von Ross' aussortierten Varianten des Motivs (Abb. 4, 5).

Neben den Kindern beobachtete Judith Joy Ross im Eurana Park auch Jugendliche an der Schwelle zum Erwachsenenalter, deren Unsicherheit und melancholische Stimmung sie berührte und an eigene frühe Erfahrungen erinnerte. Ausdruck dessen ist die Aufnahme einer jungen Frau im Badeanzug, die mit schönem langen Haar und großer Brille als Dreiviertelfigur gezeigt ist (Tafel S. 45). Sie schaut seitlich an der Kamera vorbei, und ihre Haltung drückt Verlegenheit und Schutzbedürfnis aus. Im Vergleich zu den Eis essenden Mädchen ist bei ihr nur noch wenig von kindlicher Unvoreingenommenheit, Freiheit und ungebrochenem Vergnügen zu spüren. In ihrem Portrait zeichnen sich bereits die problematischen Seiten des Lebens ab, das Abwägen von konformem und nicht konformem Verhalten sowie unausweichliche, schwer, wenn nicht gar unmöglich zu beantwortende Fragen an die Zukunft.

Diesen unterschiedlichen Lebensabschnitten und Stimmungen hat Judith Joy Ross in der Serie *Eurana Park* auch die

ground it complements the triad of girls with the portrait of a symbol of the time—an attribute that, quickly melted, encapsulates the rapid change of the situation. Some of Ross's rejected variations of the motif (ills. 4, 5) demonstrate that such a fortunate moment requires sensitivity and close attention.

Besides children, in Eurana Park Judith Joy Ross observed adolescents at the threshold to adulthood whose insecurity and melancholic mood touched her, prompting her to recall her own early experiences. This is expressed in the three-quarter portrait of a young woman in a bathing suit with long, beautiful hair and wearing large glasses (plate p. 45). She is looking past the camera to the side, and her posture expresses shyness and a need for protection. Compared with the girls with popsicles, she exhibits little sense of childish impartiality, freedom, and undaunted pleasure. Her portrait shows the problematic aspects of life, gauging conformist and nonconformist behavior, as well as unavoidable questions about the future that are difficult, if not impossible, to answer.

In *Eurana Park,* Judith Joy Ross also adapted the colors of her photographic prints to these different stages of life. While the images of her younger subjects are rendered in a warm brown tone that expresses the security of childhood, she chooses a neutral shade of gray for the adolescents. This tone change is based on the intensity of the gold toning on printing-out paper; the more intense the toning process, the more neutral gray the result; the less intense, the warmer the shades. Her photographs, which she prepares as contact sheets on printing-out paper, measure circa twenty by twenty-five cen-

Tonigkeit ihrer Photographien angepasst. Während die Aufnahmen der Jüngeren in einem warmen, die Geborgenheit der Kindheit ausdrückenden Braunton wiedergegeben werden, wählt sie für die Jugendlichen einen neutraleren Grauton. Dies basiert auf der Intensität der Goldtonung ihrer schwarzweißen Photoabzüge. Je stärker die den Herstellungsprozess abschließende Tonung ist, desto neutraler grau fällt das Ergebnis aus, je schwächer, desto wärmer werden die Bildtöne. Ihre Photographien, die sie als Kontaktabzüge auf Auskopierpapier ausarbeitet, messen circa 25x20 cm, was ungefähr der Negativgröße von 8x10 inch entspricht. Sie platziert die Negative auf das Auskopierpapier in einen Kontaktrahmen und stellt diesen ins Tageslicht. Nach einiger Zeit – zehn Minuten oder auch einigen Stunden – zeichnet sich das Bild allein durch das Licht der Sonne in einem Lila-Braun-Ton ab. Dieses Bild wird dann mit Goldchlorid getont, fixiert und gewaschen, um es haltbar zu machen.[14] Zwar handelt es sich bei diesem Arbeitsprozess um ein in der Frühzeit der Photographie verankertes Verfahren, dennoch wirken Ross' Photographien nicht antiquiert. Vielmehr ist der Prozess ein Garant für eine besonders feine Durchzeichnung ihrer Bilder. Die Brillanz des Augenblicks wird hervorgehoben und dem Anspruch einer wirklichkeitsgetreuen Abbildung in besonderer Weise Rechnung getragen.

Judith Joy Ross fühlte von jeher eine große Nähe zur Natur. Die ersten, ihrer Meinung nach fehlgeschlagenen Versuche, einzelne Bäume im Wechsel der Jahreszeiten, Pflanzen oder Landschaften zu „portraitieren", datieren aus dem Jahr 1976. Erst 1985 kam sie ihrem Ziel näher, und zwar an einem für ihren Vater bedeutsamen Ort, dem See in Dorrance, Pennsylvania, den er selbst angelegt hatte und wo er seiner Leidenschaft als Landschaftsgärtner nachgegangen war. Ihrem Vater zu Ehren photographierte Judith Joy Ross nun jene Bäume am See, die er einst gepflanzt und gehegt hatte (Abb. 6). Für sie haben diese Bilder einen persönlichen Hintergrund. Dem Außenstehenden zeigen sie verwunschen wirkende Landschaften, die zur Kontemplation wie geschaffen scheinen.

1983 nahm Judith Joy Ross zum ersten Mal Kontakt mit John Szarkowski auf, dem damaligen Direktor des Department

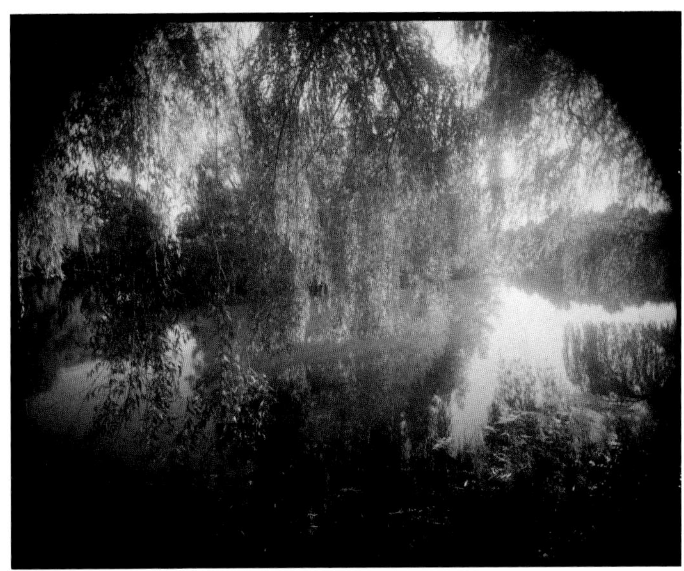

6 Ohne Titel | Untitled, Dorrance, Pennsylvania, 1985

timeters, which corresponds approximately to an eight-by-ten-inch negative. She puts the negatives on the printing-out paper in a contact frame and places this in daylight. If, after a while, be it ten minutes or hours, the image "prints out," which means it appears in a maroon-purple hue from the action of the sunlight alone, it then has to be toned in gold chloride and then fixed and washed to be made permanent.[14] Although this working process stems from the early days of photography, Ross's pictures do not look quaintly antiquated. This is because the process chosen provides a particularly fine pervasiveness of detail and meets the demand for a realistic depiction, giving the brilliance of the moment priority.

Judith Joy Ross always felt a closeness to nature. The first, in her opinion unsuccessful, attempts to make portraits of individual trees, plants or landscapes during the changing seasons, date from 1976. For Ross, something was missing from these efforts. Finally, in 1985 she came closer to her goal when she worked at a site that had been important to her father—a lake he had laid out in Dorrance, Pennsylvania, where he had long ago pursued his passion for the landscape. In order to honor him she photographed the trees he had once planted (ill. 6). These pictures show an enchanted place that seems to have been made for contemplation, far beyond the private context.

In 1983 Judith Joy Ross first contacted John Szarkowski, Director of the Department of Photography at the Museum of Modern Art, New York. Between 1962 and 1991 he exercised a decisive influence on its collection and exhibition program.

of Photography am Museum of Modern Art in New York. Sie wollte ihm ihre im Eurana Park entstandenen Aufnahmen und die ersten Portraits, die sie am Vietnam Veterans Memorial in Washington, D. C., aufgenommen hatte, vorstellen. Szarkowski leitete die photographische Abteilung am MoMA von 1962 bis 1991 und übte einen entscheidenden Einfluss auf das Ausstellungsprogramm und die museumseigene Sammlung aus. Bei einer der wöchentlichen Portfolio-Sichtungen erwarb Szarkowski zwei Werke aus der *Eurana Park*-Serie für den Bestand; später sollten weitere Bilder hinzukommen. Bei dieser Gelegenheit fragte er, ob sie das Werk von August Sander kenne. Ross erinnert sich, dass sie ihre Bewunderung für Sander nicht zugeben wollte, weil sie befürchtete, geradezu als Kopistin dazustehen. Szarkowski spürte ihr Unbehagen und griff ihrer Antwort vor: „Es ist in Ordnung, Judith, es heißt ‚Tradition‘, wenn man durch die Arbeit eines anderen beeinflusst wird.“ Rückblickend sagt sie heute: „Was für ein unglaublicher Tag das war, in diese großartige Sammlung aufgenommen zu werden und einer solchen Persönlichkeit wie John Szarkowski zu begegnen. Er war ja selbst Photograph und wusste, wie Photographen denken. Er wusste, ich hatte Angst.“[15]

1984 setzte Judith Joy Ross ihre Arbeit am Vietnam Veterans Memorial fort. Eine Auswahl daraus zeigte sie Susan Kismaric, Senior Curator am Museum of Modern Art, während eines Besuchs bei ihrem gemeinsamen Freund Larry Fink in Martin’s Creek, Pennsylvania. Kismaric war begeistert und bestand darauf, dass Ross auch diese Bilder im MoMA vorlegen sollte. John Szarkowski wählte dann für die von ihm kuratierte Gruppenausstellung *New Photography* im Jahr 1985 dreizehn Aufnahmen aus der gerade abgeschlossenen Portraitserie aus. Andy Grundberg kommentierte die Photographien in einer Ausstellungsrezension in der *New York Times*: „Was sie uns über Amerika nach Vietnam oder die Tragödie des Krieges erzählen, ist keineswegs eindeutig, aber die Photographin hat unmissverständlich ein visuelles Schauspiel geschaffen, das uns – wie das Denkmal selbst – an die bleibenden Narben des Krieges erinnert.“[16]

When Ross presented him with her pictures from Eurana Park and her first year’s work at the Vietnam Veterans Memorial, Washington, D.C., at one of the department’s scheduled weekly open portfolio reviews, he purchased two works from *Eurana Park* for the collection. Later, a number of other photographs were acquired for the museum. On this occasion he asked Ross if she was familiar with the work of August Sander. Ross recalls that she tried to deny her love for Sander’s work, fearing that she would be accused of copying, but Szarkowski, sensing her dissembling, said, “It’s okay Judith. It’s called ‘tradition’ to be influenced by the work of others.” Looking back, Ross states, “What a incredible day to be accepted into this great collection and to make the acquaintance of a person like John Szarkowski. As a photographer himself he knew how photographers think; he knew I was afraid.”[15]

Judith Joy Ross continued to work on another important series during 1984, realized at the Vietnam Veterans Memorial. She showed a selected group of these works to Susan Kismaric, Senior Curator at MoMA, while visiting the home of their mutual friend Larry Fink in Martin’s Creek, Pennsylvania. Kismaric insisted that Ross should bring these photographs to MoMA for review. Szarkowski subsequently chose thirteen images from her recently completed series for *New Photography,* the group exhibition he was curating in 1985. Andy Grundberg had the following to say about the portraits in an exhibition review he wrote for the *New York Times*: “What they tell us about post-Vietnam America or about the tragedy of the war is by no means explicit, but the photographer clearly has created a visual theater that serves to remind us—like the memorial itself—of the war’s enduring scars.”[16]

Ross had begun the series *Portraits at the Vietnam Veterans Memorial, Washington, D.C.* still with a feeling of grief and loss. She lived in a small apartment in Allentown, Pennsylvania. To contend with the circumstances of her own life, she considered asking passersby on the street “How do you manage to cope with sorrow and pain?” At about the same time, she heard on the radio about the installation of the Vietnam Veterans Memorial in Washington, D.C., designed by Maya

Ross hatte die *Portraits at the Vietnam Veterans Memorial, Washington, D.C.* immer noch mit dem Gefühl von Trauer und Verlust begonnen. Damals lebte sie in einem kleinen Appartement in Allentown, Pennsylvania. Zur Bewältigung der eigenen Lebenssituation zog sie in Erwägung, Passanten an der Straßenecke zu fragen: „Wie gehen Sie mit Trauer und Schmerz um?" Als sie etwa zur selben Zeit von der Errichtung des von Maya Lin entworfenen Vietnam Veterans Memorial in Washington D.C. hörte, stand für sie schnell fest, dass dies wohl der geeignetere Ort war, ihrer Frage nachzugehen.[17] Es entstand eine lakonische Aufnahme aus dem Fenster ihres Zimmers, der Vorhang einen Spaltbreit geöffnet (Tafel S. 49). Es ist das Schlüsselbild für den Beginn der neuen Bildserie *Portraits at the Vietnam Veterans Memorial, Washington, D.C.*

In den Jahren 1983 und 1984 fuhr Judith Joy Ross oft nach Washington. Die Bilder, die sie als Jugendliche vom Vietnamkrieg gesehen hatte, etwa von Larry Burrows im *Life*-Magazin und von Agenturphotographen in Zeitungen klangen nach. Auch Aufnahmen aus dem 19. Jahrhundert von Roger Fenton, Felice Beato und Bilder des amerikanischen Bürgerkriegs von Timothy O'Sullivan and George N. Barnard hatten sich ihr eingeprägt. Am Vietnam Veterans Memorial setzte sie sich einmal mehr mit der Grausamkeit und den über Generationen anhaltenden Folgen von Kriegen auseinander, mit nicht zu beantwortenden Fragen um Macht, Schuld und Gerechtigkeit, deren angemessener Aufarbeitung und einem adäquaten Umgang damit. Die von ihr aufgenommenen Portraits am Vietnam Veterans Memorial zeigen auch, was das Denkmal mit seinen Inschriften verdeutlichen will: Der Krieg ist kein anonymes Massensterben, sondern als der massenhafte Tod von namentlich bekannten Individuen zu verstehen. Jeder, den sie dort antraf, suchte seinen eigenen Zugang zum historischen Geschehen wie auch zur speziellen Situation am Denkmal und hatte selbst über zehn Jahre nach Ende des Vietnamkrieges noch mit Erinnerungen und seelischen Verletzungen zu kämpfen. Dabei zeigt uns die Photographin die Gesichter zwar oft aus relativ großer Nähe, dennoch ist die Distanz individuell ausgelotet. Viele der Dargestellten sind als Brustbild oder Drei-

Lin.[17] It was quickly clear to her that this was the more suitable place to pursue her question. She then produced a succinct photograph taken from the window of her room, the curtain slightly open, a prelude to the launching of a new series, *Portraits at the Vietnam Veterans Memorial, Washington, D.C,* (plate p. 49).

In 1983 and 1984, Judith Joy Ross made recurring trips to Washington. The pictures of the Vietnam War taken by Larry Burrows for *Life* magazine and those reproduced in newspapers made by wire service photographers that she had seen as a youth lingered. Nineteenth-century photographs by Roger Fenton, Felice Beato, and the U.S. Civil War photographs by Timothy O'Sullivan and George N. Barnard were major influences on her. At the Vietnam Veterans Memorial, she grappled with the atrocity of war and the lasting impact it has on generations, with its unanswerable questions with regards to power, guilt, and justice and society's attempts to adequately come to terms with them. The portraits by Judith Joy Ross also visualize what the memorial, with its inscriptions, aspires to illustrate: war is not to be regarded as anonymous widespread death but as the death on a massive scale of individuals with names. Each of the people she met there sought out personal access to the historical occurrence as well as to the special situation at the memorial, where they were compelled to struggle, ten years after the war had ended, with memories and emotional wounds. While the photographer shows us their faces relatively close, a respectful distance is nevertheless individually sounded out. Many of the people photographed are shown in half- or three-quarter-length in indistinct outdoor space. As she states herself, Judith Joy Ross was interested in the individual characters; she worked relatively quickly with an open aperture, which necessarily produces a shallow amount in focus.[18] Only occasionally does one get an impression of the Memorial itself, for instance in an image in which two Marine lieutenants in dress whites stand with their backs to the black granite slab inscribed with the name of the fallen soldiers and those missing in action (plate p. 51). While the two young men, who maintained their bearing behind the façade of their uniforms,

viertelfigur im meist unbestimmten Außenraum abgelichtet. Judith Joy Ross interessierten nach eigener Aussage die unterschiedlichen Typen, sie arbeitete verhältnismäßig schnell, mit offener Blende, so dass Unschärfebereiche entstehen.[18] Nur gelegentlich gewinnt man einen Eindruck von dem Mahnmal selbst, etwa dort, wo zwei Marine-Leutnants in weißen Paradeuniformen mit dem Rücken zur schwarzen, mit den Namen der Gefallenen und Vermissten beschrifteten Granitplatte stehen (Tafel S. 51). Während die beiden jungen Männer, hinter der Fassade ihrer Uniform auf Haltung bedacht, ihre Empfindungen zurücknehmen, erkennt man in anderen Gesichtern Unsicherheit, Trauer, Bitterkeit oder stille Wut. Zwar scheint die detailgenaue Wiedergabe der Portraitierten zum Hinschauen und genauen Studium geradezu aufzufordern, angesichts der teilweise starken Emotionalität stellt sich jedoch intuitiv das Verlangen nach Abstand und Diskretion ein, das eher im respektvoll schweigenden Miteinander aufgeht. Judith Joy Ross ließ sich von diesem denkwürdigen Ort leiten, und es war schlicht die Präsenz und die zum Ausdruck kommende Ergriffenheit der Menschen, die sie fesselten und die sie als persönliche Bekenntnisse zum Geschehenen wahrnahm: „Ich wollte einfach beweisen, dass wir diesen Krieg hatten, und dass ich Menschen begegnet bin, die darin gekämpft hatten. Ich traf Menschen, denen der Krieg vielleicht egal war. Ich traf Menschen mit vielen unterschiedlichen Meinungen. Ich bin nicht hier, um meine oder ihre Einstellungen aufzuzeigen [...]. Wir hatten den Vietnamkrieg, wir taten es, das sind wir, so sehen wir aus. Dies war eine Stunde der Bekenntnisse.“[19]

Um sich die Fragen, ob sie überhaupt das Recht hatte, mit der Kamera an diesem Ort zu sein, und ob der Schmerz, den sie in den Gesichtern der Besucher am Denkmal sah, der gleiche ist, wie ihn Menschen überall in ihrem gewöhnlichen Leben empfinden, zu beantworten, wechselte Ross die Umgebung und betrat mit ihren 1984 aufgenommenen Bildern auf dem Gelände des Supermarkts Pathmark in Allentown, Pennsylvania, eine alltägliche Welt. In diesem Umfeld traf sie auf Väter und Mütter mit ihren Kindern, auf alleinstehende Rentner, die im Einkauf eine bescheidene Abwechslung finden,

appear to hold back their feelings, in other faces one sees insecurity, sorrow, bitterness, or silent rage. The rendition of the persons in the portraits, accurate in every detail, virtually challenges the viewer to look at and study them closely. In view of the strong emotionality and intimacy, however, a longing for distance and discretion sets in that merges into a silent togetherness. This profound place guided Judith Joy Ross. It was simply the people's presence and state of emotional turmoil that captivated her and which she perceived as personal acknowledgment of what had happened. "I just wanted to prove that we had had this war and that I met people who had fought it. I met people who probably couldn't have cared less. I met people with so many different opinions. I'm not here to show mine or theirs. ... We had the Vietnam War, we did it, this is us, this is what we look like. That was one of the signature moments."[19]

Ross questioned if she had the right to be there at all with her camera. Was the pain she saw in the faces at the memorial the same as pain experienced by people in everyday life anywhere? To explore this possibility Ross shifted the setting and entered an ordinary world with her photographs taken in 1984 on the premises of the Pathmark supermarket in Allentown, Pennsylvania. In this environment she met fathers and mothers with their children, single retirees who seek diversion by shopping, and youths who kill time at the edge of miserably functional commercial buildings, people who eke out a living and have to watch every penny (plates pp. 56–57).

She recognized that even in an everyday environment a great many people are affected by sadness. In comparison with the previous portrait series, she noticed that the Vietnam Veterans Memorial itself seemed to be reflected in the faces of the visitors. She came to the conclusion that it was not necessary to show it directly in the photographs. Later she returned to the Memorial and continued to photograph with renewed confidence.

In 1986/87 Ross made portraits of members of the United States Congress or staff in their offices (plates pp. 59–63). In doing so, she extended the radius of her photographic field of

und Jugendliche, die am Rande der trist funktionalen Geschäftsbauten ihre Zeit totschlagen, auf Menschen, die ihr Auskommen mehr schlecht als recht bestreiten und jeden Cent umdrehen müssen (Tafeln S. 56–57).

Ross erkannte, dass auch im „normalen" Leben vielen Menschen eine gewisse Traurigkeit anhaftet. Das Denkmal, so kam es ihr jetzt vor, schien sich gleichsam in den Gesichtern der Besucher zu spiegeln, brauchte folglich nicht notwendigerweise selbst im Bild zu erscheinen. Sie kehrte zum Vietnam Veterans Memorial zurück und setzte ihre Arbeit mit neuem Antrieb fort.

1986/87 begann sie eine Serie über Abgeordnete des U.S. Kongresses beziehungsweise deren Mitarbeiter, die sie in ihren Büros portraitierte (Tafeln S. 59–63). Damit erweiterte sie den Radius ihres photographischen Untersuchungsfelds und begab sich an die Schaltstellen der Macht. Ihr Vorhaben entstand unter dem Eindruck der Iran-Contra-Affäre während der Amtszeit von Präsident Ronald Reagan und Enthüllungen der Presse, die Zusammenhänge mit heimlichen Waffenverkäufen der Regierung im Austausch gegen Geiseln an den Iran und Nicaragua aufdeckte.[20] Mit einer Bestätigung der Pennsylvania Academy of the Fine Arts, anlässlich der 200-Jahr-Feier der Verfassung der Vereinigten Staaten eine Ausstellung zum geplanten Portraitprojekt auszurichten,[21] bat Judith Joy Ross in den Büros im Washingtoner Kapitol um Phototermine. 117 Kongressabgeordnete gewährten ihr schließlich nach unzähligen Briefen und Telefonaten ein Treffen. Meist hatte sie pro Aufnahme nur rund 15 Minuten Zeit. Ein skizzierter Wegeplan nebst Terminliste sollte sie vom Parkplatz durch das Gewirr endloser Gänge, Aufzüge und Treppen pünktlich von Verabredung zu Verabredung bringen, auf die sie sich zu Hause mit *The Almanac of American Politics 1986* vorbereitet hatte (Abb. 7).[22] Trotz der Anspannung, in einem ihr fremden Umfeld zu agieren, gelangen ihr Aufnahmen von großer Selbstverständlichkeit und Transparenz. In den Bildnissen zeigen sich die Politiker weder als glatte Medienpersönlichkeiten oder strahlende Helden noch als machtgetriebene Betrüger. Ross fand vielmehr Menschen in ihrem beruflichen Alltag vor, mit Stär-

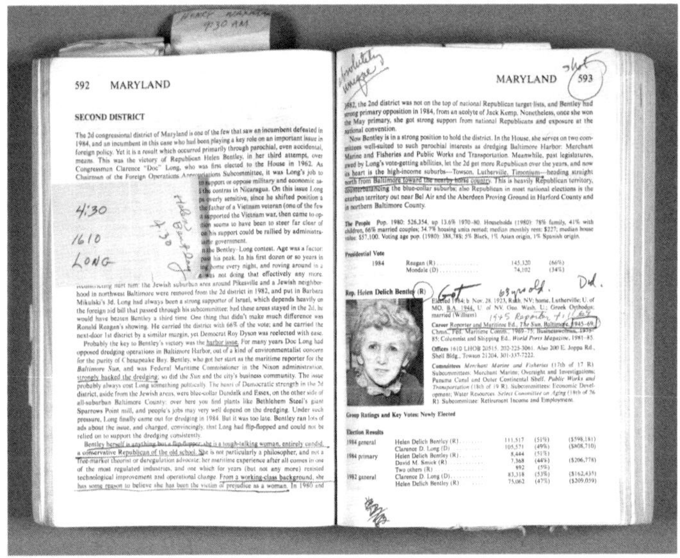
592 MARYLAND

SECOND DISTRICT

MARYLAND 593

7 *The Almanac of American Politics 1986*, Doppelseite mit Notizen von Judith Joy Ross | double page with remarks by Judith Joy Ross

investigation and engaged the interfaces of power. Her plan developed during the Iran-Contra Affair at the time of President Ronald Reagan's term of office, when press reports uncovered relationships between secret arms sales by the government in exchange for hostages in Iran and Nicaragua.[20] With a confirmation from the Pennsylvania Academy of the Fine Arts to mount an exhibition on the occasion of the bicentennial of the constitution of the United States,[21] Ross requested photo sessions with the members of Congress in their House and Senate offices surrounding the Capitol Building in Washington, D.C. After countless letters and telephone conversations, one hundred and seventeen members of Congress agreed to being photographed. She generally had only fifteen minutes for each photograph. Sketched route maps and a time schedule were meant to take her from the parking area through the maze of endless corridors, elevators, and stairs on time from appointment to appointment. She had prepared herself at home with the aid of an encyclopedia of the U.S. Congress, *The Almanac of American Politics 1986* (ill. 7).[22] Despite the tension associated with working in an unfamiliar environment, she succeeded in producing photographs of great naturalness and transparency. In the portraits, the politicians present themselves neither as smooth media personalities or radiant heroes, nor as power-driven crooks. Rather, Ross came upon people in their everyday professional surroundings, with strengths and weaknesses, completely average, in good or bad form on the day. A review of the exhibition at the Pennsylvania

ken und Schwächen, vollkommen durchschnittlich, in guter oder schlechter Tagesform. Eine 1988 im *New Art Examiner* erschienene Rezension der Ausstellung in der Pennsylvania Academy of the Fine Arts bestätigt diesen Eindruck: „Im Einzelnen verweisen die Photographien auf Menschlichkeit und zeigen so sogar die Verletzlichkeit und Fehlbarkeit derjenigen, die die höchsten Ämter einnehmen. Als Gruppe betrachtet, vermittelt diese Serie die begrenzte, aber auch unentbehrliche Leistungsfähigkeit und Verantwortung des Einzelnen innerhalb der übergeordneten sozialen Struktur." [23]

Als ein Pendant zur Reihe der Kongressabgeordneten kann die Werkgruppe *Elections* angesehen werden, die Judith Joy Ross 1990, während sie an der Serie *Jobs* arbeitete, begonnen hatte und bis zur Wahl von Barack Obama 2008 fortsetzte (Tafeln S. 117–119). In Bethlehem, Pennsylvania, und anderen umliegenden Orten suchte sie zunächst die Parteilokale der Demokraten auf, später auch die Wahlbüros. Während die Parteizugehörigkeit der Dargestellten im ersten Fall klar ist, bleibt sie bei den Wählern an den Urnen naturgemäß offen. Insgesamt führt die Serie nicht die bekannten Gesichter der Politik vor Augen, sondern anonyme Wählerinnen und Wähler, Wahlhelfer und -aufseher, Einzelkämpfer oder interessierte Zaungäste des Geschehens; kurz all jene, die mehr oder weniger aktiv ihre demokratischen Rechte wahrnehmen. Auch bei dieser Bildreihe geht es Judith Joy Ross darum, menschliche Verhaltensweisen vorzustellen, die sich fern der Medienrealität – wie sie sich etwa auf Wahlplakaten oder in -spots darstellt – aus dem eigenen unprätentiösen Leben heraus entwickelt haben. Das Phänomen Wahlen und Wahlkampf wird von Judith Joy Ross von der Basis her beobachtet, mit Fokus auf den persönlichen Einsatz, sei es, dass jemand mündliche Überzeugungsarbeit leistet, Gespräche und Telefonate führt, Flyer verteilt oder Buttons an seiner Kleidung befestigt – Meinungsäußerungen, die trotz öffentlichkeitswirksamer Berichterstattung durch Radio, Fernsehen und Werbung bei Wahlen ein entscheidender Faktor sind. Aus deutscher Sicht formulierte das Wolfram Brunner in seinen Ausführungen zum Wahlkampf in den USA wie folgt: „Die in deutschen Medien gern

Academy of the Fine Arts published in 1988 in the *New Art Examiner* confirmed this impression: "Individually, these photographs establish the humanness, and hence the vulnerability and fallibility, of those holding even the highest office. Taken as a group this series conveys the limited but indispensable effectiveness and responsibility of the individual within the larger social order."[23]

Elections, a cycle of works Judith Joy Ross began in 1990 while she was working on the series *Jobs* and continued until Barack Obama was elected in 2008, can be regarded as a companion piece to the series of members of Congress (plates pp. 117–119). In Bethlehem, Pennsylvania, and other surrounding locations she went to the local headquarters of the Democratic Party, and later on also to the voting polls. Whereas in the first case the political leanings are obvious, in the images of the voters there was no way of determining which party they belonged to. As a whole the series does not show the well-known faces of politics; instead, we can see anonymous voters, poll workers and monitors, lone wolves, or onlookers interested in what was happening—in short, all of those who more or less actively exercised their democratic rights. In this case as well, Ross is concerned with presenting human modes of behavior that develop out of an individual's own unpretentious life, far from any media reality—as shown on, for instance, election posters or in commercial spots. Judith Joy Ross records the phenomenon of elections and election campaigns from the grass roots, with a focus on personal involvement, whether that be someone who does a great deal of verbal persuading, conducts conversations or makes phone calls, distributes flyers, or attaches campaign buttons to their clothing—each expresses an opinion that is a decisive factor during elections, whatever the high-publicity reporting on radio, television, or in the form of advertising. From a German point of view, Wolfram Brunner made the following remarks on the election campaign in the United States: "The catchwords of the 'candidate centering,' 'media-relatedness,' 'marketing orientation,' and 'professionalization' of American political campaigns readily used in German media only partially describe reality. ... And if you take a

benutzten Schlagwörter von der Kandidatenzentrierung, Medienbezogenheit, Marketingorientierung und Professionalisierung amerikanischer Politik-Kampagnen beschreiben die Realität [...] nur partiell. [...] Und wenn man genau hinblickt, zeigt sich, daß häufig die scheinbar kleinen Dinge eine wesentlichere Rolle spielen: Das Rekrutieren von Freiwilligen zum Beispiel, die Pflege von Datenbanken oder die pünktliche Versendung eines Mailings. Die Wirklichkeit des US-Wahlkampfs ist oftmals grauer als sein Image."[24]

Im Jahr 1988 erhielt Judith Joy Ross von der Stadt Easton, Pennsylvania – von wo aus Walker Evans 1935 die Brücke über den Delaware River photographiert hatte – ein Stipendium in Höhe von 3.000 Dollar, um ein künstlerisches Projekt im öffentlichen Raum zu realisieren. Da kein Thema vorgegeben war, entschied sie sich für photographische Portraits von Kindern und Jugendlichen, die in der Stadt lebten. Schon zu Projektbeginn war es ihr Wunsch, die Photographien im Gebäude der Young Women's Christian Association in Easton auszustellen, und zwar erstmals in Vergrößerungen im Format 50x60 cm. In dieser Größe – so Ross' Gedanke – würden sie von den Nutzern des Gebäudes eher wahrgenommen, die sich aus ganz unterschiedlichen Personenkreisen zusammensetzten, etwa Teilnehmer dort angebotener Kurse oder obdachlose Frauen und Kinder, die im oberen Stockwerk wohnen durften. Ross wollte allen die Möglichkeit geben, sich die Bilder anzuschauen.[25] Insgesamt zwölf Photographien wurden damals ausgestellt und von der Stadt Easton angekauft. „Ich wollte zeigen, wie wundervoll Kinder sind, einfach so, wie sie sind"[26], sagt sie und meint damit ein entschieden anderes Bild von Kindern als das in der Werbung oder im Fernsehen vermittelte. Entstanden ist ein umfangreiches Konvolut an Aufnahmen von Kindern und Jugendlichen unterschiedlichen Alters. In diesen Portraits bleibt es eher den Jüngeren vorbehalten, sich mit spielerischer Freude vor der Kamera zu zeigen, so bescheiden, zuweilen berührend erfinderisch ihr Auftritt auch ist (Tafeln S. 66–67). Die älteren Jungen hingegen üben sich bereits in starken Posen, versuchen möglichst cool zu wirken, wie die Aufnahme eines jungen Mannes im Hawaii-

close look, you will see that it is the apparently small things that frequently play an important role: recruiting volunteers, for example, maintaining databases, or distributing mailing on time. The reality of the election campaign in the US is often grayer than its image."[24]

In 1988, Judith Joy Ross received a $3,000 grant from the city of Easton, Pennsylvania—the place where in 1935 Walker Evans had taken a photograph of the bridge over the Delaware River—in order to realize an artistic project in public space. As there was no prescribed theme, she decided on photographic portraits of children and youths who lived in the city. From the outset of the project, it was her wish to exhibit the pictures in the building of the Young Women's Christian Association and to make for the first time prints enlarged from eight-by-ten negatives to twenty-by-twenty-four-inch prints. In this format, she believed that they would be more likely to be noticed by the persons who utilized the building. Very different kinds of people spent time in the YWCA building in question, including participants in courses offered there or homeless women and children who were allowed to live on the upper floor. Ross wanted to give all of them the opportunity to view the pictures.[25] A total of twelve images were exhibited at that time and commissioned by the City of Easton. She states: "I wanted kids to see how wonderful they are, just as they are."[26] Her idea was to create images of children as they really are, not as projected by advertising and television imagery. What developed was an extensive body of photographs that is comprised of images of children and youths of different ages. In these portraits, the younger children are more likely to present themselves to the camera and the photographer with playful delight, often modest and sometimes touchingly inventive (plates pp. 66–67). In contrast, the older boys indulge in strong airs as they try to look as cool as possible, which is exemplified by the photograph of a young man in a Hawaiian shirt (plate p. 65). The photographer nevertheless succeeds in glimpsing behind the poses they assume to capture something of the vulnerability and the living situation of the town's children. The threadbare second-hand clothes with their out-of-

Hemd zeigt (Tafel S. 65). Der Photographin gelingt es gleichwohl, hinter die eingenommenen Posen zu blicken und etwas von der Verletzlichkeit und der Lebenssituation der Stadtkinder einzufangen. Die abgetragenen Secondhand-Kleidungsstücke mit ihren verfehlten Emblemen oder merkwürdigen Mustern mögen ein Verweis darauf sein. Vermutlich sind die Kinder auf Kleiderspenden angewiesen – an einen eigenen Geschmack kann man oft nur schwer glauben.

Ein für Judith Roy Ross heute sehr bekanntes Motiv aus der Reihe der *Easton Portraits*, drei junge Mädchen in Badeanzügen, bildet den Abschluss der Publikation, die 1989 die von John Szarkowski präsentierte Ausstellung *Photography Until Now* begleitete.[27] Das Bild, das 1995 auch für den Titel von Susan Kismarics Monographie gewählt wurde, kann als Auftakt und Beispiel für eine neue Phase im Umgang mit dem Medium gelten (Abb. 8). So dürften beispielsweise die drei Mädchen – eine moderne, eher lakonische Variante der drei Musen – einen exemplarischen Bildtypus begründet haben, der in den zwischen 1992 und 1998 entstandenen Strandportraits von Rineke Dijkstra eine weitere Reflexion und Stilisierung erfährt.[28] Auch Thomas Struths Einzelportraits und seine Familienbilder aus den vergangenen 25 Jahren haben eine ähnliche psychologische Dichte wie die Arbeiten von Judith Joy Ross – authentisch, einfühlsam, individuell und allgemeingültig.[29]

Ende der 80er Jahre fanden weitere Gruppenausstellungen in Amerika statt, die die Arbeiten von Judith Joy Ross verstärkt in das Licht der Öffentlichkeit rückten. Das Philadelphia Museum of Art zeigte 1987 in *Twelve Photographers Look at US* Arbeiten aus der Serie *Portraits at the Vietnam Veterans Memorial*. Die Ausstellung konzentrierte sich auf das Portrait und bezog amerikanische Künstler wie Larry Fink, Nan Goldin, Nicholas Nixon oder Joel Sternfeld ein.[30] Ein Jahr später führte Max Kozloff in der Schau *Real Faces*, die im Whitney Museum of American Art in New York stattfand, vier Positionen zusammen. Neben Judith Joy Ross waren Bill Burke, Nan Goldin und Birney Imes vertreten. Beide Ausstellungen wurden in der Tagespresse sowie in Kunst- und Kulturmagazinen besprochen. So erschienen beispielsweise in der *New York Times*

place emblems or odd patterns may be a reference to this. The young people may have to depend on clothing donations; it is difficult to believe their outfits reflect their own taste.

A motif from the *Easton Portraits* series featuring three girls in bathing suits is a picture for which Judith Joy Ross is very well known. It is the last photograph in the publication that accompanied the exhibition *Photography Until Now* presented by John Szarkowski in 1989.[27] The image, which was also selected for the cover of Susan Kismaric's monograph, can be regarded as the prelude to and an example for a new phase in the treatment of the medium (ill. 8). For example, the three girls—a modern, more succinct variation of the three muses—may have founded an exemplary type of photographic image. It experiences further reflection and stylization in the beach portraits Rineke Dijkstra produced between 1992 and 1998.[28] Thomas Struth's solo portraits and family pictures from the past twenty-five years also possess a psychological density that is similar to the works of Judith Joy Ross—authentic, perceptive, and individual yet general.[29]

Further group exhibitions took place in America in the late 1980s and continued to place works by Ross in the public spotlight. In the exhibition *Twelve Photographers Look at US* mounted in 1987, the Philadelphia Museum of Art presented works from the series *Portraits at the Vietnam Veterans Memorial*. The show concentrated on the portrait and included American artists such as Larry Fink, Nan Goldin, Nicholas Nixon, and Joel Sternfeld.[30] A year later, Max Kozloff assembled the work of four photographers for the exhibition *Real Faces* at the Whitney Museum of American Art in New York. In addition to Judith Joy Ross, it presented Bill Burke, Nan Goldin, and Birney Imes. Both of these exhibitions were extensively reviewed in the daily press as well as in art and culture magazines. *The New York Times*, for example, published two reviews of *Real Faces* by Andy Grundberg and John Gross that mention the photographs by Judith Joy Ross.[31] Grundberg writes that "Ross' ... pictures are the most delicate."

In 1998 and 2004, Ross again extensively dealt with specific localities and their residents in two series. In the late

zwei Rezensionen über *Real Faces* von Andy Grundberg und John Gross, in denen auch die Aufnahmen von Judith Joy Ross Erwähnung finden.[31] „Ross' [...] Bilder sind die feinfühligsten", so Grundberg.

Judith Joy Ross hat sich 1998 und 2004 in zwei Serien nochmals eingehend mit bestimmten Ortschaften und deren Bewohnern befasst. Zunächst fuhr sie Ende der 90er Jahre nach Northeast Philadelphia, jenen Teil der größten Stadt Pennsylvanias, in dem einst die weiße Mittel- und Arbeiterschicht vorherrschend war und der heute überwiegend von Afroamerikanern, Hispanics sowie Immigranten aus unterschiedlichen Ländern und Kontinenten bewohnt wird. Kein ungefährliches Terrain, was bedeutete, dass die Photographin bei ihren ersten Arbeitsaufenthalten von einem Vertreter der Stadt begleitet wurde. Erneut richtete sie ihr Augenmerk auf Kinder und Jugendliche. Sie spiegeln die gemischte Bewohnerschaft, und auf den Photographien gibt es immer wieder verhaltene Hinweise, die auf den schwierigen sozialen Kontext schließen lassen. Das Trio der ein wenig zu alt wirkenden kleinen Mädchen – eines trägt für ihr Alter völlig ungeeignete Kunststoffschläppchen mit schiefen Plateausohlen – oder das Handzeichen eines Jungen weisen in diese Richtung (Tafeln S. 122–123). Judith Joy Ross führt die jungen Menschen in ihrer ganz eigenen Existenz vor Augen, wie sie trotz widriger Lebensbedingungen ihren persönlichen Kosmos entfalten.

Zwar hat Judith Joy Ross den größten Teil ihres Werkes in Pennsylvania erarbeitet, dennoch existieren Bildreihen, die andernorts aufgenommen wurden und sie mehrmals bis nach Europa führten. In der Serie *Washington Square Park* begegnet sie Menschen, die schon früh mit einem schweren Schicksal konfrontiert wurden. Es sind vorwiegend ehemalige afrikanische Kindersoldaten, die 2001 zu einer UN-Konferenz in New York eingeladen waren (Tafel S. 126). Ihre Gesichter erzählen von bitteren Erfahrungen und lassen auf psychische Verletzungen schließen. Tragischerweise fiel ihr Aufenthalt in die Zeit der Terroranschläge des 11. September 2001, was ihnen im vermeintlich sicheren Gastland vollkommen unerwartet eine andere Form des Schreckens vor Augen führen sollte.

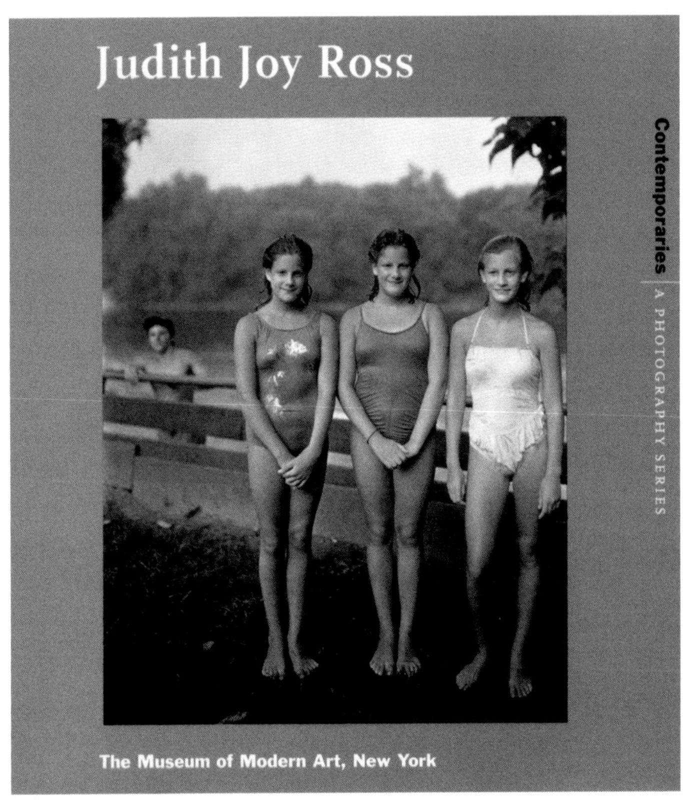

8 *Judith Joy Ross*, The Museum of Modern Art, New York, 1995

1990s, she drove to Northeast Philadelphia, that part of Pennsylvania's largest city in which the white middle- and working class were once predominant and which is today largely inhabited by Afro-Americans and Hispanics as well as immigrants from various countries and continents. This was not safe territory, which meant that a representative of the city accompanied the photographer on her first working sessions. She again turned her attention to children and youths. They mirror the mixed population, and the photographs time and again feature cautious references that allow us to draw conclusions about the difficult social context, such as the trio of slightly old-looking little girls with one wearing completely inappropriate plastic clogs with worn-down platform soles, or the hand signs being made by a boy (plates pp. 122–123). Judith Joy Ross shows these young people in their very own existence, how they unfold their personal cosmos within adverse living conditions.

While Judith Joy Ross created the major part of her oeuvre in Pennsylvania, there are series of photographs that were taken elsewhere and which several times took her as far as Europe. In the series *Washington Square Park* she encounters people who were confronted with a harsh fate early on in their

Wiederum scheint die Photographin mit diesen Bildern der existentiellen Frage nachzugehen, wie der Mensch mit Trauer und Schmerz umgeht.

Für die Bildreihe *Paris*, 2003–2006, spielt die Gegenüberstellung unterschiedlicher Lebensmodelle und Kulturen eine entscheidende Rolle. Als Amerikanerin wollte Ross ein Paris zeigen, das, fernab des Klischees, mehr ist als eine Stadt, in der weiße Amerikaner ihre Hochzeitsreise verbringen. Sie nahm Kontakt zu Menschen afrikanischer Herkunft auf, die sich zwar in Paris zu Hause fühlen, aber mit einer Menge von Schwierigkeiten zu kämpfen haben und zudem nach wie vor ihren Traditionen verbunden sind. So kam sie beispielsweise in der Metro mit einer Passantin ins Gespräch und verabredete sich mit ihr für den nächsten Tag zu einer Aufnahme (Tafel S. 88). Bald musste sie jedoch feststellen, dass ihre Französischkenntnisse nicht ausreichten, um eine für die photographische Aufnahme notwendige nähere Verbindung zu den Afrikanern aufzubauen. Ihr Bruder Edward, der in Paris lebt, kam ihr zu Hilfe, und so stammt die überwiegende Zahl der portraitierten Afrikaner vor allem aus seinem Bekanntenkreis oder aus dem seines damaligen Mitbewohners Seydou Camera (Tafel S. 87). In einem übergreifenden Kontext gesehen, veranschaulicht die Bildreihe aus Paris Aspekte der Migration und Integration, die nicht nur für die westliche Welt zutreffen.

In den Entstehungszeitraum der *Paris*-Serie fallen auch die Photographien, die Judith Joy Ross 2004 in dem rund 170 km nördlich von Philadelphia gelegenen Ort Freeland aufnahm. Wie viele andere Städte der Region lebte Freeland einst vom Kohleabbau, einer heute nicht mehr existierenden wirtschaftlichen Struktur.[32] Die Stadt war dafür bekannt, genauso viele Bars wie Kirchen zu haben. Ross' Interesse an Freeland ist auch mit ihrer persönlichen Geschichte verbunden: Es ist der Geburtsort ihres Vaters. Zunächst plante sie Portraits von Schülern einer Privatschule zusammen mit Einheimischen. Das Vorhaben scheiterte aber nicht zuletzt daran, dass Freeland im Wesentlichen eine Arbeiterstadt und der Anteil wohlhabender, gut situierter Einwohner eher gering ist. Schließlich entstanden Portraits von Kindern, die in einer

lives. They are especially former African child soldiers who were invited to a conference organized by the United Nations in New York in 2001 (plate p. 126). Their faces tell of bitter experiences and suggest emotional wounds. Tragically, their visit coincided with the terrorist attacks of 9/11, which would unexpectedly bring home to them another form of horror in what was allegedly their safe host country. Nevertheless, with these pictures the photographer seems to pursue again the existential question of how human beings deal with sorrow and pain.

The comparison of different life styles and cultures plays a crucial role in the series *Paris*, 2003–2006. As an American, Ross wanted to show a Paris, far from the usual clichés, that is not just a city where white American tourists come for a honeymoon visit. For this reason she contacted people of African heritage. Many of them feel at home in Paris, yet must often struggle with difficulties to establish themselves and still cling to their traditions. What Ross did, for example, was to start a conversation with a passerby in the Metro and then make an appointment for a photo session on the following day (plate p. 88). After a while she found that her French language skills were too poor to readily establish closer contact, necessary for taking photographs. For this reason, many of the Africans in her portraits are friends of her brother Edward, who lives in Paris, or of his African roommate, Seydou Camera (plate p. 87). The series can be read in an overarching context, as it addresses aspects of migration and integration that not only pertain to the Western world.

The photographs that Judith Joy Ross took in 2004 in Freeland, a town about a hundred miles north of Philadelphia, also date from this period. Like many other towns in the region, Freeland was once characterized by coal mining, an economic structure that no longer exists.[32] It was once known to have as many bars as churches. Ross's interest in Freeland is also bound to her personal history: it is her father's place of birth. She initially planned to produce portraits of students at a private school along with the townsfolk. Her plan failed, not least because Freeland is essentially a blue-collar town, and the share of well-to-do residents is minor. What Ross ultimately

ärmlichen Siedlung leben und zumeist bei Pflegefamilien untergebracht sind. Der Lebensweg dieser Kinder scheint vorgezeichnet, die Aussichten auf eine Zukunft mit besseren Bedingungen eher unwahrscheinlich. Noch sind sie zu jung, um ihre Situation bewusst zu reflektieren. Ein anschauliches, fast fatalistisch anmutendes Beispiel ist die Aufnahme von einem Jungen, der mit seinem Kettcar einen Unfall simuliert. Auf den ersten Blick lässt sich die Situation nicht einschätzen, doch sein Grinsen verrät das kindliche Spiel um Aggression und Schmerz. Den womöglich ausgelösten Schreck und die Zuwendung im Moment des Photographierens scheint er als kleinen Erfolg zu genießen (Tafel S. 108). Außer Kinder und Jugendliche photographierte Ross auch ältere Bürger von Freeland, woraus sich eines ihrer nächsten Projekte entwickelte, das sie Kirchenbesuchern widmete (Tafel S. 107).

Judith Joy Ross entschied sich für eine der zahlreichen Kirchen in der Region und photographierte die Menschen nach dem Besuch der Messe. Da sie selbst nicht besonders religiös ist, bestand ihr Interesse in erster Linie darin, mit den Menschen in Kontakt zu kommen. Sie traf hier viele Eltern mit ihren Kindern, ein familiäres Miteinander an, das ihr im alltäglichen Straßenbild nicht so sehr aufgefallen war (Tafel S. 91). Bei Betrachtung der Bilder stellt sich zudem die Frage, ob sich auf den Gesichtern möglicherweise eine besonders beseelte oder befreite Stimmung abzeichnet, oder ob hier eher eigene Projektionen hineinspielen, denen man beim Anschauen von Bildern ohnehin kaum entkommen kann.

Ein weiteres gesellschaftliches Ereignis, das die Amerikaner generationenübergreifend fasziniert, ist Baseball. Die Popularität dieses Mannschaftsspiels ist so groß, dass der Sportsoziologe Peter Dewald gar von einem „Nationalsport mit religiöser Bedeutung" spricht.[33] Judith Joy Ross nahm zwischen 1989 und 1991 einige Portraits von Baseballspielern auf, denen sie zufällig an verschiedenen Orten Pennsylvanias begegnet war (Tafeln S. 75–77). In den Aufnahmen drückt sich Freude am Spiel und an der körperlichen Bewegung aus. Eines der Bilder zeigt einen Mann, der, den Baseballschläger über der Schulter, hochkonzentriert vor der Kamera posiert, als würde

produced were portraits of children who live in a poor neighborhood, for the most part in foster families. Their journey through life seems predestined and their prospects poor for a future in better circumstances. They are still too young to consciously reflect on their situation. A descriptive, almost fatalistic example is the photograph of a boy who simulates an accident with his pedal car. At first glance, it is difficult to assess the situation, but his grin bespeaks the childish game of pretending aggression and pain. He seems to enjoy the shock he may have caused and the attention he received the moment his picture was being taken was a small triumph (plate p. 108). Besides children and youths, Ross also took photographs of elderly citizens of Freeland, from which one of her subsequent projects developed that she devoted to churchgoers (plate p. 107).

Ross decided in favor of one of the numerous churches in the region and took photographs of people after they had attended church service. As she is not particularly religious, her main interest was just to get in contact with these people. She encountered many sets of parents with their children, a family life, which was not so much in evidence in everyday street scenes (plate p. 91). Looking at the resulting portraits, the question occurs of whether an especially inspired or liberated atmosphere is reflected in their faces after church, or whether it is more one's own projection which might play a role—this can hardly be escaped when viewing pictures.

Another social event that fascinates entire generations of Americans is baseball. The popularity of this team game is so great that the sports sociologist Peter Dewald even speaks of a "national sport with religious significance."[33] Between 1989 and 1991, Judith Joy Ross produced portraits of baseball players she chanced upon in different places in Pennsylvania (plates pp. 75–77). The pictures exude a sense of delight in the game and in physical activity. One can interpret the picture of a man with a baseball bat on his shoulder—highly concentrated as he poses in front of the camera, as if the victory of his team depended solely on the decisive swing.

Besides religion and sports, work or the workplace is a fundamental social constant: a recipe for one's standard of

der Sieg seiner Mannschaft einzig von seinem entscheidenden Schlag abhängen.

Neben Religion und Sport ist die Arbeit beziehungsweise der Arbeitsplatz eine fundamentale gesellschaftliche Konstante: Garant des Lebensstandards, identitätsstiftend und zur Verantwortung auffordernd. So stehen Beruf und Berufung im Zentrum der von Judith Joy Ross 1990 erarbeiteten Serie *Jobs*, die sie vor allem auch deshalb begann, um eine engere Beziehung zu ihrem Wohnort zu bekommen. Zu sehen sind Portraits von Menschen in unterschiedlichen Berufen und Jobs – etwa ein Polizist, ein Koch oder ein Autovertreter (Tafeln S. 69–73), denen die Photographin in ihrer Nachbarschaft, bei der Erledigung alltäglicher Aufgaben begegnet war. Unmittelbar stellen sich hier Assoziationen zum Werk von August Sander ein, der für seine Darstellungen verschiedener gesellschaftlicher Schichten und Berufe berühmt ist.[34]

Von einigen Personen, die sie im Zusammenhang mit der Werkreihe *Jobs* photographierte, erfuhr Judith Joy Ross, dass sie als Reservisten der Armee dienten, was ihnen auch in Friedenszeiten ein regelmäßiges Einkommen sicherte. Als sie die Armory in Bethlehem besuchte, um dort weitere Reservisten aufzunehmen, realisierte sie plötzlich, dass Alarmstufe Rot herrschte und sich die Einheit für den Krieg rüstete. Irakische Streitkräfte waren in Kuwait einmarschiert, was ab Januar 1991 Luft- und Bodenangriffe insbesondere der US-Armee nach sich zog.[35] Judith Joy Ross bewegten diese Ereignisse. Sozusagen am Vorabend des Krieges portraitierte sie zumeist jüngere Männer und Frauen, die von heute auf morgen damit konfrontiert waren, zu den Waffen greifen zu müssen (Tafeln S. 79–81). Ihre zivile Kleidung hatten sie kurz vor der Aufnahme gegen Uniformen getauscht – ein symbolischer Akt, der einen neuen Lebensabschnitt markierte, in dem der Arbeitsplatz, die Familie und Freundschaften zurückgestellt werden mussten und eine unberechenbare Zukunft begann.

Anfang der 90er Jahre fand das photographische Werk von Judith Joy Ross seinen Weg nach Europa. Eine erste Station bildete 1993/94 die Gruppenausstellung *Photographs from the Real World*, die im Rahmen des kulturellen Programms

life, crucial for the creation of a sense of identity, and something that requires people to take on responsibility. Thus, career and calling are the focus of *Jobs*, a series Judith Joy Ross began in 1990, because she was seeking to create for herself a stronger sense of the community in which she lived. It features portraits of people in different professions or jobs—such as a police officer, a cook, or a car salesman (plates pp. 69–73) whom the photographer encountered in her neighborhood as they attended to everyday tasks. In this case, one immediately makes associations with August Sander's work, famous for the depiction of different social classes, professions, and trades.[34]

Within the context of the *Jobs* series, Judith Joy Ross had photographed people who served as army reservists, which in times of peace is a part-time job that guarantees a supplemental income. She had casually returned to the local armory to continue photographing and to her dismay discovered the unit was on Red Alert, mobilizing for war. Iraqi forces had invaded Kuwait, which would result in aerial and ground assaults, in particular by the U.S. Army, beginning in January 1991.[35] It was in this situation, so to speak on the eve of war, that Ross portrayed for the most part young men and women in the armory who were suddenly confronted with having to take up arms (plates pp. 79–81). Just prior to having their pictures taken, they had exchanged their civilian clothing for uniforms—a symbolic act that marked a new chapter in their lives in which the workplace, the family, and friendships had to be put aside, and the beginning of an unpredictable future.

In the early 1990s, Judith Joy Ross's photography found its way to Europe. A first milestone was set by the group exhibition *Photographs from the Real World*, which took place within the scope of the cultural platform of the 17th Winter Olympic Games in Lillehammer, Norway. The photographer Dag Alveng presented sixteen international photographers, for each of whom he invited an author to write a contribution to the accompanying catalogue. The esteemed photographer Robert Adams wrote about Judith Joy Ross.[36] The exhibition included several of the pictures of children and youths she had taken

der XVII. Olympischen Winterspiele in Lillehammer/Norwegen stattfand. Der Photograph Dag Alveng stellte 16 internationale Positionen vor und lud zu jeder einen Autor ein, einen Text für den begleitenden Katalog zu verfassen. Über Judith Joy Ross schrieb der von ihr sehr geschätzte Photograph Robert Adams.[36] In der Ausstellung wurden unter anderem einige der Bilder von Kindern und Jugendlichen gezeigt, die sie zwischen 1992 und 1994 an verschiedenen Schulen in Hazleton und Cleveland aufgenommen hatte. Die Reihe *Portraits of the Hazleton Public Schools* konnte sie mit Hilfe des Charles Pratt Memorial Award 1992 realisieren, eine großzügige Förderung, die es ihr erlaubte, die Serie über öffentliche Erziehung anzufertigen (Tafeln S. 93–101). Die Arbeit nahm drei Jahre in Anspruch und wurde im letzten Jahr durch ein Stipendium vom *Double Take Magazine* unterstützt. Mit dem Thema Schule verweist Judith Joy Ross auf die zentrale Bedeutung von Bildung. Gleichzeitig setzt sie sich erneut mit ihren eigenen Kindheitserinnerungen und ihren Erfahrungen als Schülerin in Hazleton auseinander. Dazu wählte sie Schulen aus, die sie selbst, ihre Brüder und schon ihre Mutter besucht hatten. „Ich will nicht, dass die Bilder im dokumentarischen Sinn Schule erklären. Ich möchte den Betrachter auf eine emotionale Reise schicken, die ihn in die eigene Kindheit zurückführt"[37], lautet das persönliche Credo der Künstlerin. Wie in einer Zeitmaschine begibt sich der Betrachter auf eine Reise in seine eigene Geschichte.

Die Aufnahmen, die Judith Joy Ross in Schulen in Cleveland erarbeitete, sind im Auftrag der George Gund Foundation entstanden und waren für deren Jahresbericht vorgesehen (Tafeln S. 103–105). Im Vergleich zu ihrer Tätigkeit an den Schulen in Hazleton war sie mit der Schulsituation an diesem Ort weniger vertraut. Dies führte dazu, dass sie sich in ihren Bildern mehr auf die Persönlichkeit und Präsenz der einzelnen Schüler konzentrierte, während die Umgebung, die Klassenzimmer oder situativen Momente eher zurückstehen. Die Schulen, an denen sie photographierte, zeichneten sich durch eine besonders gemischte Schülerschaft aus, die Kinder und Jugendlichen kamen aus vielen verschiedenen Nationen

between 1992 and 1994 in various schools in Hazleton and Cleveland. The series *Portraits of the Hazleton Public Schools* was made possible with the aid of the Charles Pratt Memorial Award she received in 1992. It was a major grant allowing Ross to devote herself to photographing a series about public education (plates pp. 93–101). This work took three years to complete, and in the last year was supported by a grant from *Double Take Magazine*. By choosing the school theme, Judith Joy Ross highlights the pivotal significance of education. At the same time, she again grapples with her own childhood memories and her experiences as a schoolgirl in Hazleton. For this purpose, she chose schools that she, her brothers, and even her mother had attended. The artist's personal credo: "I don't want the pictures to explain school in some documentary sense. [I] want it be an emotional journey. I want the viewer to reconnect with what it is to be a kid."[37] As if in a time machine, viewers embark on a journey into their own biographies.

The photographs that Judith Joy Ross compiled in schools in Cleveland were done as a commission to create an annual report for the George Gund Foundation (plates pp. 103–105). Compared to her work in the schools in Hazleton, she was not so familiar with those of the city of Cleveland. This motivated her to focus more on the personality and presence of the individual students than on their surroundings, the classrooms, or situative moments. The schools in which she photographed were chosen for their exceptionally varied body of students, with children from many different countries in the same class. Ross was granted permission by the school authorities, worked together with an assistant, and all the shooting was done in two weeks. She states, "For me, Cleveland was the easiest of all projects, Hazleton was the most challenging."[38] Far beyond the fact that Ross enables us to gain insight into the lives of these young people, it is apparent that despite similar external conditions, the ideal of equality can apparently hardly be carried through in the light of an increasingly limited education system.

The series *2046* from 1996 is also based on questions about the future (plates pp. 111–115). Judith Joy Ross took the

zusammen. Ross photographierte mit offizieller Erlaubnis, arbeitete gemeinsam mit einem Assistenten, und alle Aufnahmen wurden innerhalb von zwei Wochen realisiert. „Cleveland war für mich das einfachste aller Projekte, Hazleton war die größte Herausforderung"[38], so die Künstlerin. Über die primäre Tatsache hinaus, dass Ross mit ihren natürlichen Portraits mittelbar die Begegnung mit diesen jungen Menschen ermöglicht, wird erkennbar, dass sich an den Schulen trotz vergleichbarer äußerer Bedingungen das Ideal der Gleichberechtigung, noch dazu vor dem Hintergrund eines immer weiter limitierten Bildungswesens, offenbar kaum durchsetzen lässt.

Die Frage nach der Zukunft liegt auch der Serie *2046* von 1996 zugrunde (Tafeln S. 111–115). Judith Joy Ross nahm ihren 50. Geburtstag zum Anlass eines imaginären Ausblicks. Die Reihe umfasst neben Bildern von Kindern und Jugendlichen auch Portraits von Erwachsenen und lädt zu Visionen und Spekulationen über individuelle wie allgemeine Perspektiven ein.

1997 entstand erneut eine Serie in ihrem Wohnort Bethlehem. Zu dieser Zeit – und auch heute noch – zählte Judith Joy Ross häufig zu den Besuchern der öffentlichen Bibliothek (Tafeln S. 83–85). Für sie stellte sich die städtische Einrichtung als besonderer Ort dar, als privater Raum innerhalb eines öffentlichen Raums, der die Menschen in ruhiger Atmosphäre zum Beobachten, Studieren und Reflektieren einlädt und in dem viel „zwischen den Zeilen" geschieht. Und so fesselten nicht zuletzt die Besucher, Angestellten und Kinder die Aufmerksamkeit der Photographin. Eine Auswahl der Bilder wurde im Jahr 2000 zusammen mit Aufnahmen von Adam Bartos in einem Bildbericht über öffentliche Bibliotheken im amerikanischen Magazin für Literatur und Photographie *Double Take* publiziert.[39]

Die Bethlehem Public Library ist einige Jahre später erneut Ausgangspunkt einer photographischen Serie. Auf dem Gelände des Gebäudes wurde 2006 die von Quäkern organisierte Ausstellung *Eyes Wide Open* eröffnet, die zwischen 2004 und 2007 durch Amerika tourte. Gezeigt wurden Stiefel von amerikanischen Soldaten, die im Irak und in Afghanistan gefallen waren.[40] Ross war von den Gesichtern der Menschen, die die

occasion of her fiftieth birthday to produce an imaginary outlook. Besides pictures of children and youths, the series also includes portraits of adults and calls on one to visualize and speculate about one's personal prospects as well as perspectives in general.

In 1997 the artist focused on another place in Bethlehem. Then, as now, she often visited the public library. What attracted her was that the library can be seen as a very private space within a public one, a quiet place that inspires people to observe, to study, to reflect, and where a lot of things happen "between the lines" (plates pp. 83–85). The people there—visitors, employees, and children—drew her attention as a photographer. In 2000, a selection of the pictures was published alongside photographs by Adam Bartos in a photo reportage on public libraries in *Double Take,* an American magazine for literature and photography.[39]

Several years later, the Bethlehem Public Library again served as the point of departure for a photographic series. In 2006, the Quaker traveling exhibition *Eyes Wide Open,* which toured through America between 2004 and 2007, opened on the premises of the building. It presented boots that had been worn by American soldiers who had been killed in action in Iraq and Afghanistan.[40] Ross was struck by the faces of the people who were viewing the exhibition. *Eyes Wide Open* provided a public space for people to contemplate the war. This gave rise to the portrait series *Protest the War,* which until 2006 would take her to other cities where *Eyes Wide Open* was exhibited and to demonstrations and marches against the war. In this case as well, Ross concentrated on the individual and not on a protest by the masses. The portraits are imbued with great seriousness; the protesters' faces evince a lack of understanding of and resistance against the political decision in favor of war, as well as anxiety about the future and grief over the dead—understandable human feelings that underscore the dimension of the protest (plates pp. 129–131). In 2009, the art critic Kenneth Baker wrote the following in his review of the group exhibition *Face of Our Time*[41] at the San Francisco Museum of Modern Art, for which the curator Sandra

Ausstellung besuchten, zutiefst beeindruckt. *Eyes Wide Open* bot ein öffentliches Forum, des Krieges und seiner Folgen zu gedenken. So begann sie die Portraitserie *Protest the War*, die sie bis 2006 zu weiteren Stationen von *Eyes Wide Open* führen sollte ebenso wie zu damit einhergehenden Anti-Kriegs-Demonstrationen im Land. Die Photographin konzentriert sich auch hier auf den einzelnen Menschen und nicht auf einen Protest der Masse. Die Portraits sind von großer Ernsthaftigkeit erfüllt, aus den Gesichtern der Demonstranten sprechen Unverständnis und Widerstand gegen die politische Entscheidung für den Krieg, auch Angst vor der Zukunft und Trauer um die Toten – nachvollziehbare menschliche Gefühle, die die Dimension des Protests unterstreichen (Tafeln S. 129–131). Der Kunstkritiker Kenneth Baker schreibt 2009 in seiner Rezension der Gruppenausstellung *Face of Our Time*[41] im San Francisco Museum of Modern Art, für die die Kuratorin Sandra S. Phillips eine Auswahl aus den *Protestors* getroffen hat: „Judith Joy Ross' stille Portraits der Anti-Kriegs-Demonstranten konfrontieren uns mit Individuen, deren Gesichtsausdruck uns vermittelt, dass wir uns – ungeachtet ihrer Biographien – privilegiert fühlen können, sie zu kennen."[42] Ross hatte die Aufnahmen dem *New York Times Sunday Magazine* zur Veröffentlichung angeboten, um die Anti-Kriegs-Haltung der amerikanischen Bürger verstärkt vor Augen zu führen, hatte damit jedoch keinen Erfolg. Waren ihre Bilder zu direkt und persönlich? Das Thema zu unbequem? Heute stellt sie sich die Frage, ob die Serie nicht zu stark von ihrer eigenen Protesthaltung beeinflusst ist, Ausdruck ihres persönlichen Feldzugs gegen den Krieg, wenn auch gerade darin eine Motivation für sie lag. Grundsätzlich erscheint es ihr inzwischen angemessener, eine distanziertere Haltung einzunehmen, die eine möglichst freie Lesart der Bilder erlaubt. Insofern ist es verständlich, wenn Judith Joy Ross in ihren jüngsten Arbeiten, in denen sie sich mit dem Verhältnis des Menschen zur Natur und zum Tier befasst, größeren Abstand zu den Motiven wahrt. Auch hier hinterfragt sie Wechselwirkungen und Anpassungsprozesse (Tafel S. 133).

In den drei Jahrzehnten ihres photographischen Schaffens ist das Œuvre von Judith Joy Ross in über 20 Einzel- und

S. Phillips had made a selection from *Protest the War:* "Judith Joy Ross' quiet portraits of anti-war protestors put before us individuals of whose mien makes us imagine we might feel privileged to know them, whatever the facts of their lives."[42] Ross had offered the pictures to the *New York Times, Sunday Magazine* in order to draw more attention to the stand against the war by the American people, yet the newspaper declined. Were the photographs too direct and personal? Was the subject too uncomfortable? Today, this begs the question of whether the series is not too strongly influenced by the artist's own rebellious stance, an expression of her personal crusade against the war, even though it was precisely this that motivated her to produce the series. In principle it seems to be more reasonable for her to take up a more impersonal stance, one that preferably allows an open interpretation of the pictures. In this respect it is understandable that in her most recent works, which deal with the human being's relationship to nature and to animals, Judith Joy Ross maintains greater distance to her motifs. Here, too, she scrutinizes interdependencies and processes of adaptation (plate p. 133).

In the three decades of her photographic activity, Judith Joy Ross's oeuvre has been recognized in more than twenty solo and in excess of sixty group exhibitions. It is predominately received in the United States, followed by Germany and the Benelux countries. The last extensive solo exhibition was mounted in 2009 at the Davison Art Center, Wesleyan University, in Middleton, Connecticut, and featured over fifty photographs. The number of group exhibitions to include works by Ross has been on the increase since about 2000. In Europe, the radius encompasses cities such as Lisbon, Vienna, Lausanne, and London.[43] As different as the concepts of the group exhibitions are, the portraits they present consistently attract attention due to their sovereignty and their very individual, enchanting aura, which alternates between document, individual portrait, and snapshot in time.

Judith Joy Ross's work proves to be an important chapter in portrait photography. Each of the series heterogeneously addresses major historical or political issues of the time, social

mehr als 60 Gruppenausstellungen gewürdigt worden. Der Schwerpunkt der Rezeption liegt auf den Vereinigten Staaten, gefolgt von Deutschland und den Beneluxländern. Die letzte Einzelausstellung größeren Umfangs fand 2009 mit über 50 Photographien im Davison Art Center, Wesleyan University in Middleton, Connecticut, statt. Seit etwa dem Jahr 2000 nimmt die Zahl der Gruppenausstellungen, in die Werke von Judith Joy Ross einbezogen sind, mehr und mehr zu. Der Radius umfasst in Europa Städte wie Lissabon, Wien, Lausanne und London.[43] Wie unterschiedlich die Gruppenausstellungen auch konzipiert sind, ihre Bildnisse fallen immer wieder durch ihre Souveränität und ganz eigene Aura auf, die zwischen Dokument, Individualportrait und Momentaufnahme changiert.

Judith Joy Ross' Schaffen erweist sich als ein bedeutendes Kapitel photographischer Portraitarbeit. Jede der Bildreihen spricht facettenreich und themenübergreifend wichtige historische oder politische Zeitfragen, gesellschaftliche Wertesysteme und existentielle Prozesse an, die sie mit Blick auf den einzelnen Menschen und seinen Lebensweg zur Debatte stellt. Im Fokus stehen dabei weder die Privilegierten noch diejenigen, die sich am unteren Ende der gesellschaftlichen Skala befinden. Durchgängig ist Ross am Leben all jener Menschen gelegen, die die sogenannte breite Bürgerschaft bilden und ihren Alltag fern des „amerikanischen Traums" bewältigen, also all jene, denen die Medien gemeinhin wenig Aufmerksamkeit schenken – zu „normal" verläuft ihr Leben, zu wenig Spektakuläres gibt es zu berichten. Deutlich wird Ross' Gespür für natürliche Posen und im Profanen gefundene Schönheit ebenso wie ihre Faszination an feinen Nuancen und Details, sei es ein Augenaufschlag oder das Pflaster auf dem Knie eines Kindes. Schließlich tragen auch die unterschiedlichen Farbtöne ihrer Abzüge zur abgestimmten Atmosphäre und Gesamtwirkung bei. Wenn Judith Joy Ross für ihre Bilder in Anlehnung an Julia Margaret Cameron das Kriterium „Taken from Life"[44] [Aus dem Leben gegriffen] anführt, so zeigt sich darin nicht allein ihr geerdeter Realitätsbezug, sondern auch der Anspruch eines künstlerischen Transfers und eine Nobilitierung erlebter Wirklichkeit.

value systems, and existential processes. She puts up for consideration these various themes with an eye toward the individual and his or her journey through life. The focus is placed neither on the wealthy nor on the other end of the social scale. She is undeviatingly interested in the lives of all those people who make up the so-called broad middle classes and master their everyday lives at a distance from the "American dream"—all of those to whom the media generally pay little attention because their lives are too "normal" and supply nothing spectacular to report about. What becomes manifest is Judith Joy Ross's feeling for natural poses and the beauty she discovers in the ordinary, as well as her fascination for fine nuances and details, be it a glance or the band-aid on a child's knee. Finally, the various tones of her prints also contribute to the harmonized atmosphere and overall effect. When, for her photographs, Judith Joy Ross alludes to Julia Margaret Cameron, citing Cameron's inscription for her own photographs "Taken from Life,"[44] this is not only an indication of her relationship to reality but also demonstrates her ambition of achieving an artistic transfer and an ennoblement of experienced reality.

Anmerkungen

[1] Vgl. Julian Cox: „frequently inscribed on the mounts of her prints variants of the phrases ‚from life, registered photograph, copyright' and titled each work in her flowing script", in: *Julia Margaret Cameron*, Photographs from the J. Paul Getty Museum, Los Angeles, 1996, S. 8, [In Focus].
[2] Judith Joy Ross: *Portraits of the Hazleton Public Schools,* Text: Jock Reynolds, New Haven: Yale University Press, 2006, S. 84.
[3] Judith Joy Ross im Gespräch mit den Autorinnen, Bethlehem, Pennsylvania, Juni 2010.
[4] *Judith Joy Ross*, The Museum of Modern Art, New York, Essay: Susan Kismaric, New York: Harry N. Abrams, Inc., 1995 [Contemporaries: A Photography Series].
[5] August Sanders erste Publikation trug den Titel *Antlitz der Zeit* und wurde oft mit dem Terminus „Spiegel" assoziiert, beispielsweise von Otto Mente, der darüber hinaus eine Wirkungsweise von Sanders Portraits anspricht, die weitaus später und im anderen kulturellen Kontext auch für Judith Joy Ross in Anspruch genommen werden kann: „Er [August Sander] hält seiner Zeit den Spiegel vor und sagt mit den Mitteln seiner Kunst ganz schlicht: So bist du Mensch! Das klingt je nach dem Ohr, zu dem diese Worte dringen, je nach dem Auge, das in die Offenbarungen dieser Aufnahmen blickt, nach Gesellschafts- und Zeitkritik, oder vermittelt den bitteren Geschmack der Enttäuschung, ist aber immer eine unverkennbare Anleitung zur Selbsterkenntnis." Otto Mente: „Neue Aufgaben für die Photographie", in: *Das Atelier des Photographen und Deutsche Photographische Kunst*, Halle/Saale, 35. Jahrg., 1928, Heft 2, Sonderdruck, S. 23–24.
[6] N.N.: „Menschen des 20. Jahrhunderts. Eine Lichtbildausstellung in Köln", in: *Rheinische Tageszeitung,* Köln, Ausgabe Nr. 329, 29. November 1927.
[7] „Dokumentarisch? Das ist ein sehr komplexer und irreführender Begriff. Und er ist nicht wirklich klar. [...] Der richtige Ausdruck wäre *dokumentarischer Stil*. Das Polizeifoto vom Tatort eines Mordes ist ein echtes Dokument. Dokumente dienen einem Zweck, die Kunst dagegen ist zweckfrei. Daher ist die Kunst nie Dokument, aber sie kann natürlich den Stil übernehmen." Leslie Katz: „An Interview with Walker Evans (1971)", in: *Photography in Print*, Hrsg.: Vicki Goldberg, Albuquerque: University of New Mexico Press, 1981, S. 364, zitiert nach: *New Topographics, Texte und Rezeption,* Hrsg.: Landesgalerie Linz am Oberösterreichischen Landesmuseum, Die Photographische Sammlung/SK Stiftung Kultur, Köln, Salzburg: Fotohof edition, 2011, S. 21.
[8] Vgl. *Walker Evans. Photographs for the Farm Security Administration 1935–1938*, Library of Congress, New York: Da Capo Press, 1973, Catalog of Photographs, S. 52–67.
[9] Vgl. *Lewis Hine. Die Kamera als Zeuge. Fotografien 1905–1937*, Hrsg.: Karl Steinorth, Kilchberg/Zürich: Edition Stemmle, 1996; Vicki Goldberg: *Lewis W. Hine. Children at Work*, München, London, New York: Prestel, 1999.
[10] *Life's Picture History of Western Man*, Hrsg.: Henry R. Luce, New York: Time Inc., 1951.
[11] Judith Joy Ross im Gespräch mit den Autorinnen, Bethlehem, Pennsylvania, Juni 2010.
[12] Vgl. *Calendar of Events*, Allentown Art Museum, Januar/Februar 1985. 1997 zeigte das Allentown Art Museum die erste Retrospektive von Judith Joy Ross.
[13] Der noch heute genutzte Park wurde urspünglich von dem Stahlmagnaten Charles M. Schwab und seiner Ehefrau Eurana gestiftet. Charles Schwab (1862–1939) war Teilhaber des Hüttenwerks Bethlehem Steel, Pennsylvania, auf ihn gehen weitere Stiftungen wie eine Schule in Weatherly zurück. Seine Bedeutung für die Stadt Bethlehem vgl. http://www.bethlehempaonline.com/schwab_bio.html (Stand April 2011).
[14] Eine Art Gelatinesilberpapier, das hier ähnlich wie Albuminpapier funktioniert und von Kodak bis in die 80er Jahre und von Chicago Albumen Works bis 2009 hergestellt wurde.
[15] Judith Joy Ross in einer E-Mail an die Autorinnen, Juni 2011.
[16] Andy Grundberg: „Photography View; the modern focuses in contemporary visions", in: *The New York Times*, 15. September 1985.

Notes

[1] Cf. Julian Cox, "frequently inscribed on the mounts of her prints variants of the phrases 'from life, registered photograph, copyright' and titled each work in her flowing script." In *Julia Margaret Cameron, Photographs from the J. Paul Getty Museum* (Los Angeles: J. Paul Getty Museum, 1996), p. 8 [In Focus].
[2] Judith Joy Ross, *Portraits of the Hazleton Public Schools,* text by Jock Reynolds (New Haven: Yale University Press, 2006), p. 84.
[3] Judith Joy Ross in conversation with the authors in Bethlehem, Pennsylvania, June 2010.
[4] *Judith Joy Ross,* The Museum of Modern Art, New York, essay by Susan Kismaric (New York: Harry N. Abrams, Inc., 1995) [Contemporaries: A Photography Series].
[5] August Sander's first publication bore the title *Antlitz der Zeit* (Face of Our Time) and was often associated with the term "mirror", for example by Otto Mente, who beyond this addresses an effect produced by Sander's portraits that can also be applied to Judith Joy Ross, albeit far later and in a different cultural context: "He [August Sander] held up a mirror to his time and, using the means of his art, very simply says: This is you! Depending on the ear in which these words resound, depending on the eye that gazes into the revelations of these photographs, this sounds like a criticism of society and the time, or it communicates the bitter taste of disappointment, yet it is always an unmistakable guide to self-awareness." Translated from Otto Mente, "Neue Aufgaben für die Photographie," in *Das Atelier des Photographen und Deutsche Photographische Kunst,* 35th ed., vol. 2, (Halle/Saale, 1928), pp. 23–24.
[6] Author unknown: "Menschen des 20. Jahrhunderts: Eine Lichtbildausstellung in Köln," *Rheinische Tageszeitung,* Cologne, no. 329, November 29, 1927.
[7] "Documentary? That's a very sophisticated and misleading word. And not really clear. . . . The term should be 'documentary style.' An example of a literal document would be a police photograph of a murder scene. You see, a document has a use, whereas art is really useless. Therefore art is never a document, though it certainly can adopt that style." Leslie Katz, "An Interview with Walker Evans" (1971), in *Photography in Print,* ed. Vicki Goldberg (Albuquerque: University of New Mexico Press, 1981), p. 364. Cited in *New Topographics,* ed. Center for Creative Photography, Tucson, in cooperation with George Eastman House, Rochester (Göttingen: Steidl, 2009), p. 16.
[8] Cf. *Walker Evans: Photographs for the Farm Security Administration 1935–1938,* ed. Library of Congress (New York: Da Capo Press, 1973), catalog of photographs 52–67.
[9] Cf. *Lewis Hine: Die Kamera als Zeuge; Fotografien 1905–1937,* ed. Karl Steinorth (Kilchberg and Zurich: Edition Stemmle, 1996); Vicki Goldberg, *Lewis W. Hine: Children at Work* (Munich et al.: Prestel, 1999).
[10] *Life's Picture History of Western Man,* ed. Henry R. Luce (New York: Time Inc., 1951)
[11] Judith Joy Ross in conversation with the authors in Bethlehem, Pennsylvania, June 2010.
[12] Cf. *Calendar of Events,* Allentown Art Museum, January/February 1985. In 1997, the Allentown Art Museum presented the first retrospective of photographs by Judith Joy Ross.
[13] The park, which is still used today, can be traced back to a work of charity by the steel magnate Charles M. Schwab and his wife, Eurana. Charles Schwab (1862–1939) ran Bethlehem Steel in Pennsylvania; further foundations as well as a school in Weatherly can also be traced back to him. For his importance for the city of Bethlehem, cf. http://www.bethlehempaonline.com/schwab_bio.html (status: April 2011).
[14] This is a gelatin silver paper that works much as an albumen paper and was manufactured by Kodak until the 1980s and by Chicago Albumen Works 2009.
[15] Judith Joy Ross via mail to the authors, June 2011.
[16] "Photography View; the modern focuses in contemporary visions," *The New York Times,* September 15, 1985.
[17] The memorial was dedicated in 1982, seven years after the official end of the Viet-

[17] Das Denkmal wurde 1982, sieben Jahre nach dem offiziellen Ende des Vietnamkrieges eingeweiht. „Der Entwurf dazu stammte von der Yale-Studentin Maya Lin. Er sah zwei in den Boden eingelassene Wände von je 76 m Länge aus poliertem schwarzen Granit vor, die ansteigend keilförmig aufeinander zulaufen. Auf den Granitplatten sollten alle 57.939 Namen der im Krieg gefallenen oder vermissten Soldaten eingraviert werden", aus: Agnes Matthias: *Die Kunst, den Krieg zu fotografieren. Krieg in der künstlerischen Fotografie der Gegenwart*, Marburg: Jonas Verlag, 2005, S. 215. „[...] jeder einzelne von ihnen namentlich und chronologisch nach seinem Sterbedatum aufgeführt, ohne dass letzteres jedoch angegeben ist", aus: Agnes Matthias, 2005, S. 217.
[18] Judith Joy Ross im Gespräch mit den Autorinnen, Paris, Dezember 2010.
[19] Judith Joy Ross im Gespräch mit den Autorinnen, Bethlehem, Pennsylvania, Juni 2010.
[20] Vgl. http://www.brown.edu/Research/Understanding_the_Iran_Contra_Affair/index.php (Stand: April 2011).
[21] Realisiert 1987, mit einer zweiten Station 1989 in der Lehigh University Art Galleries in Bethlehem, Pennsylvania.
[22] Michael Barone, Grant Ujifusa: *The Almanac of American Politics 1986*, Washington, D.C.: National Journal Group Inc., 1985.
[23] Robert Raczka: „Judith Joy Ross", in: *New Art Examiner*, Chicago, Bd. 15, Nr. 6, 1988, S. 62.
[24] Wolfram Brunner: *Projekt Politische Kommunikation. Wahlkampf in den USA, V: Finanzierung, Organisation, Planung*, Hrsg.: Konrad-Adenauer-Stiftung, Sankt Augustin, 2002, S. 10.
[25] Judith Joy Ross im Gespräch mit den Autorinnen, Paris, Dezember 2010.
[26] Judith Joy Ross in einer E-Mail an die Autorinnen, Juni 2011.
[27] Vgl. John Szarkowski: *Photography Until Now*, The Museum of Modern Art, New York, Boston, Toronto: Bulfinch Press, Little, Brown and Company, 1989, S. 312.
[28] Vgl. *Rineke Dijkstra. Beach Portraits*, Hrsg.: LaSalle Bank Photography Collection Chicago, Carol Ehlers, James Rondeau, Texte: Carol Ehlers, Thomas C. Heagy, James Rondeau, James N. Wood, New York: D.A.P., 2002.
[29] Vgl. *Thomas Struth. Portraits*, Hrsg.: Stiftung Niedersachsen, Texte: Benjamin H. Buchloh, Norman Bryson, Thomas Weski, München, Paris, London: Schirmer/Mosel, 1997.
[30] Vgl. „Twelve Photographers Look at US", *Philadelphia Museum of Art Bulletin*, Text: Martha Chahroudi, Bd. 83, Nr. 354/355, Frühling 1987, zu Judith Joy Ross siehe S. 24/25.
[31] Andy Grundberg: „Portraits Return in a New Perspective", in: *The New York Times*, 26. Juni 1988, Sektion 2, S. 31; John Gross: „About the Arts: New York; How different are the Famous from the Faces in the Crowd?", in: *The New York Times*, 18. September 1988, S. 2/39.
[32] Vgl. die eher historisch ausgerichtete Homepage www.andrew.cmu.edu/user/ct0u/news.html (Stand: April 2011).
[33] Peter Dewald: „Baseball in den USA: Nationalsport mit religiöser Bedeutung", in: *Sport und Gesellschaft – Sport and Society*, Stuttgart, 2009, Jahrgang 6, Heft 3, S. 234–258.
[34] *August Sander. Menschen des 20. Jahrhunderts. Ein Kulturwerk in Lichtbildern eingeteilt in sieben Gruppen,* bearbeitet und neu zusammengestellt von Susanne Lange, Gabriele Conrath-Scholl und Gerd Sander, Hrsg.: Die Photographische Sammlung/SK Stiftung Kultur, München, Paris, London: Schirmer/Mosel, 2002.
[35] Vgl. *Erfahrungen des Golfkrieges*, Hrsg.: Bruce W. Watson, Düsseldorf: Verlag Karl-Heinz Dissberger, 1991 (Originalausgabe bei Greenhill Books, London, 1991).
[36] Vgl. Robert Adams: „Shared Truths", in: *Photographs from the Real World*, Hrsg.: Dag Alveng, Oslo: De Norske Bokklubbene [The Cultural Program of the XVII Olympic Winter Games at Lillehammer], 1993, S. 52. Der Text wurde ein Jahr später in den Essayband von Robert Adams *Why People photograph*, erschienen bei Aperture, New York, aufgenommen. „Die Photographien sind ein Ausdruck des Mitfühlens, geteilten

nam War. "The design for it stemmed from the Yale student Maya Lin. It envisaged two walls embedded in the ground, each of which was seventy-six meters long and made of polished black granite and which cuneiformly converged upward. All 57,939 names of the soldiers either killed in the war or missing in action were to be inscribed into the granite slabs." Translated from Agnes Matthias, *Die Kunst, den Krieg zu fotografieren: Krieg in der künstlerischen Fotografie der Gegenwart* (Marburg: Jonas Verlag, 2005), p. 215. ". . . each one of their names is listed chronologically according to the date of death, without mention of the latter." In ibid., p. 217.
[18] Judith Joy Ross in conversation with the authors in Paris, December 2010.
[19] Judith Joy Ross in conversation with the authors in Bethlehem, Pennsylvania, June 2010.
[20] Cf. http://www.brown.edu/Research/Understanding_the_Iran_Contra_Affair/index.php (status: April 2011).
[21] Realized in 1987, with a second station in 1989 at the Lehigh University Art Galleries in Bethlehem, Pennsylvania.
[22] Michael Barone and Grant Ujifusa, *The Almanac of American Politics 1986* (Washington, D.C.: National Journal Group Inc., 1985).
[23] Robert Raczka, "Judith Joy Ross," *New Art Examiner* 15, no. 6 (1988), p. 62.
[24] Translated from Wolfram Brunner, *Projekt Politische Kommunikation: Wahlkampf in den USA V; Finanzierung, Organisation, Planung,* ed. Konrad-Adenauer-Stiftung (Sankt Augustin, 2002), p. 10.
[25] Judith Joy Ross in conversation with the authors in Paris, December 2010.
[26] Judith Joy Ross via mail to the authors, June 2011.
[27] Cf. John Szarkowski, *Photography Until Now,* The Museum of Modern Art, New York (Boston and Toronto: Bulfinch Press, Little, Brown and Company, 1989), p. 312.
[28] Cf. *Rineke Dijkstra: Beach Portraits,* ed. LaSalle Bank Photography Collection Chicago, Carol Ehlers, and James Rondeau, texts by Carol Ehlers, Thomas C. Heagy, James Rondeau, and James N. Wood (New York: D.A.P., 2002).
[29] Cf. *Thomas Struth: Portraits,* ed. Stiftung Niedersachsen, texts by Benjamin H. Buchloh, Norman Bryson, and Thomas Weski (Munich et al.: Schirmer/Mosel, 1997).
[30] Cf. "Twelve Photographers Look at US," *Philadelphia Museum of Art Bulletin* 83, nos. 354/355 (Spring 1987), text by Martha Chahroud; on Judith Joy Ross see pp. 24/25.
[31] Andy Grundberg, "Portraits Return in a New Perspective," *The New York Times,* June 26, 1988, section 2, p. 31; John Gross, "About the Arts: New York; How Different Are the Famous from the Faces in the Crowd?" *The New York Times,* September 18, 1988, pp. 2/39.
[32] Cf. the more historically oriented website www.andrew.cmu.edu/user/ct0u/news.html (status: April 2011)
[33] Peter Dewald, "Baseball in den USA: Nationalsport mit religiöser Bedeutung," *Sport und Gesellschaft–Sport and Society*, vol. 6, no. 3 (2009), pp. 234–258.
[34] August Sander, *People of the 20th Century: A Cultural Work of Photographs Divided into Seven Groups,* ed. Die Photographische Sammlung/SK Stiftung Kultur, revised and newly compiled by Susanne Lange, Gabriele Conrath-Scholl, Gerd Sander (Munich, Paris, London: Schirmer/Mosel, 2002).
[35] Cf. Bruce W. Watson et al., *Military Lessons of the Gulf War* (London: Greenhill Books, 1991).
[36] Cf. Robert Adams, "Shared Truths," in *Photographs from the Real World,* ed. Dag Alveng (Oslo: De Norske Bokklubbene, 1993) [The Cultural Program of the XVII Olympic Winter Games at Lillehammer], p. 52. The text was included a year later in the anthology by Robert Adams *Why People Photograph,* published by Aperture in New York. He writes the following about the portraits of children by Judith Joy Ross: "The photographs are a record of compassion, of shared suffering. We observe it in the sympathetic identification that brings Ross to her work, and in the children's tentative smiles, their brave impulse to trust her, to sense themselves in her.", p. 104.

Leids. Wir erkennen dies in der sympathisierenden Identifikation, die Ross zu ihrer Arbeit antreibt, und auch in dem vorsichtigen Lächeln der Kinder, ihrem Mut, der Photographin zu vertrauen, sich selbst in ihr zu erkennen", so Adams über die Kinderportraits von Judith Joy Ross, zitiert nach: Heinz Liesbrock, 2008, S. 7.

[37] Zitiert nach: Jock Reynolds: „Class Notes", in: *Judith Joy Ross. Portraits of the Hazleton Public Schools. Hazleton, Pennsylvania 1992–1994*, Yale University Art Gallery, New Haven & London: Yale University Press, 2006, S. 82.

[38] Judith Joy Ross in einer E-Mail an die Autorinnen, Juni 2011.

[39] N.N.: „Ex Libris. Photographers Adam Bartos and Judith Joy Ross celebrate public libraries / The Bethlehem, Pennsylvania, Public Library by Judith Joy Ross", in: *Double Take*, Boulder, 6:2, Frühling 2000, S. 87–91.

[40] Vgl. http://afsc.org/campaign/eyes-wide-open (Stand: März 2011).

[41] Benannt nach der ersten Publikation von August Sander, *Antlitz der Zeit*, erschienen 1929 im Kurt Wolff/Transmare Verlag, München. Weitere Ausgaben: München: Schirmer/Mosel, 1976, 1990, 2003; französische Ausgabe: München: Schirmer/Mosel, 1990; englische Ausgabe: München: Schirmer/Mosel, 1994, 2003.

[42] Kenneth Baker: „SECA Art Award show, as usual, disappoints", in: *San Francisco Chronicle*, 7. März, S. E–10. In der Ausstellung waren neben Photographien von Judith Joy Ross auch Arbeiten von Yto Barrada, Guy Tillim und Leo Rubinfien zu sehen.

[43] Vgl. Ausstellungsverzeichnis, S. 136ff.

[44] Vgl. Anmerkung 1.

[37] Cited in Jock Reynolds, "Class Notes," in *Judith Joy Ross: Portraits of the Hazleton Public Schools. Hazleton, Pennsylvania 1992–1994*, Yale University Art Gallery (New Haven and London: Yale University Press, 2006), p. 82.

[38] Judith Joy Ross via mail to the authors, June 2011.

[39] N.N., "Ex Libris: Photographers Adam Bartos and Judith Joy Ross celebrate public libraries / The Bethlehem, Pennsylvania, Public Library by Judith Joy Ross," *Double Take* 6, Boulder, no. 2 (Spring 2000), pp. 87–91.

[40] Cf. http://afsc.org/campaign/eyes-wide-open (status: March 2011).

[41] Named after the first publication by August Sander, *Antlitz der Zeit*, published in 1929 by the Kurt Wolff/Transmare Verlag, Munich. Further editions: Munich: Schirmer/Mosel, 1976, 1990, and 2003; French edition: Munich: Schirmer/Mosel, 1990; English edition: Munich: Schirmer/Mosel, 1994 and 2003.

[42] Kenneth Baker, "SECA Art Award Show, as Usual, Disappoints," *San Francisco Chronicle*, March 7, 2009, p. E–10. Besides photographs by Judith Joy Ross, the exhibition also featured works by Yto Barrada, Guy Tillim, and Leo Rubinfien.

[43] Cf. the list of exhibitions, pp. 136–138.

[44] Cf. note 1.

TAFELN | PLATES

Eurana Park, Weatherly, Pennsylvania, 1982

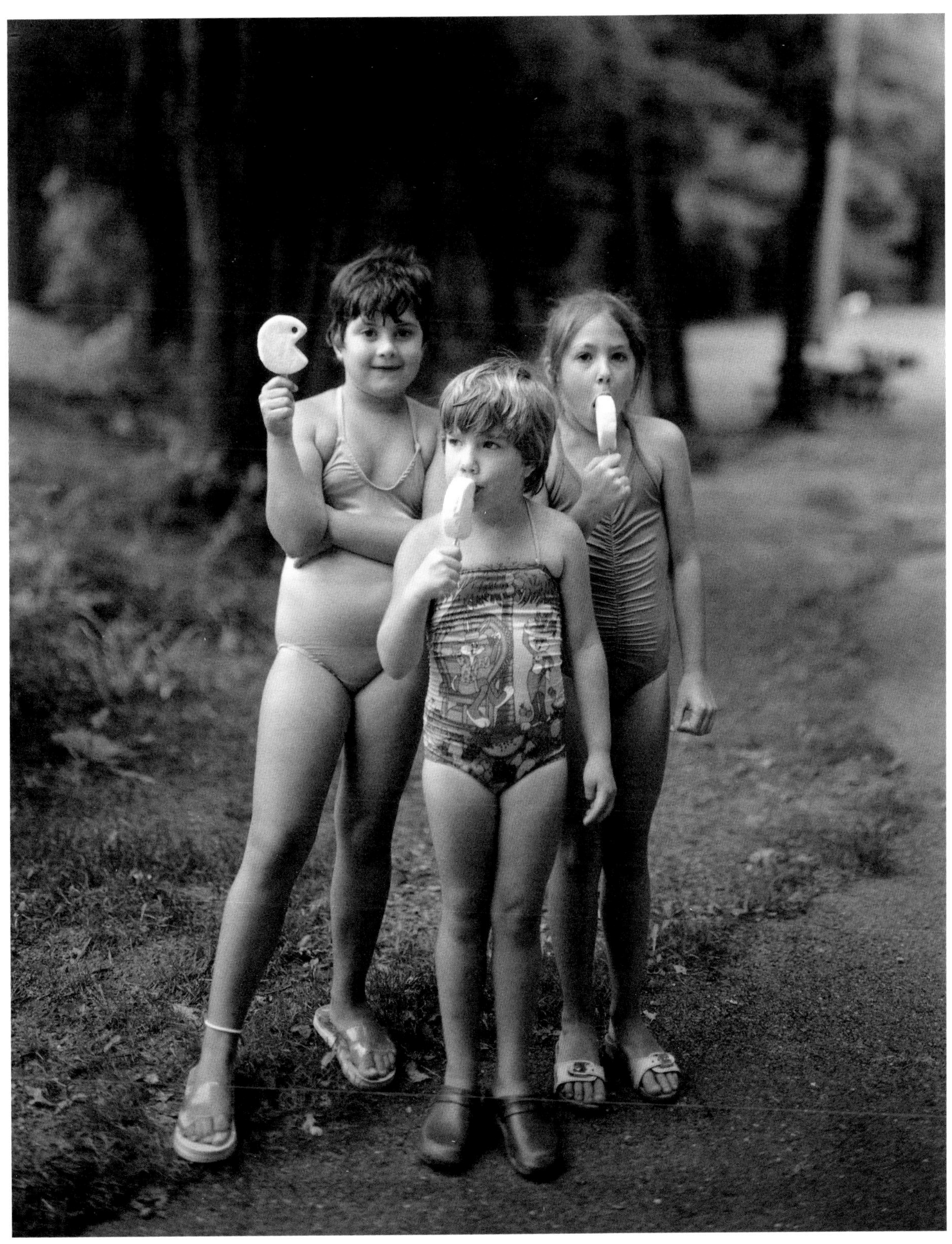

Ohne Titel | Untitled

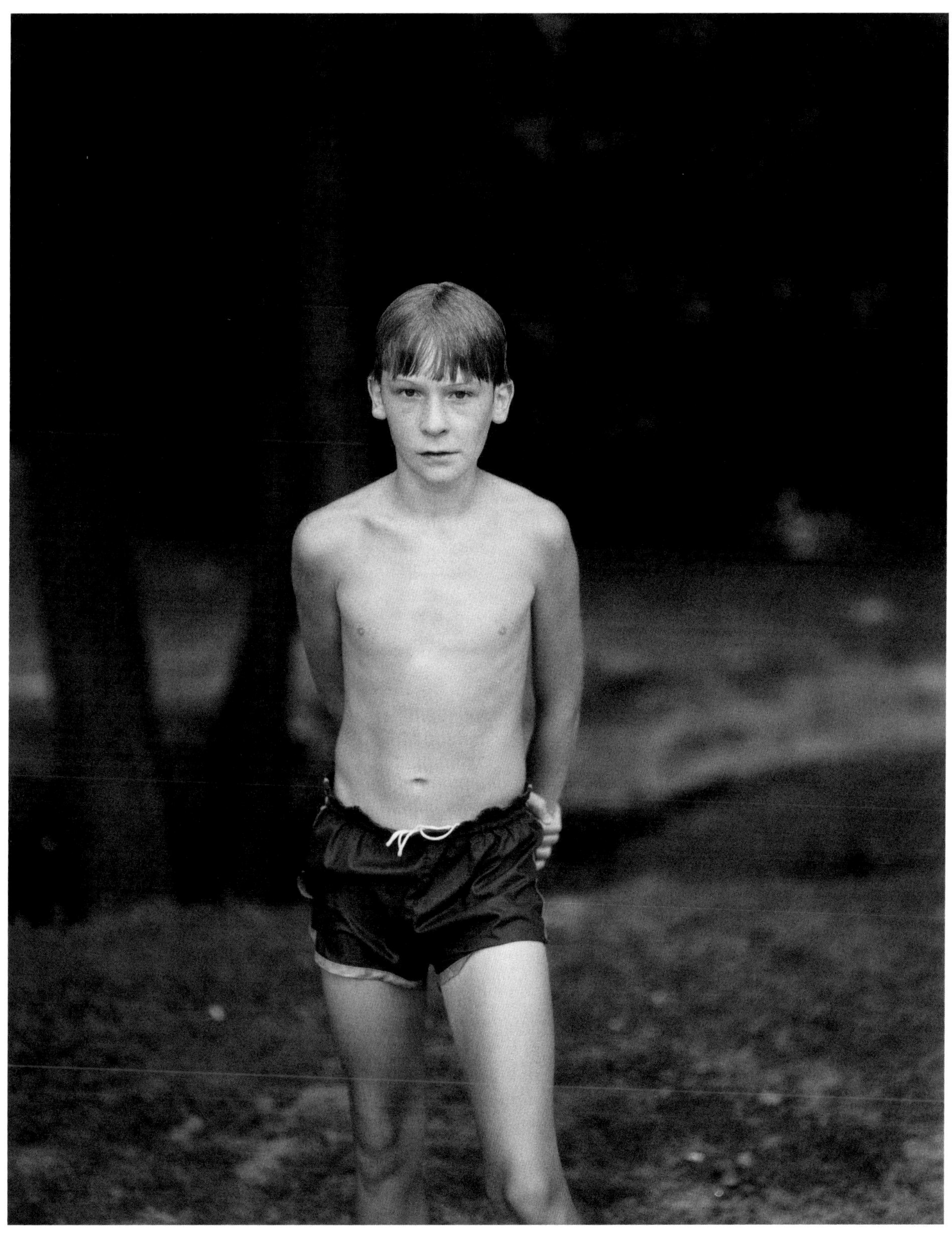

Ohne Titel | Untitled

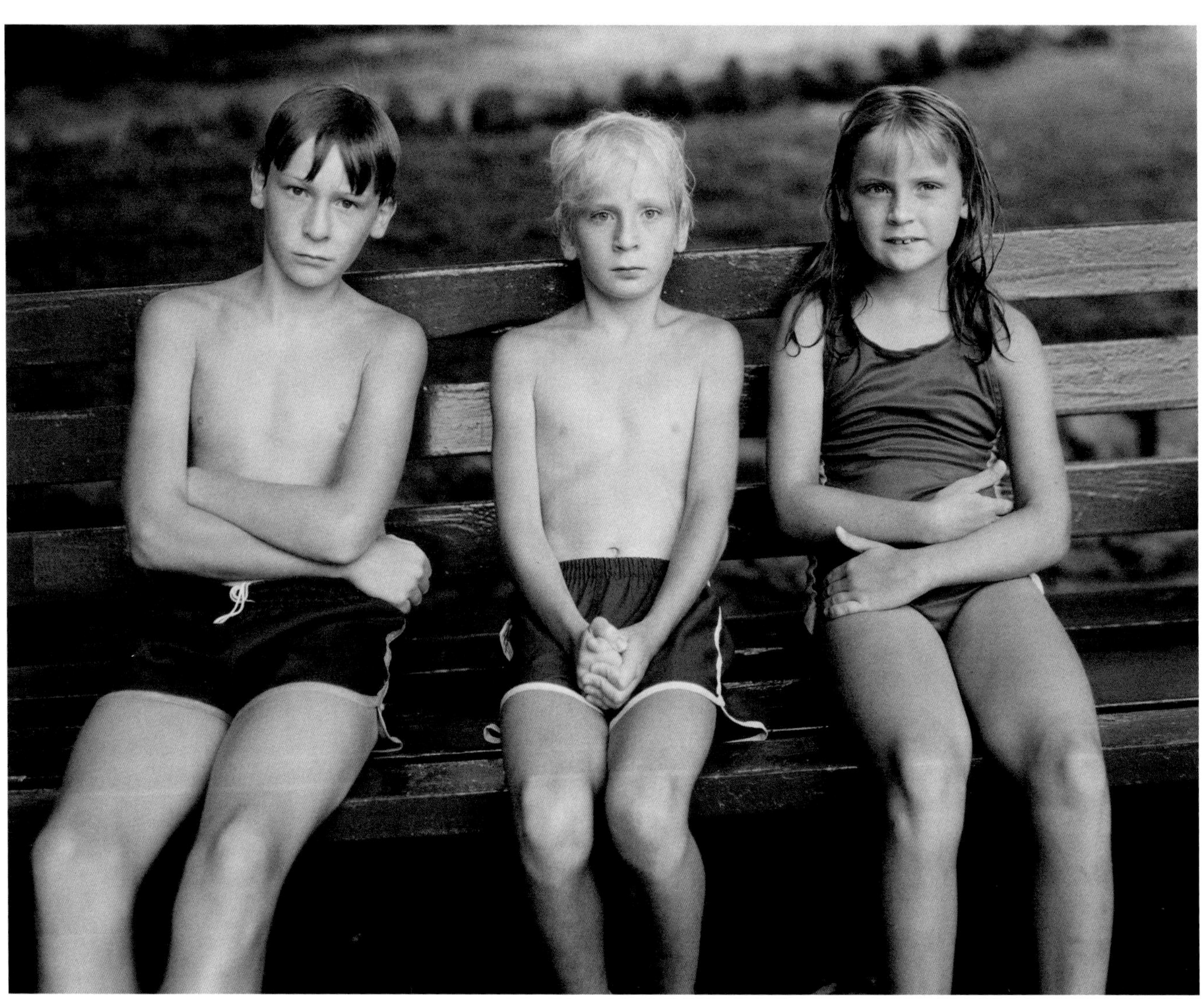

Ohne Titel | Untitled

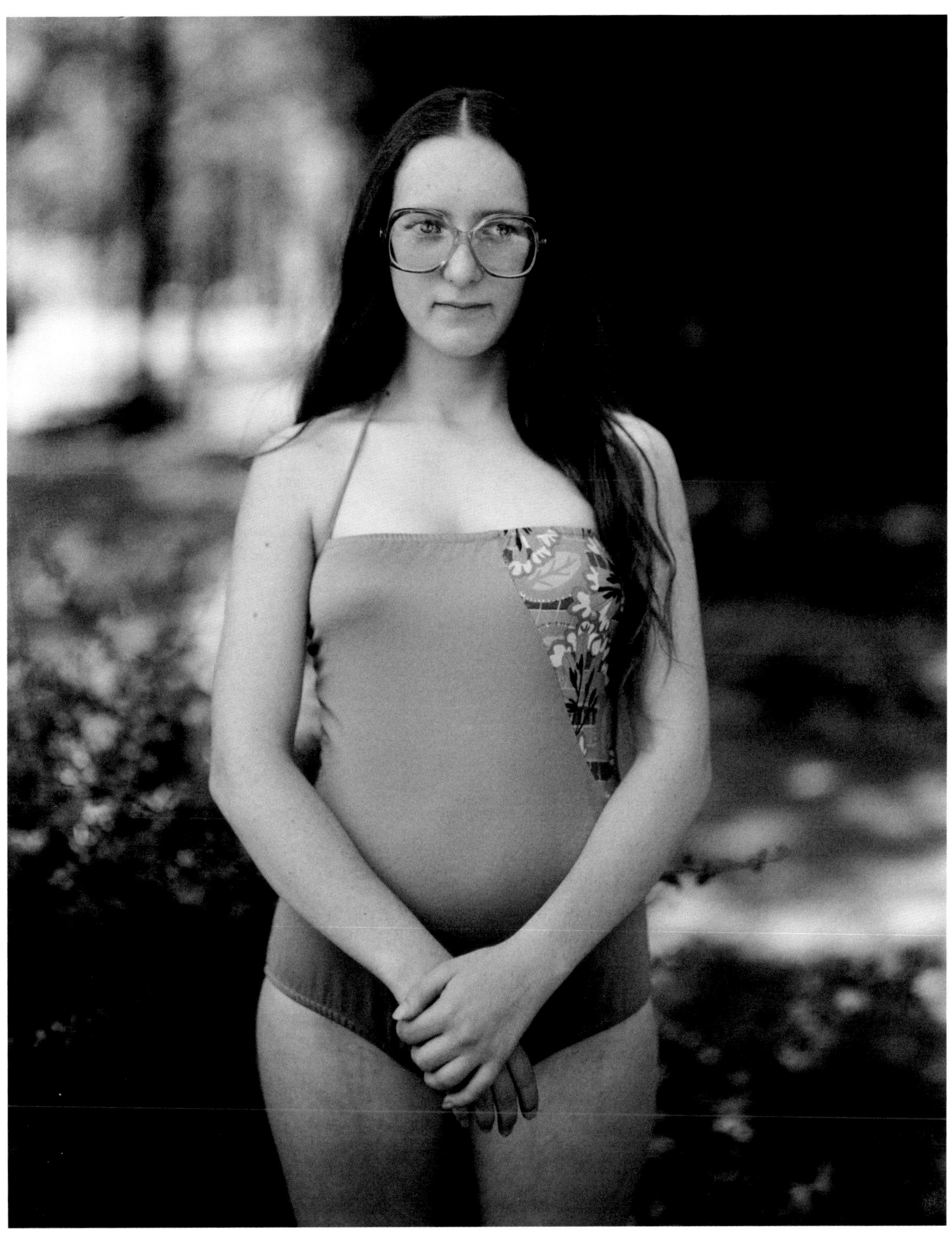

Ohne Titel | Untitled

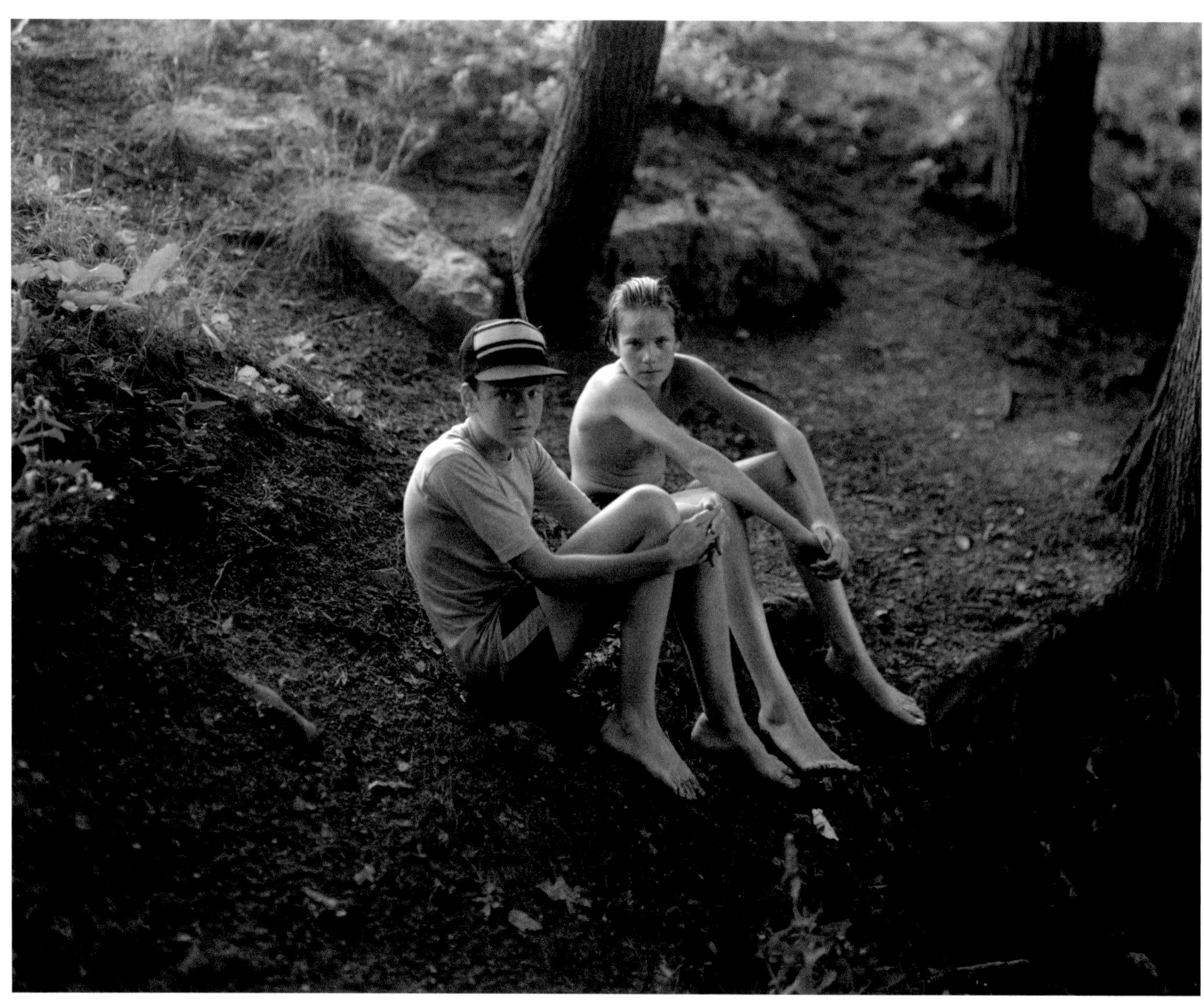

Ohne Titel | Untitled

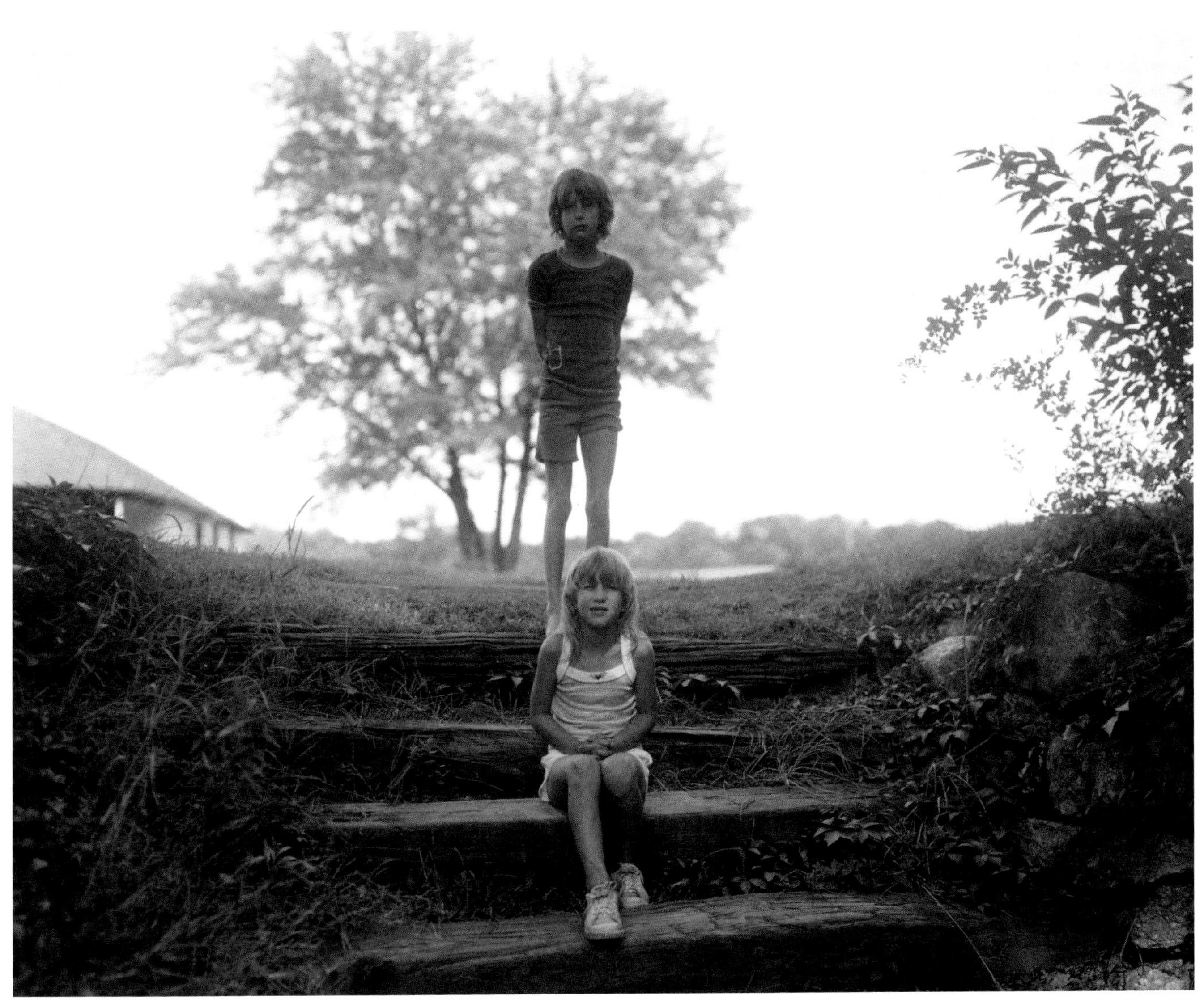

Ohne Titel | Untitled

Portraits at the Vietnam Veterans Memorial, Washington, D.C., 1983/1984

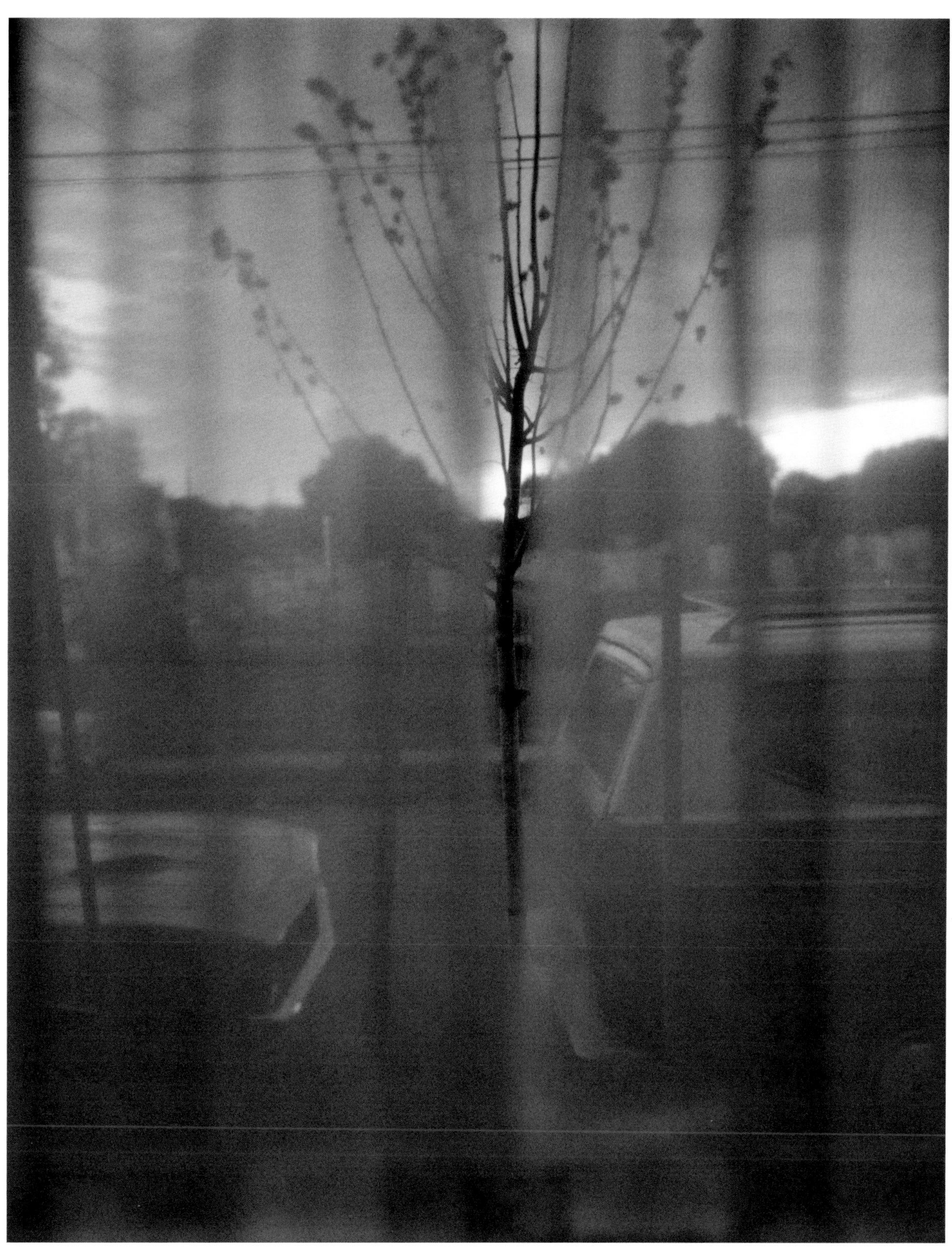

305 North 10th Street, Allentown, Pennsylvania, 1983

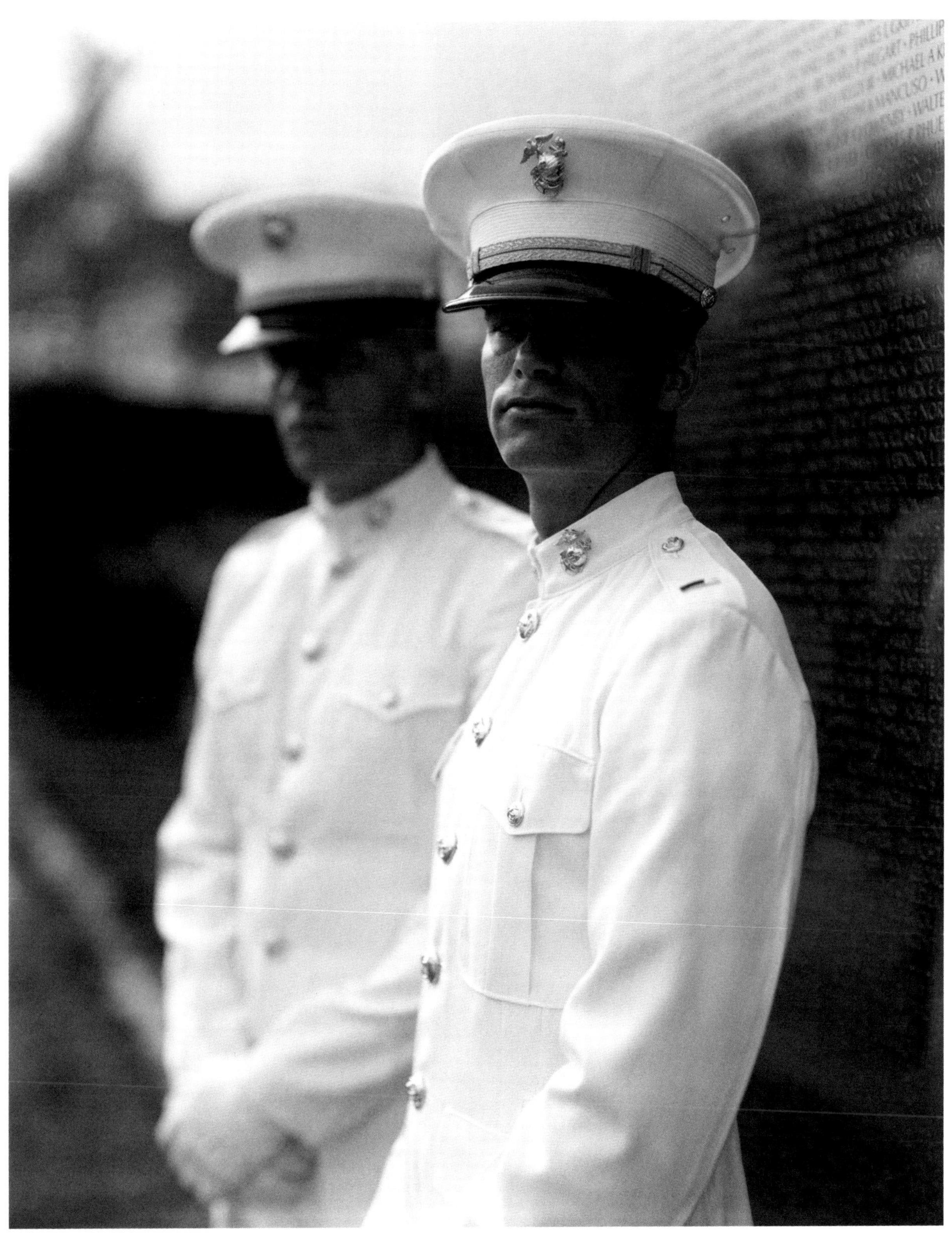

Ohne Titel | Untitled, 1983

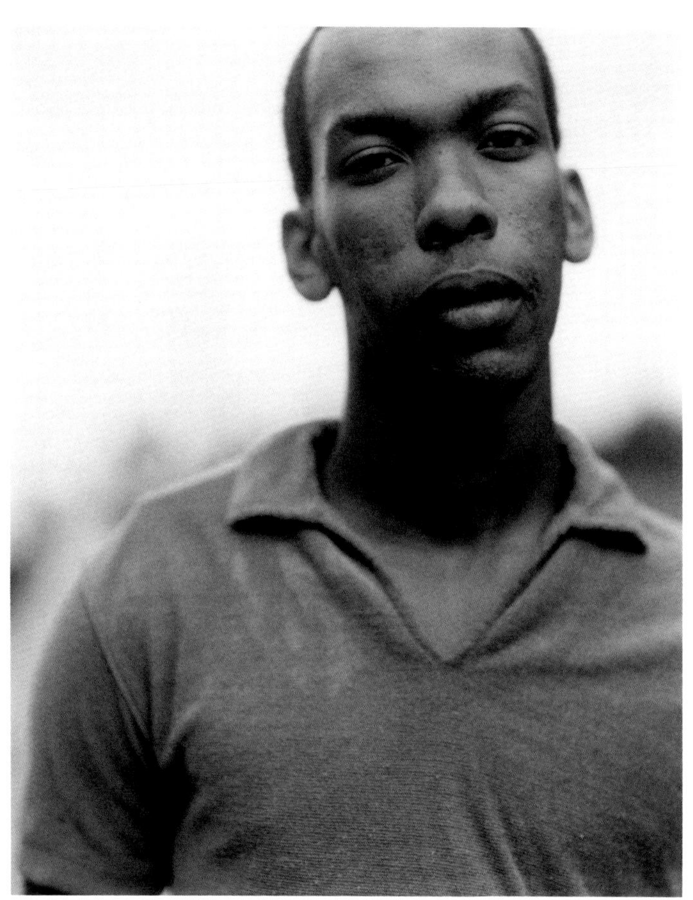

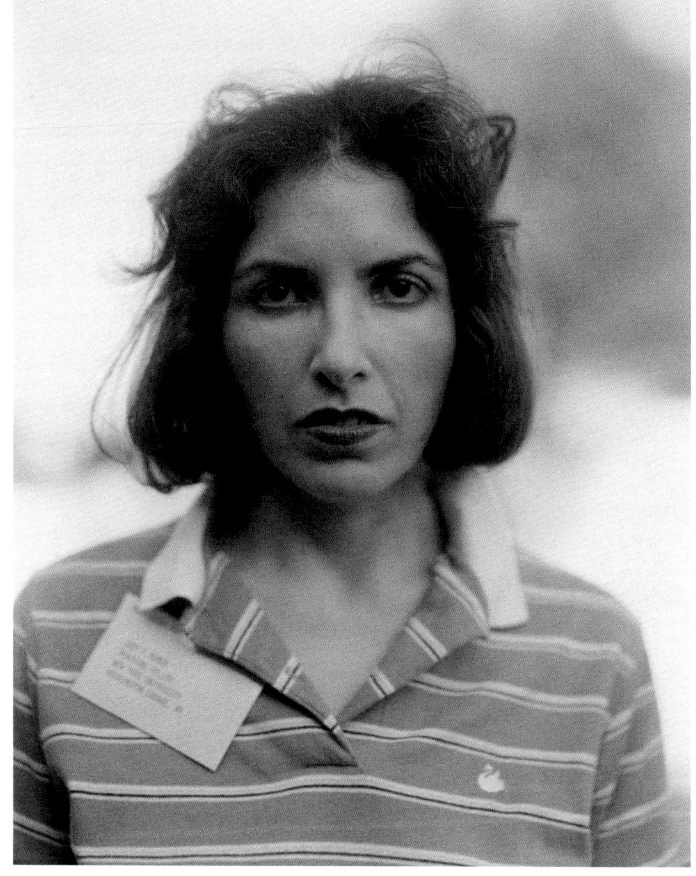

Ohne Titel | Untitled, 1984

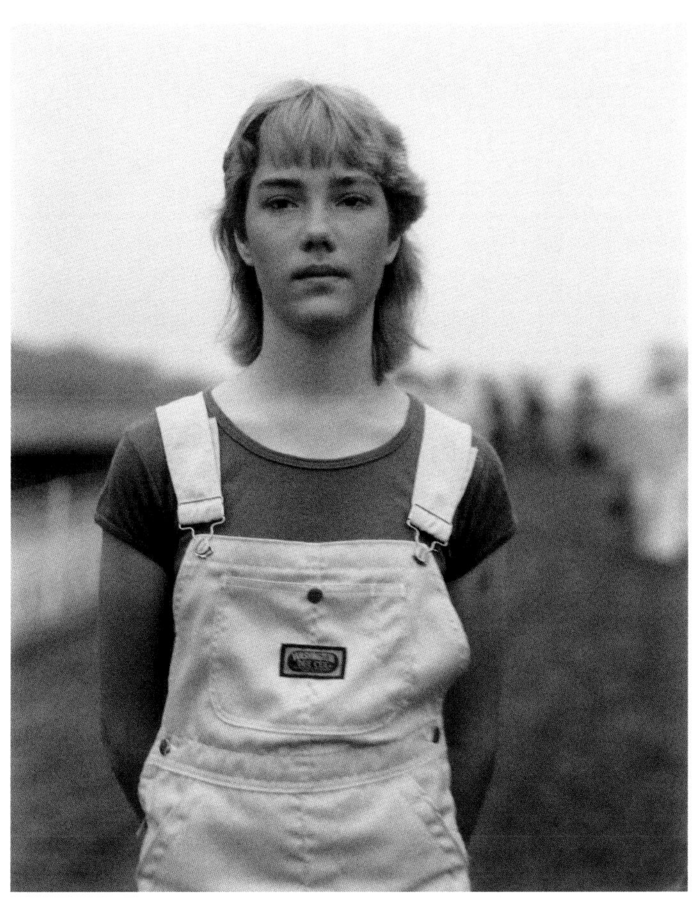

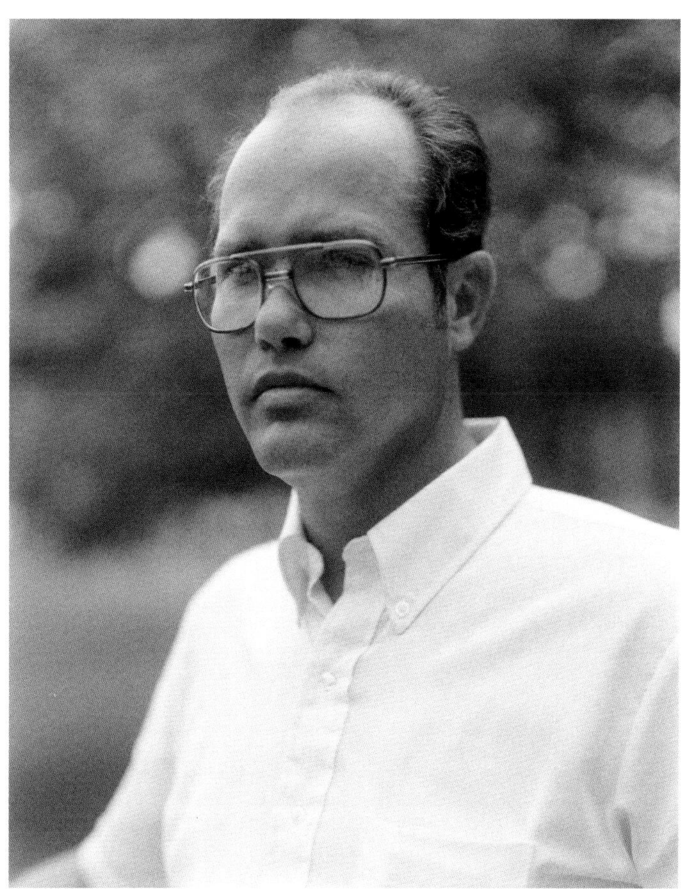

Ohne Titel | Untitled, 1984

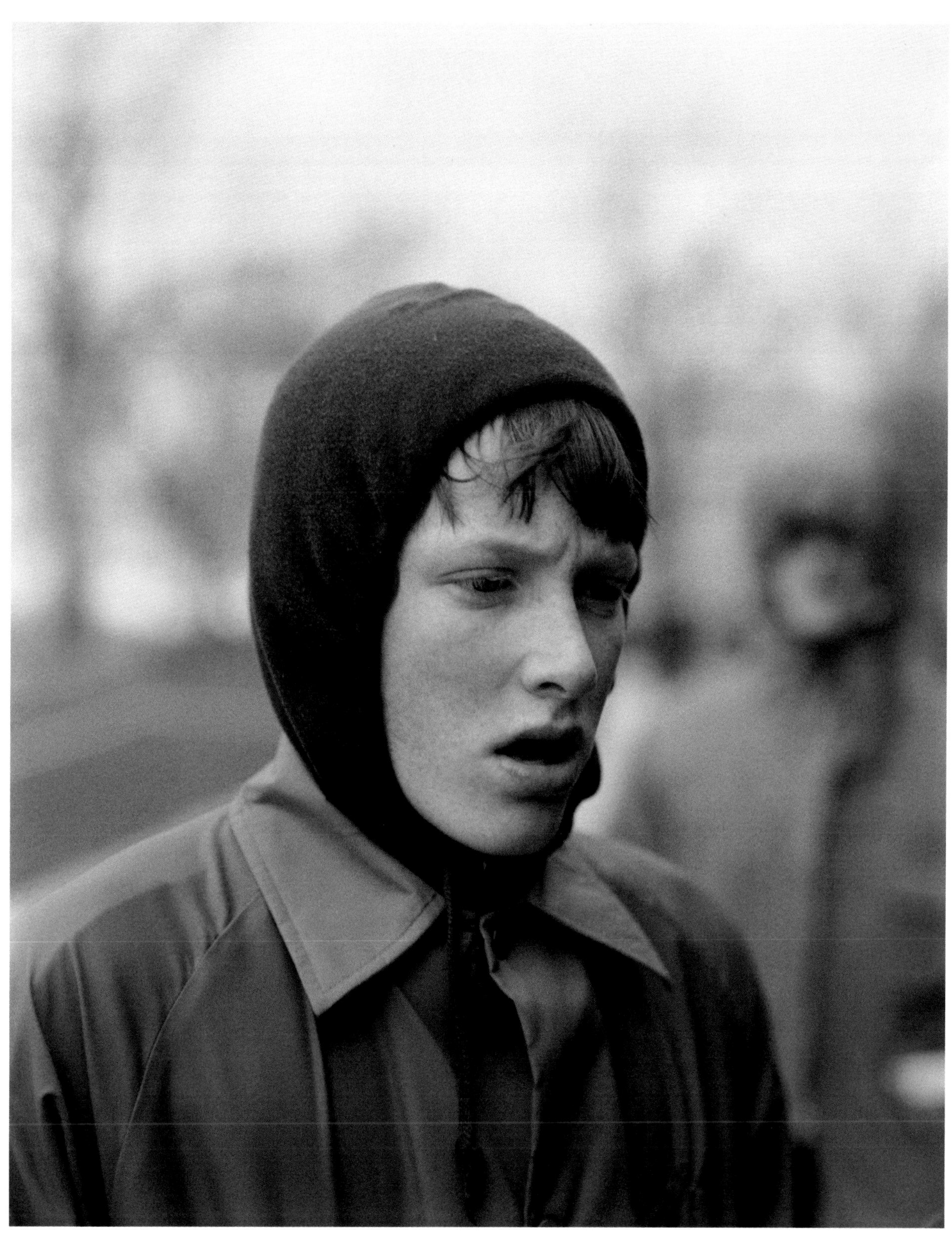

Ohne Titel | Untitled, 1984

Pathmark, Allentown, Pennsylvania, 1984

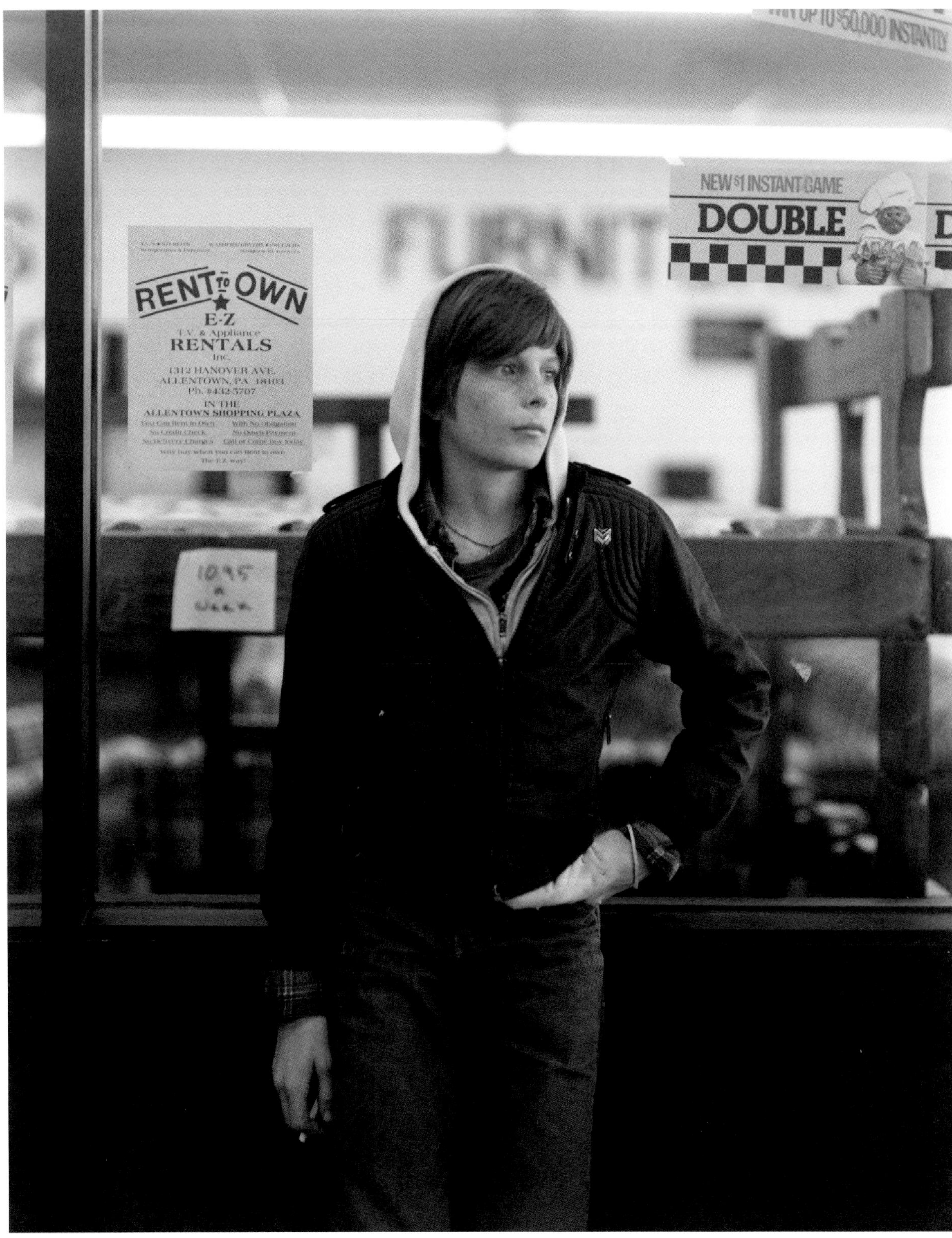

Ohne Titel | Untitled

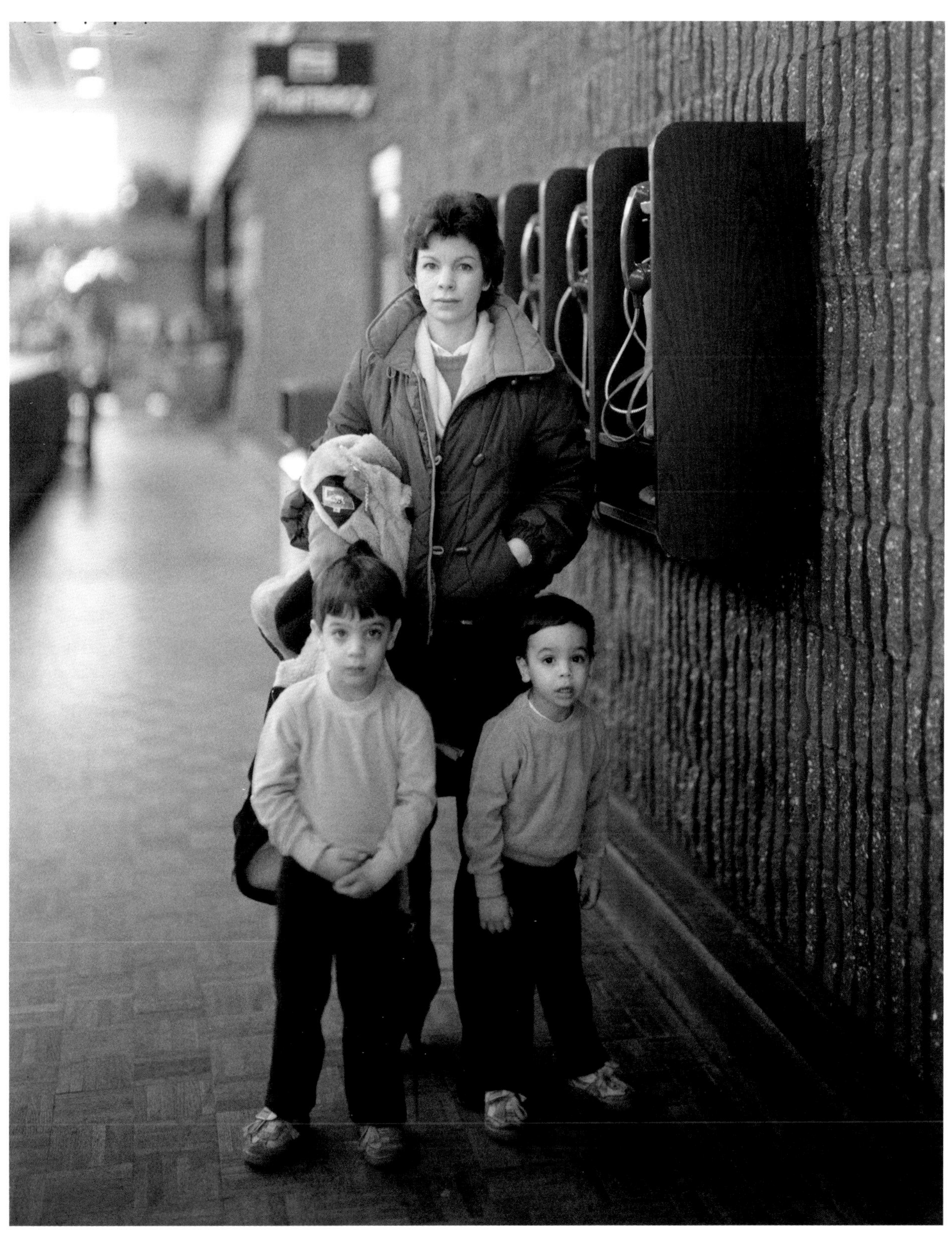

Ohne Titel | Untitled

Portraits of the U.S. Congress, 1986/1987

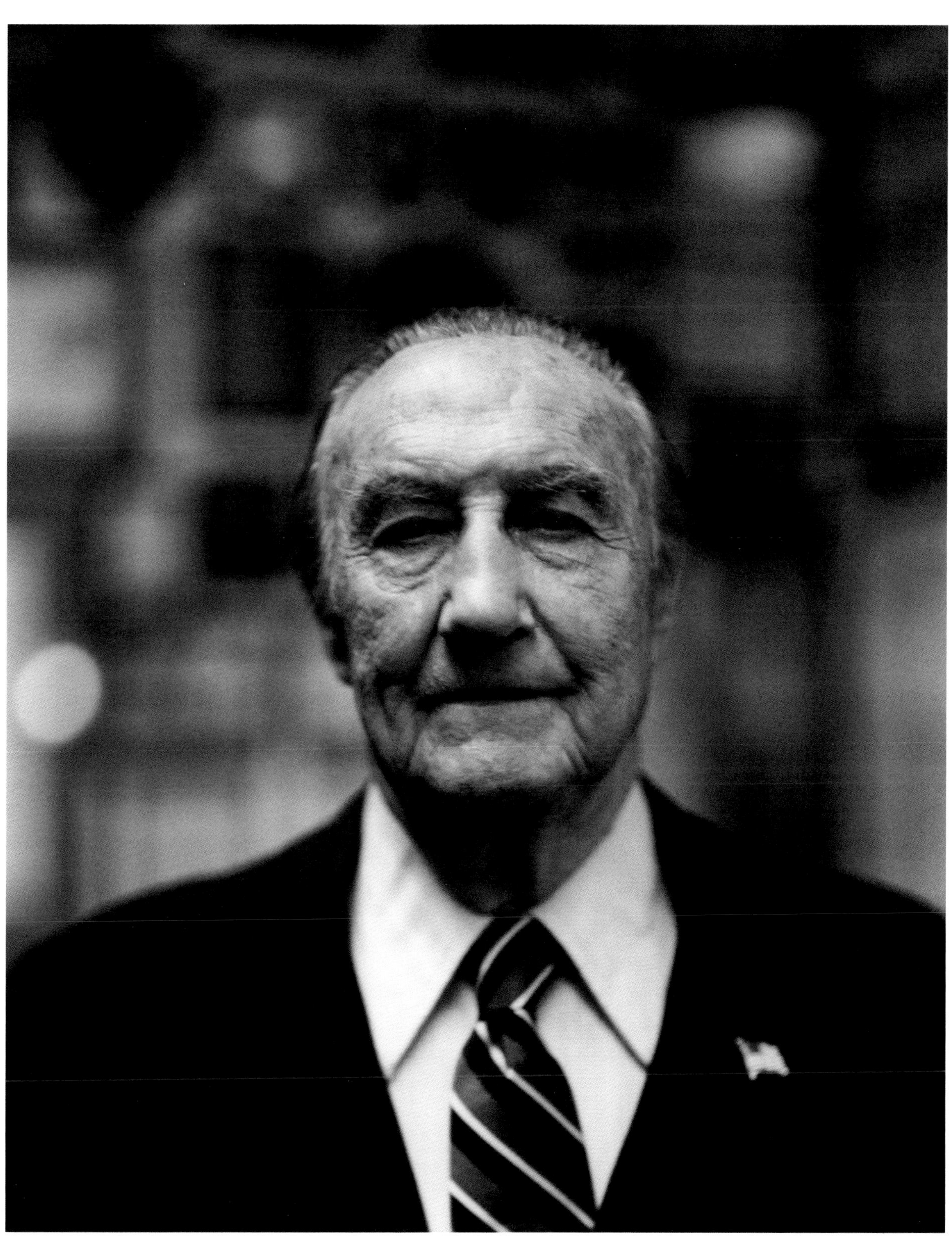

Senator Strom Thurmond, Republican, South Carolina, 1987

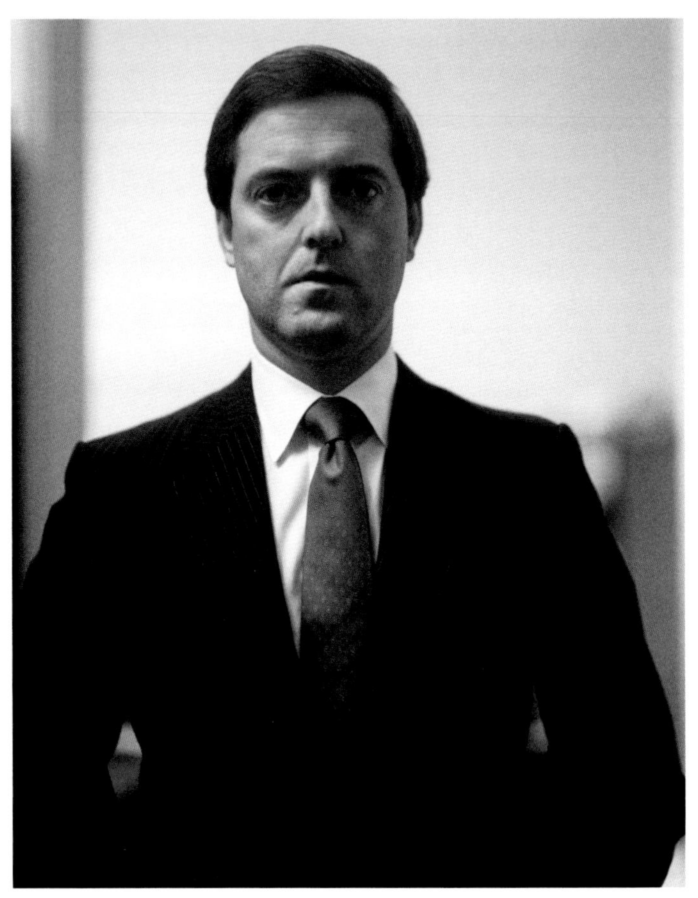

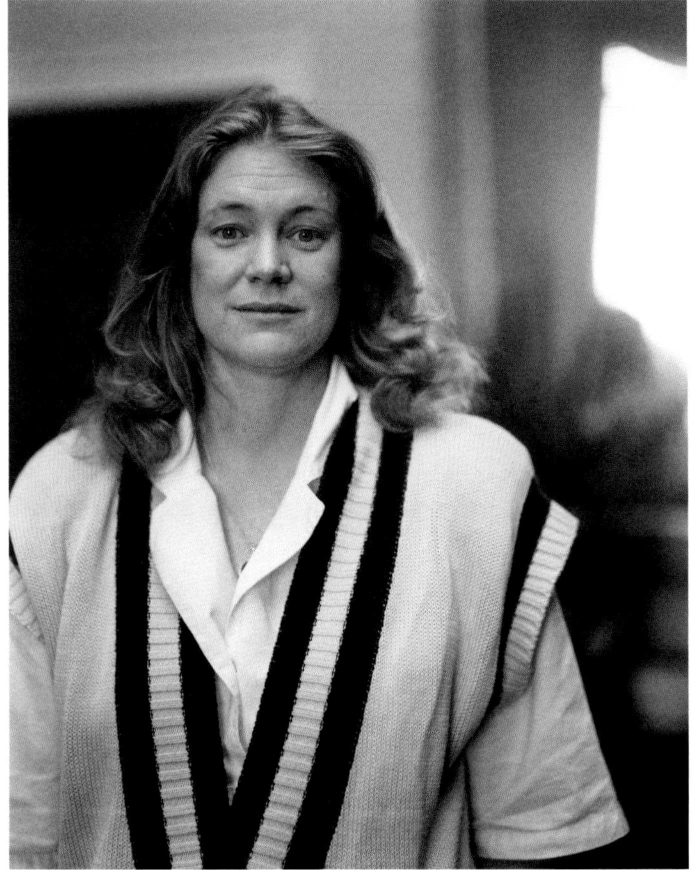

Abgeordneter des Repräsentantenhauses | Congressman John P. Hiler, Republican, Indiana, 1986

Susan Stoudt Elving, Verwaltungsassistentin von Norman Y. Mineta, Abgeordneter des Repräsentantenhauses | Administrative Assistant to Congressman Norman Y. Mineta, Democrat, California, 1986

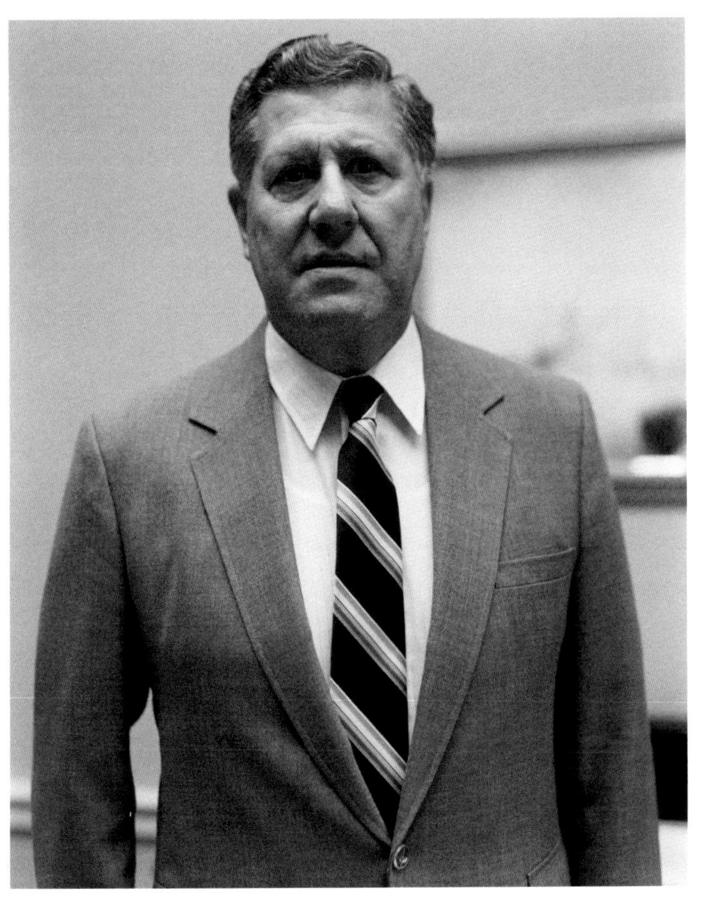

Abgeordneter des Repräsentantenhauses | Congressman Gus Yatron, Democrat, Pennsylvania, 1986

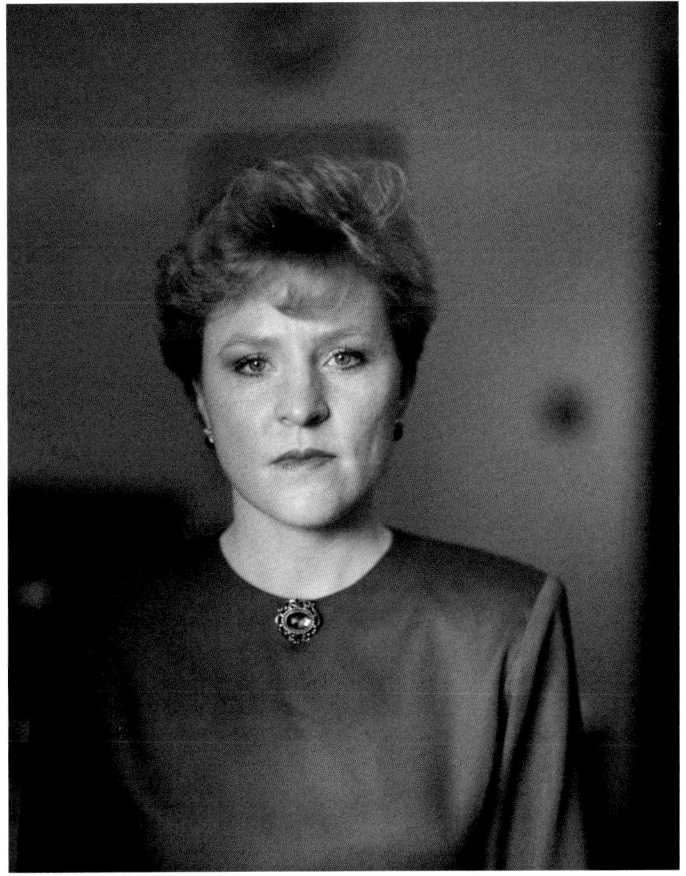

Laurie Snow, Kommunikationsleiterin von Senator Jake Garn | Communicative Director to Senator Jake Garn, Republican, Utah, 1987

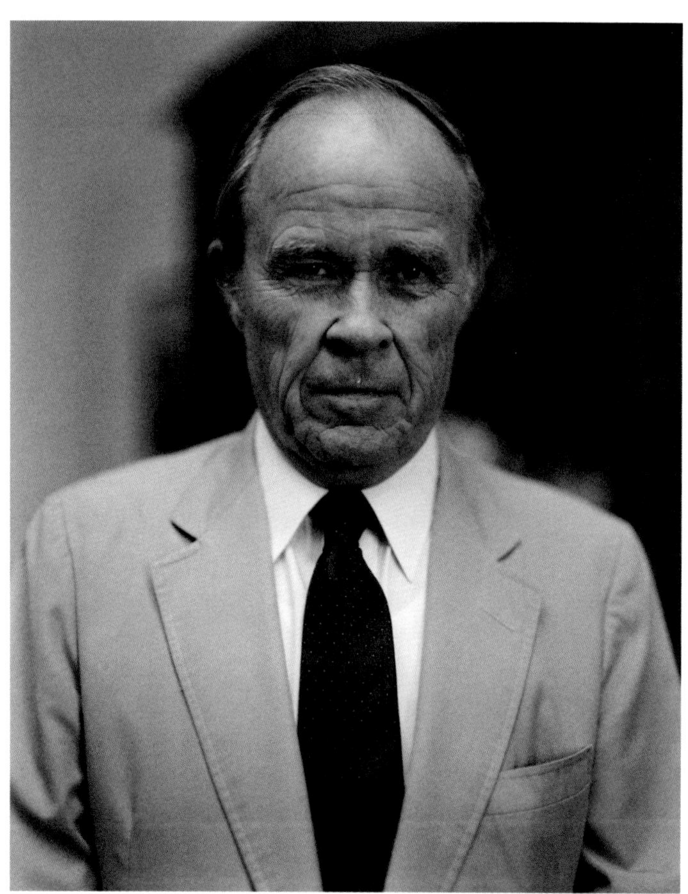

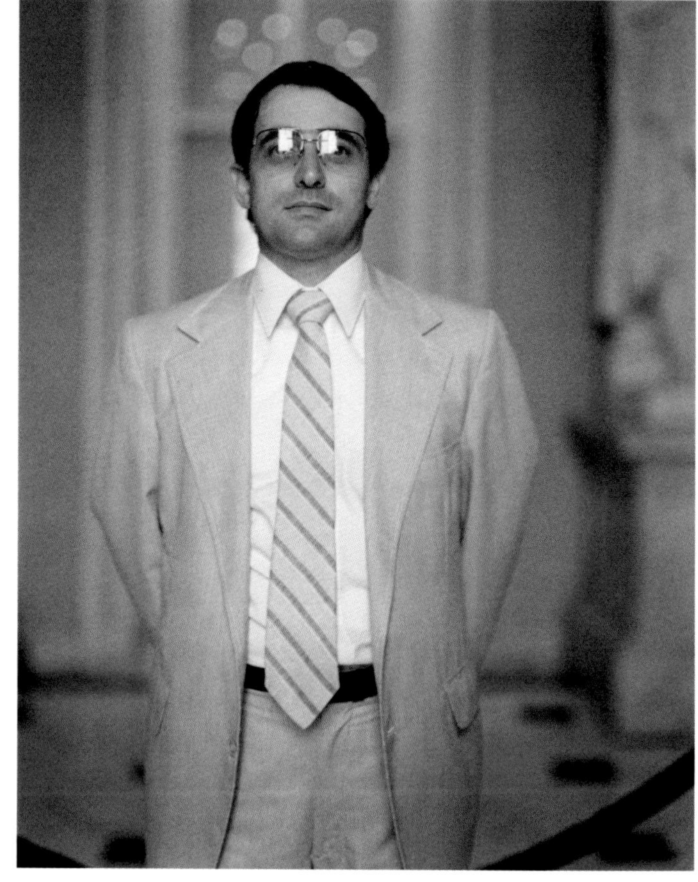

Abgeordneter des Repräsentantenhauses | Congressman Elwood (Bud) Hillis, Republican, Indiana, 1987

Phil Rotundi, Verwaltungsassistent von Thomas M. Foglietta, Abgeordneter des Repräsentantenhauses | Administrative Assistant to Congressman Thomas M. Foglietta, Democrat, Pennsylvania, 1986

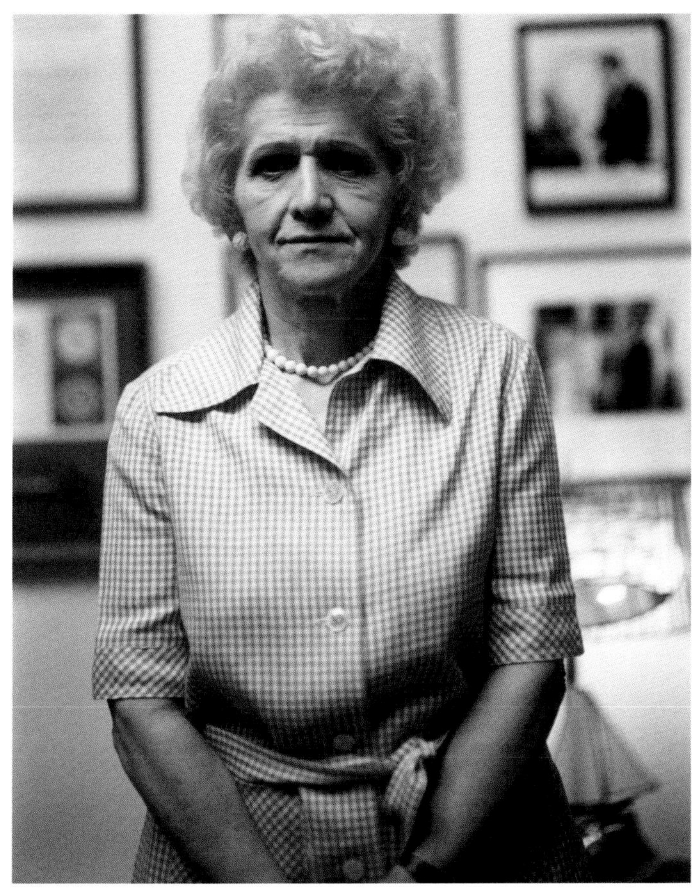

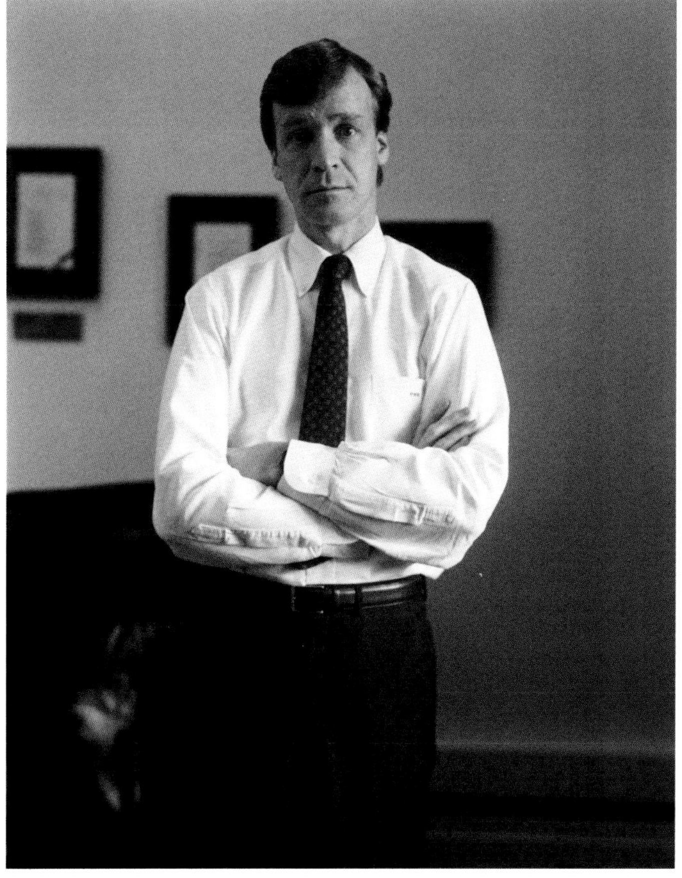

Abgeordnete des Repräsentantenhauses | Congresswoman
Helen Delich Bentley, Republican, Maryland, 1986

Abgeordneter des Repräsentantenhauses | Congressman
Peter H. Kostmayer, Democrat, Pennsylvania, 1986

Easton Portraits, 1988

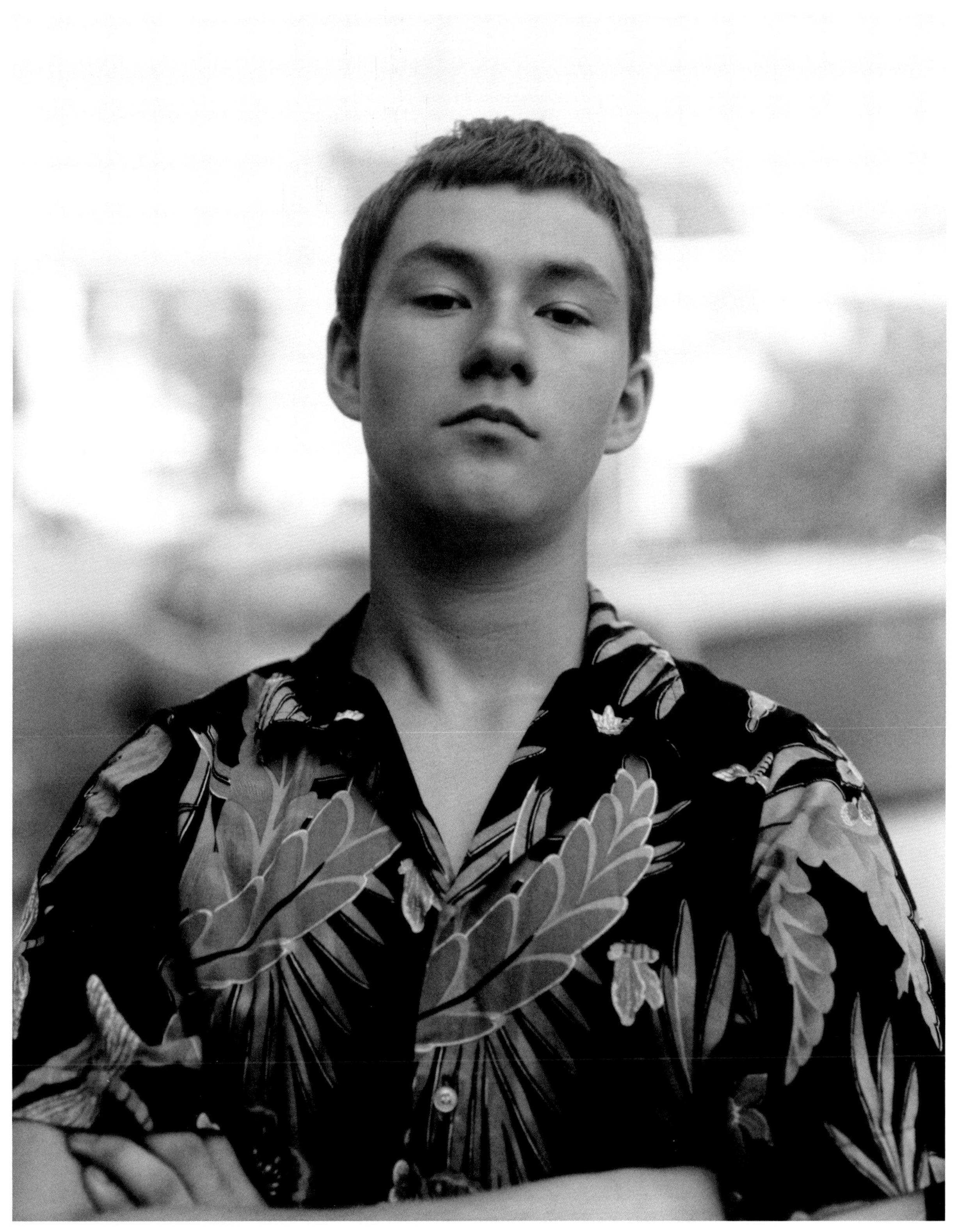

Ohne Titel | Untitled

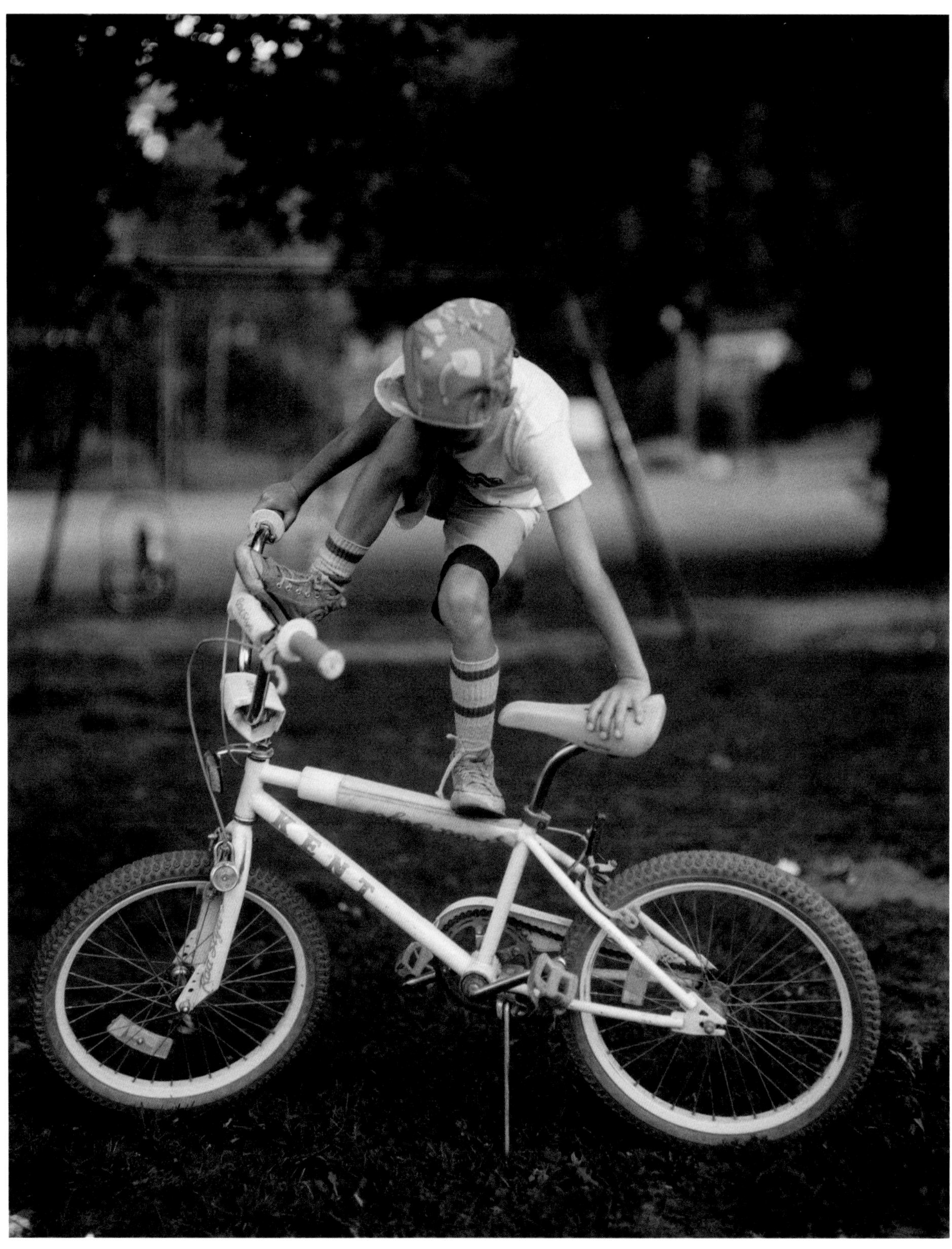

Ohne Titel | Untitled

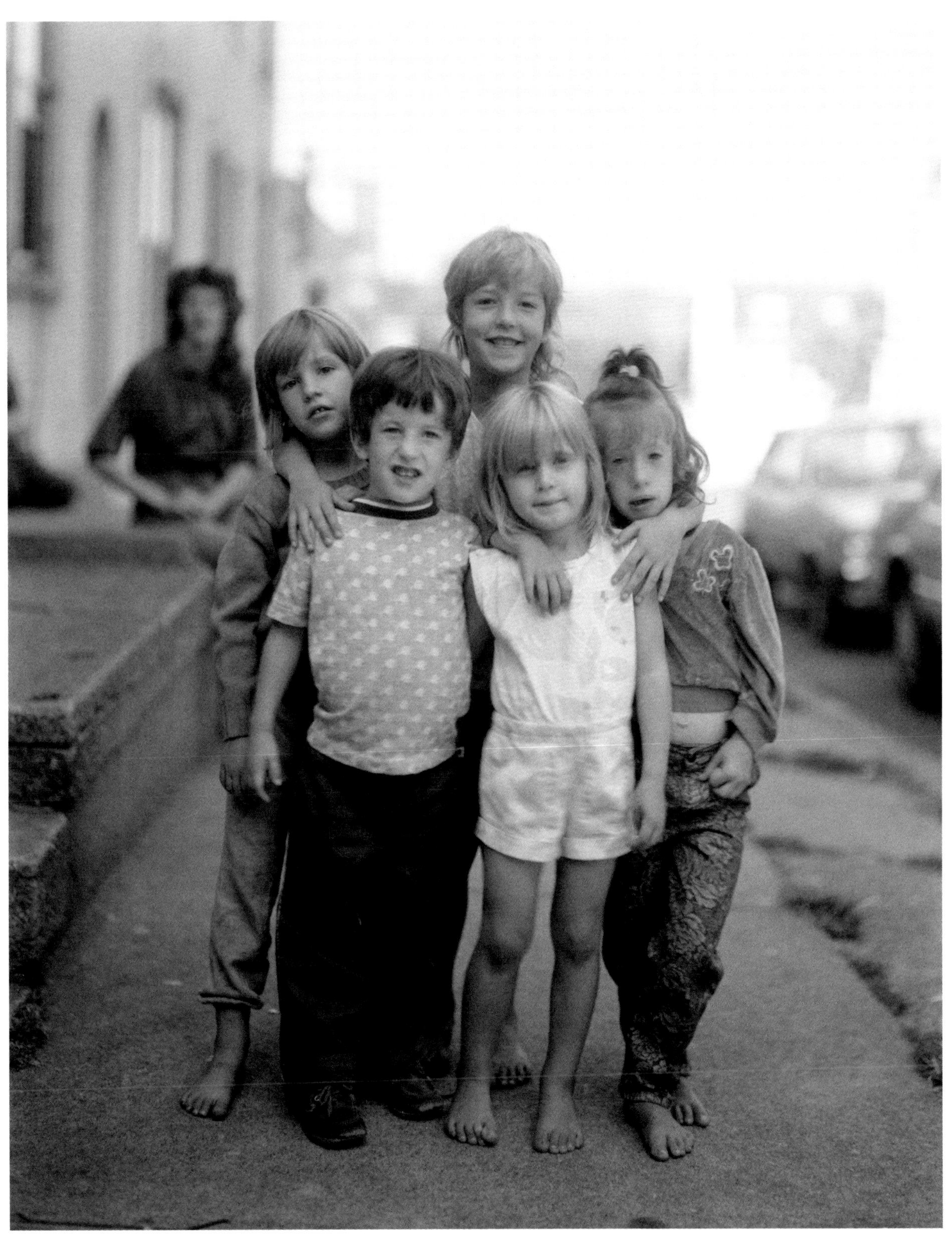

Ohne Titel | Untitled

Jobs, 1989/1990

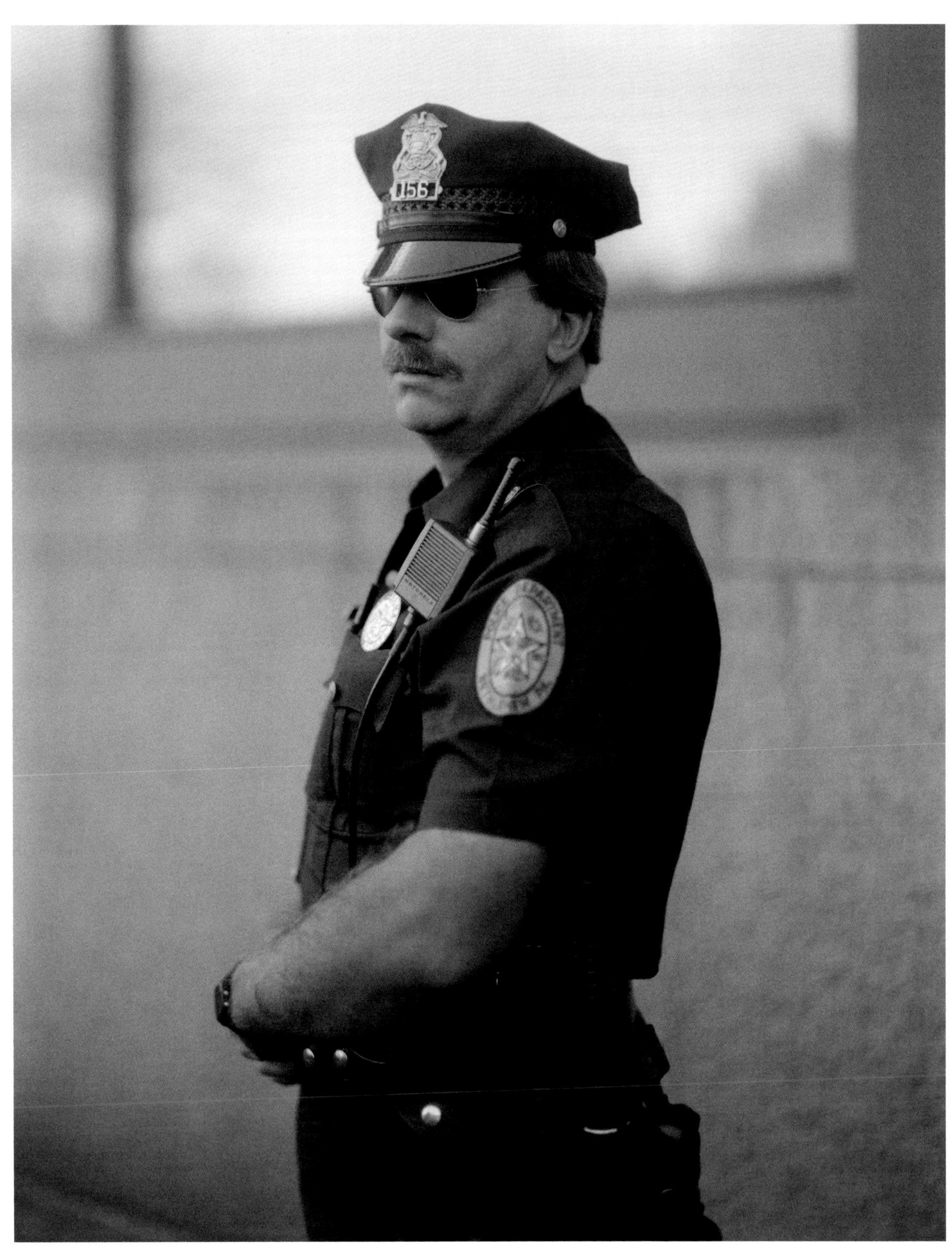

Polizist | Policeman, Bethlehem, Pennsylvania, 1990

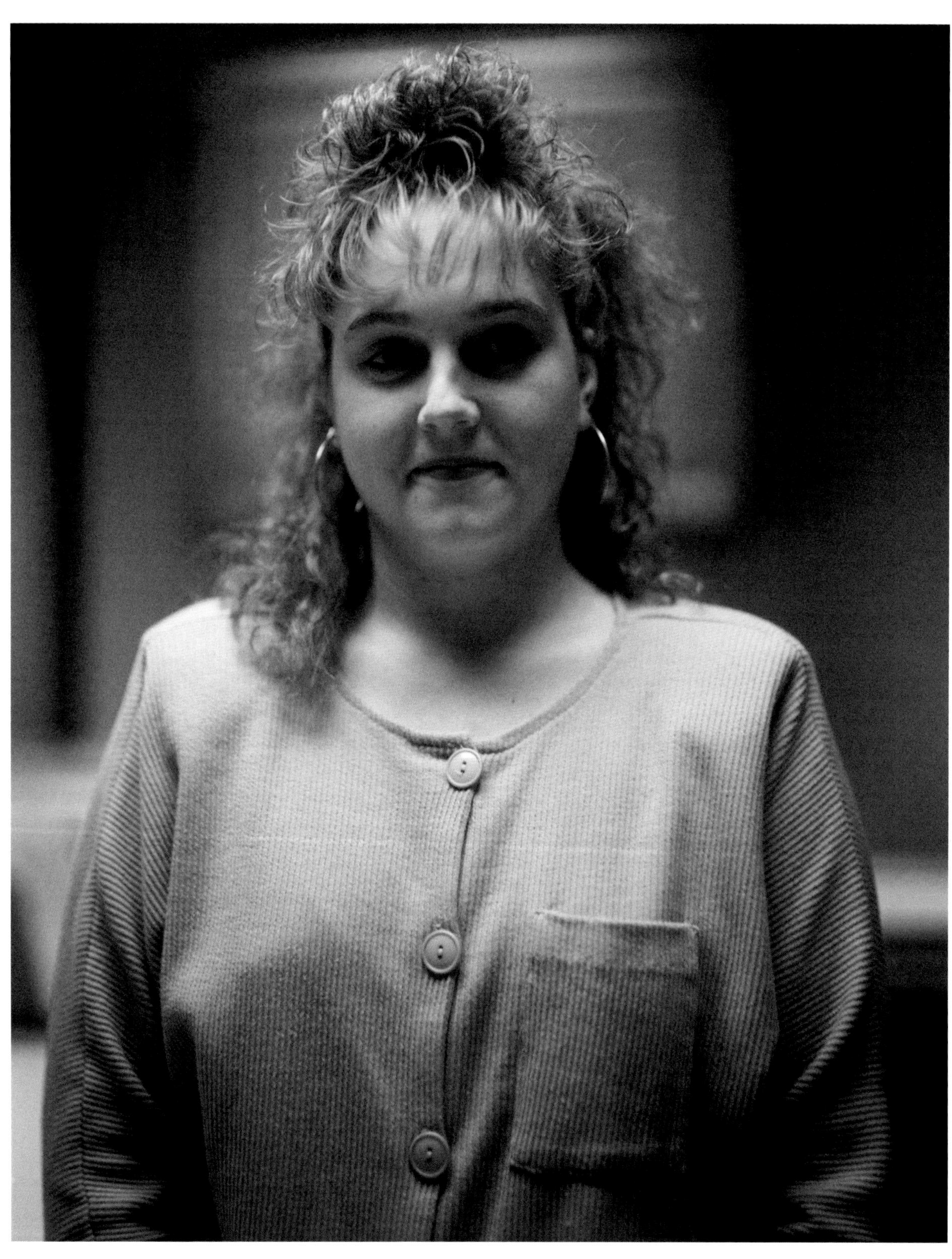

Medizinische Assistentin | Medical Assistant,
Bethlehem, Pennsylvania, 1990

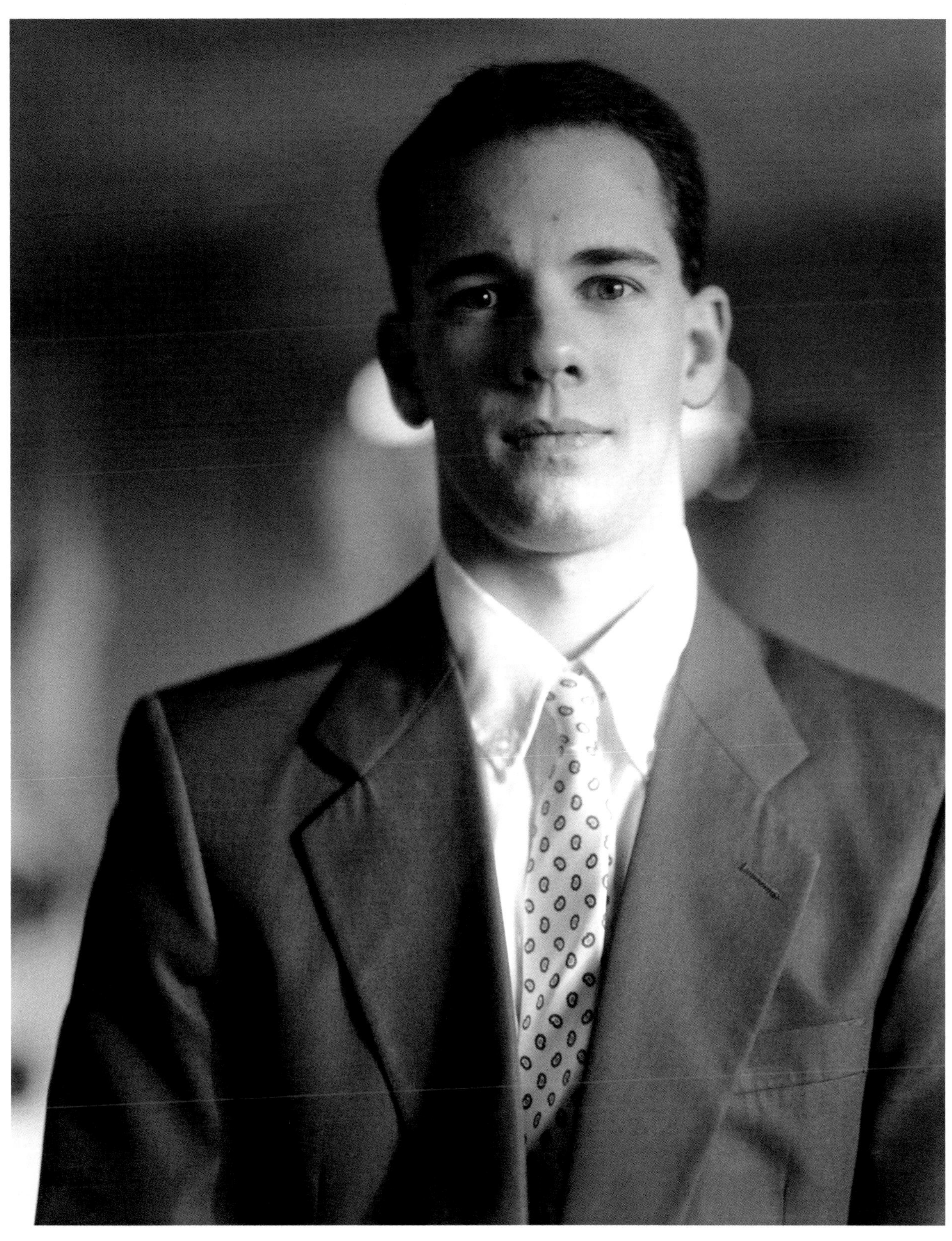

Vertreter für Ersatzteile von Toyota | Traveling Toyota Auto Parts Salesman, Fogelsville, Pennsylvania, 1989

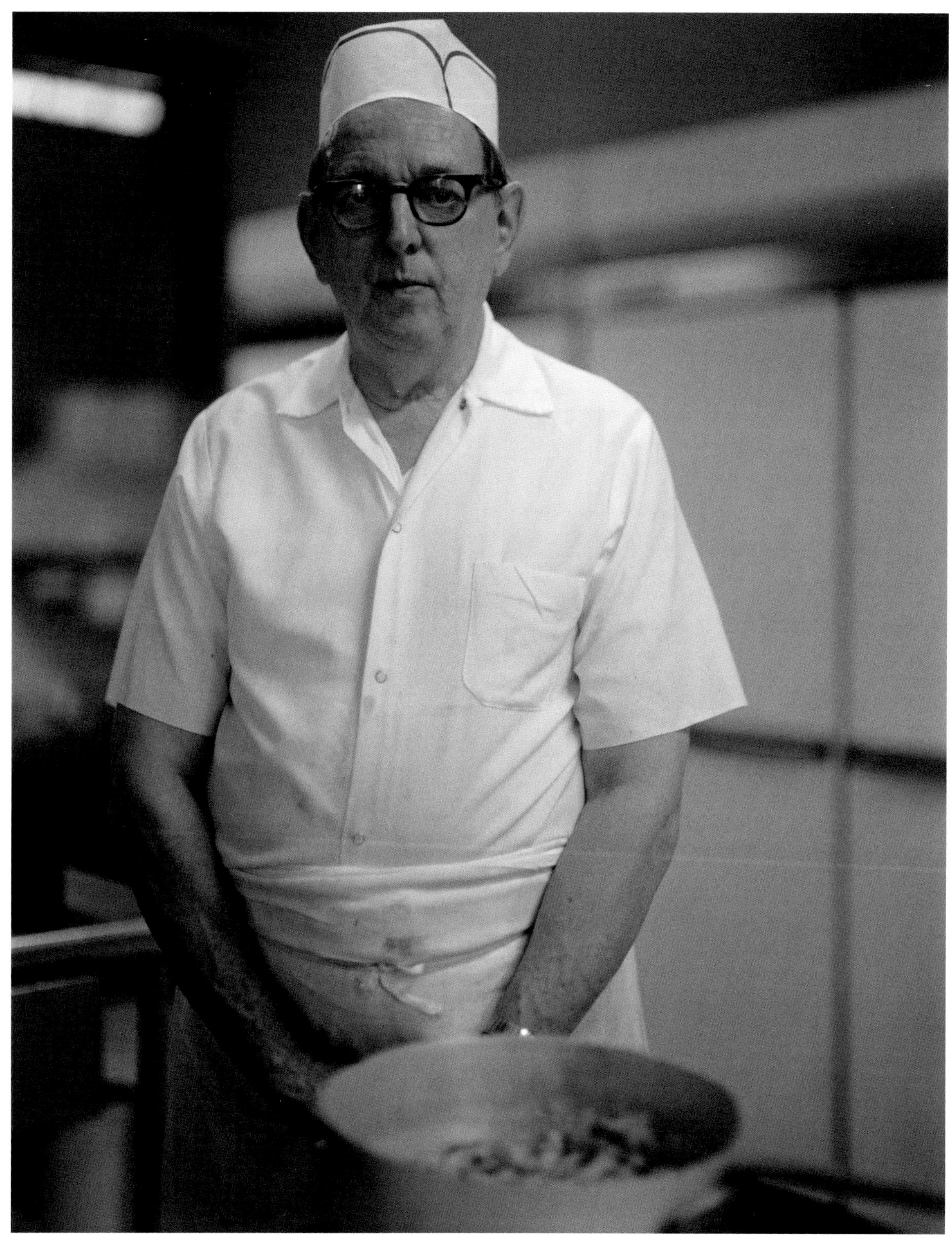

Koch | Cook, Bethlehem, Pennsylvania, 1990

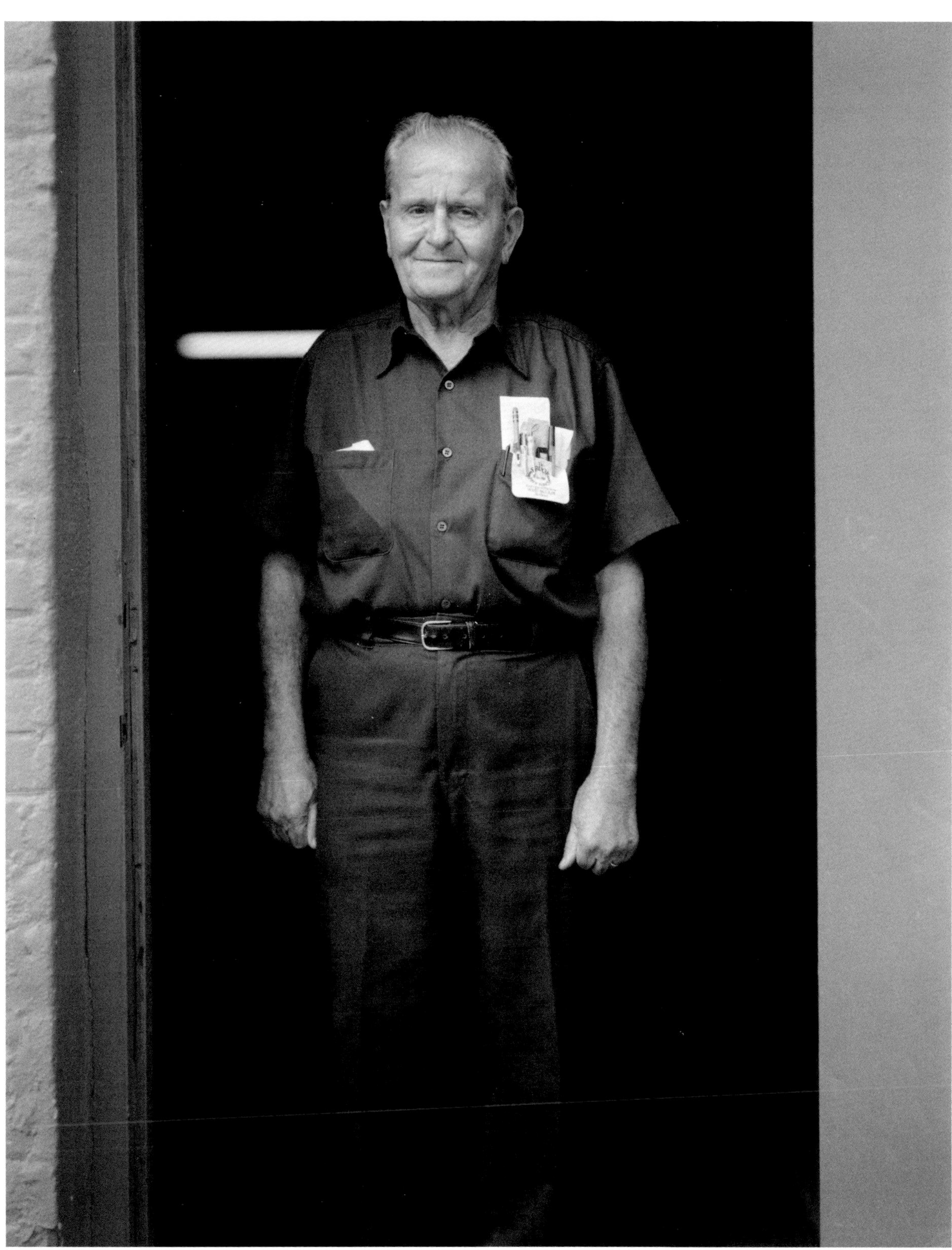

Klempner | Plumber, Bethlehem, Pennsylvania, 1990

Baseball, 1989–1991

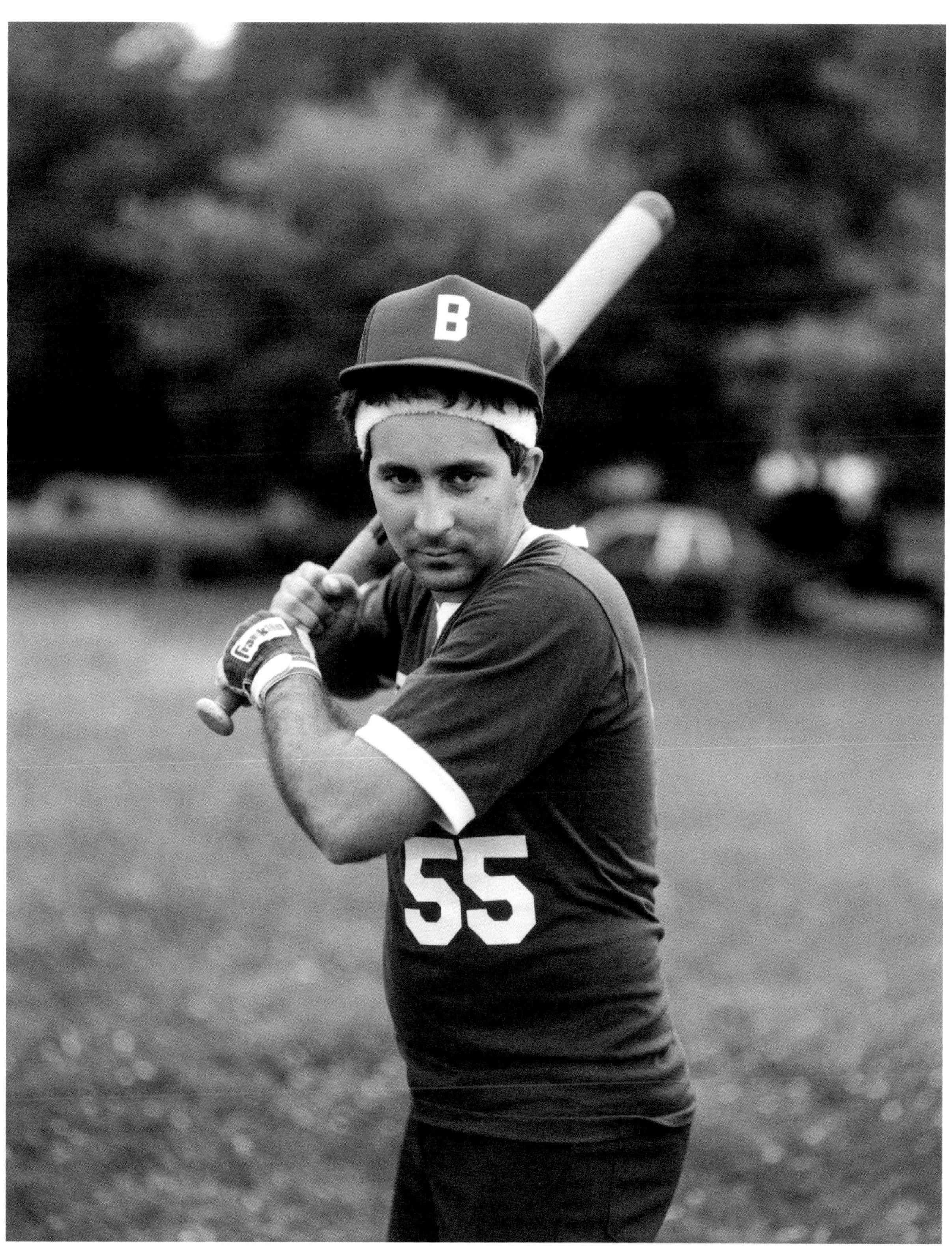

Ohne Titel | Untitled, Hellertown, Pennsylvania, circa 1991

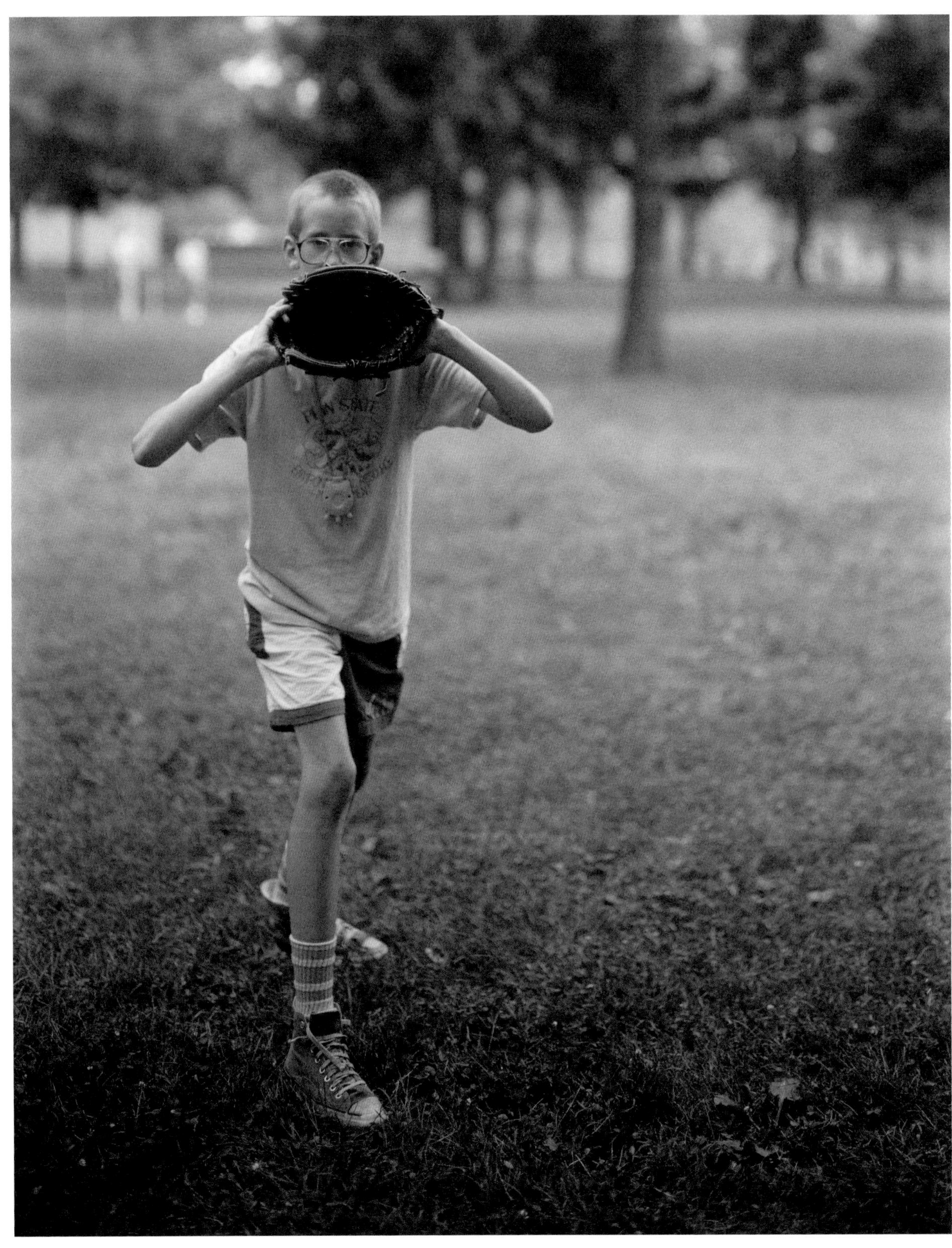

Ohne Titel | Untitled, Emmaus, Pennsylvania, 1989

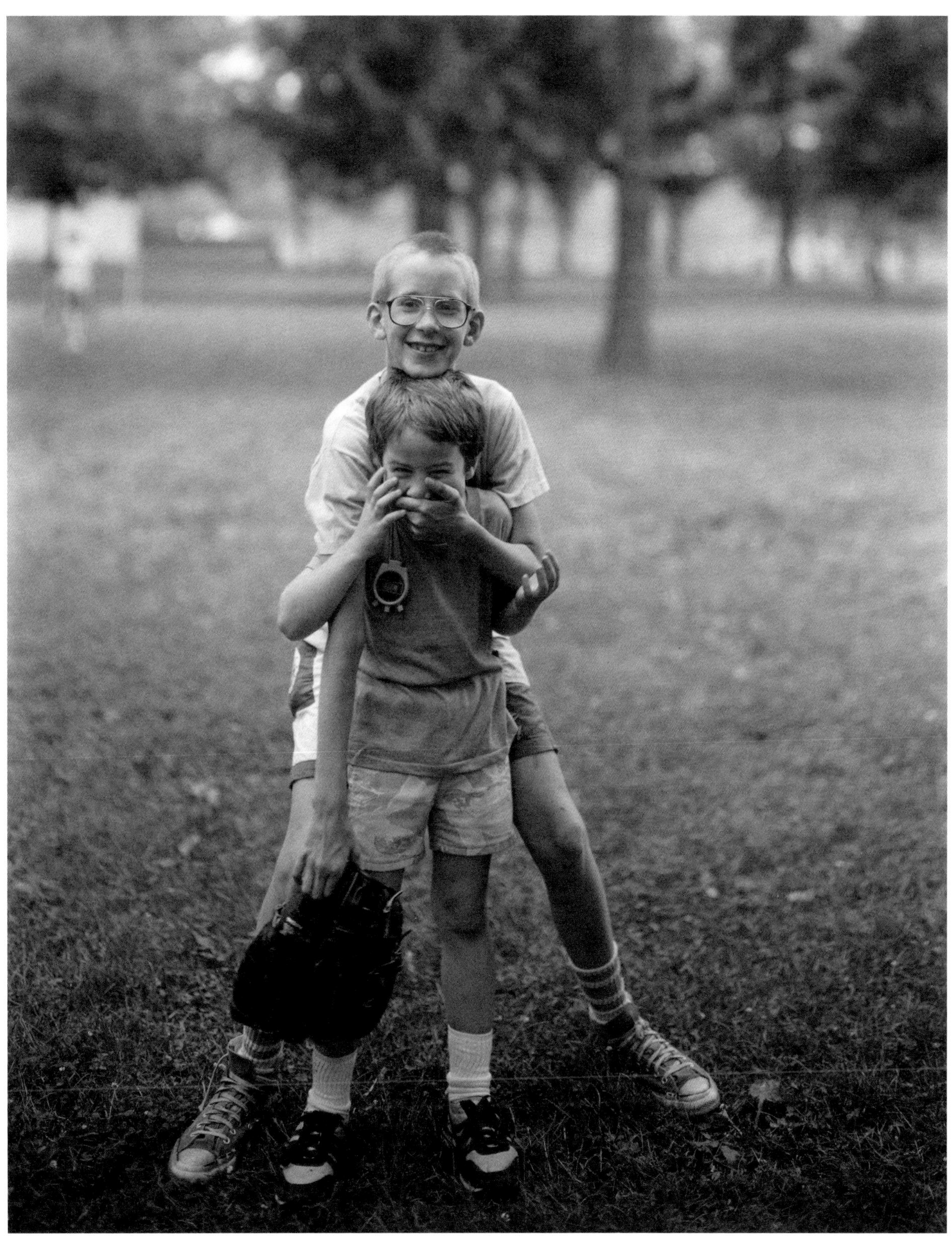

Ohne Titel | Untitled, Emmaus, Pennsylvania, 1989

U.S. Army Reserves on Red Alert. Gulf War Rallies, 1990

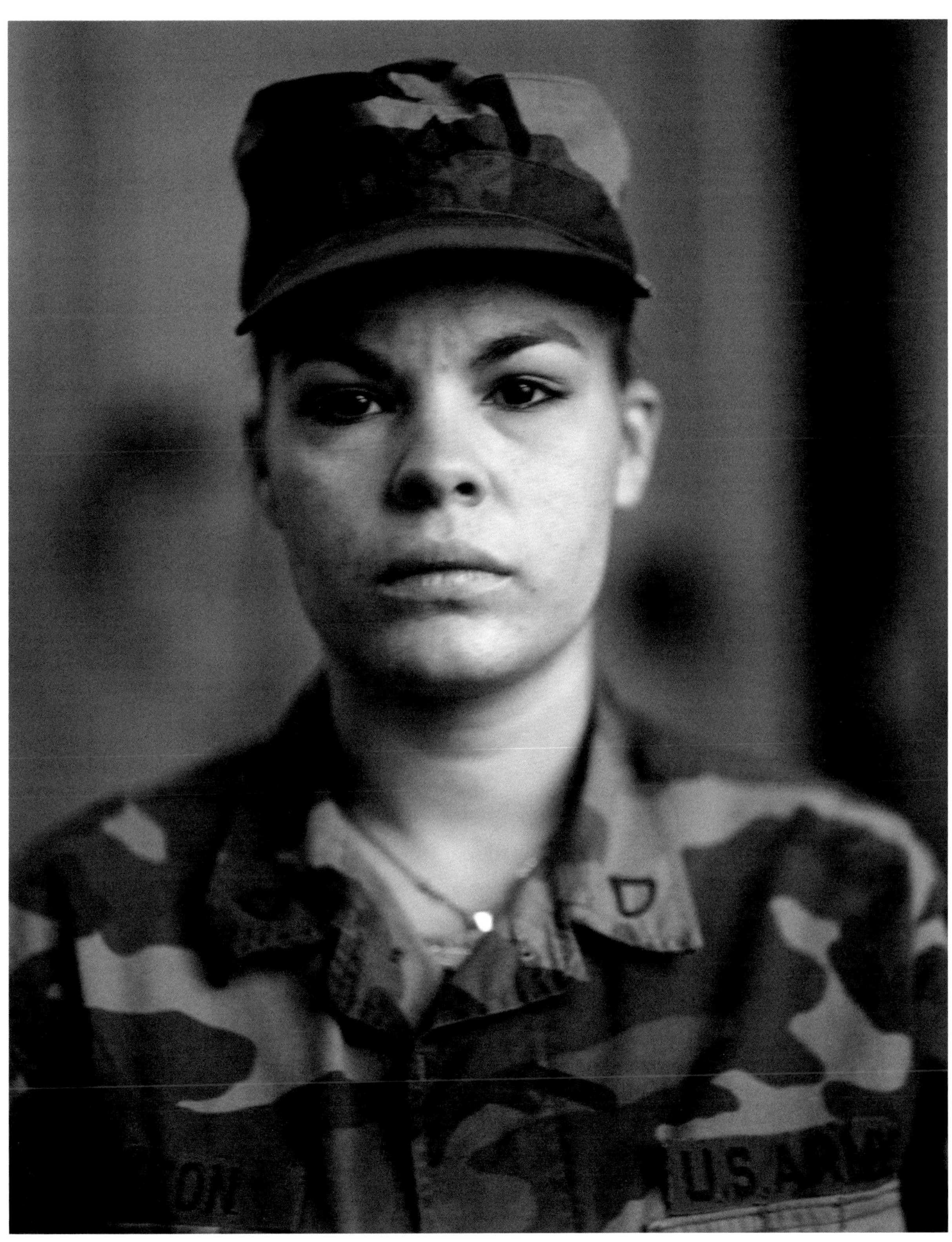

P.F.C. Maria I. Leon, Bethlehem, Pennsylvania

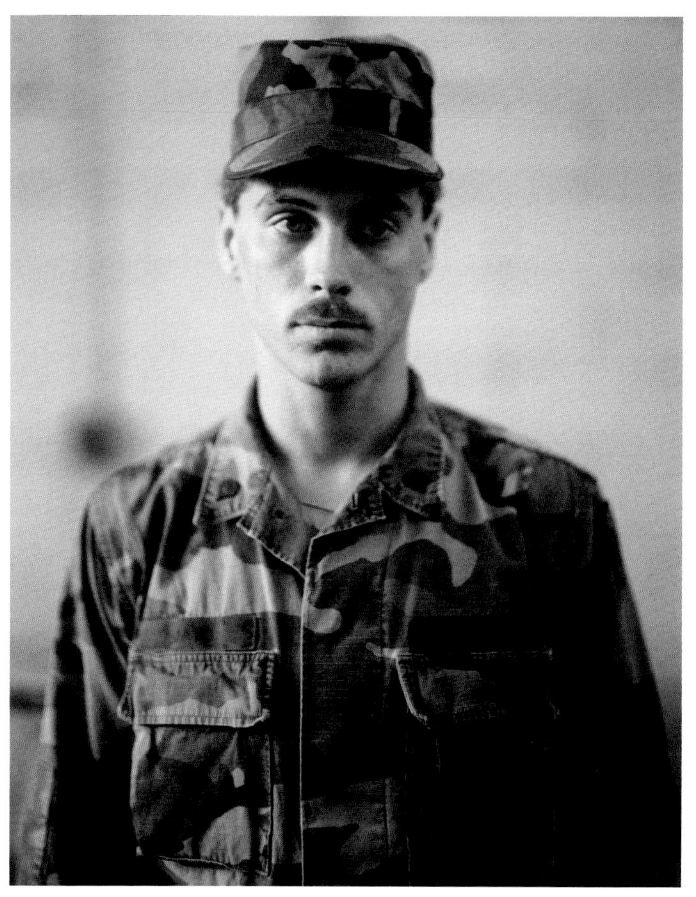

Specialist Lawrence Jani, Bethlehem, Pennsylvania

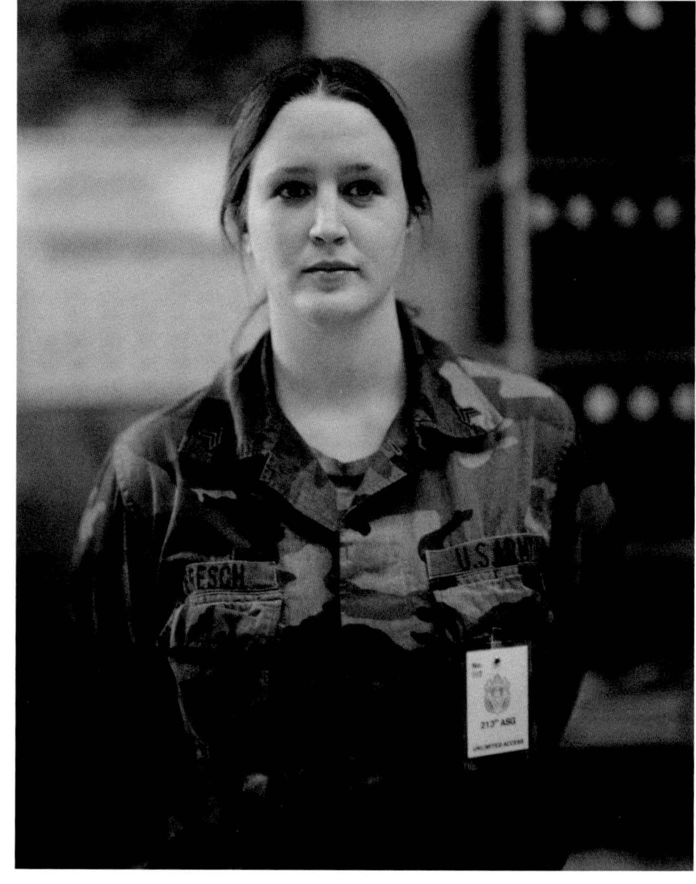

Unit Administrator, Karen J. Bresch, Bethlehem, Pennsylvania

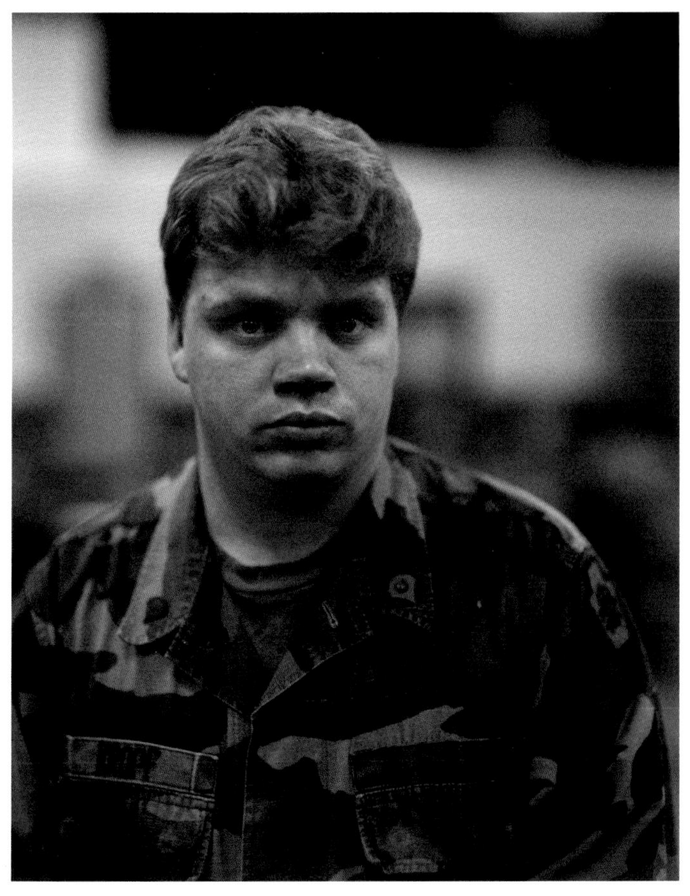

Specialist John P. Knopf, Bethlehem, Pennsylvania

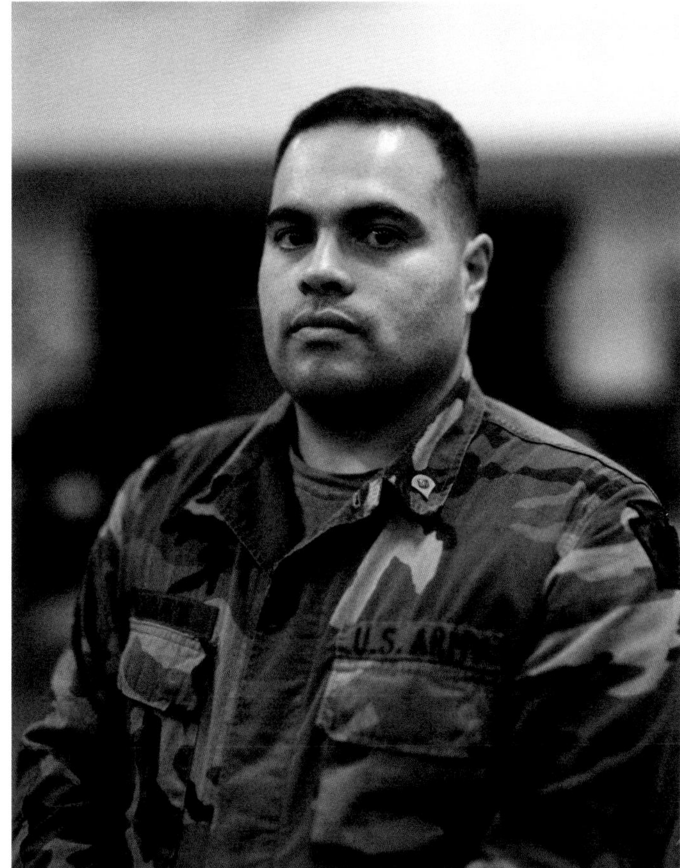

Specialist Dennis Cintron, Bethlehem, Pennsylvania

Bethlehem Public Library, Bethlehem, Pennsylvania, 1991

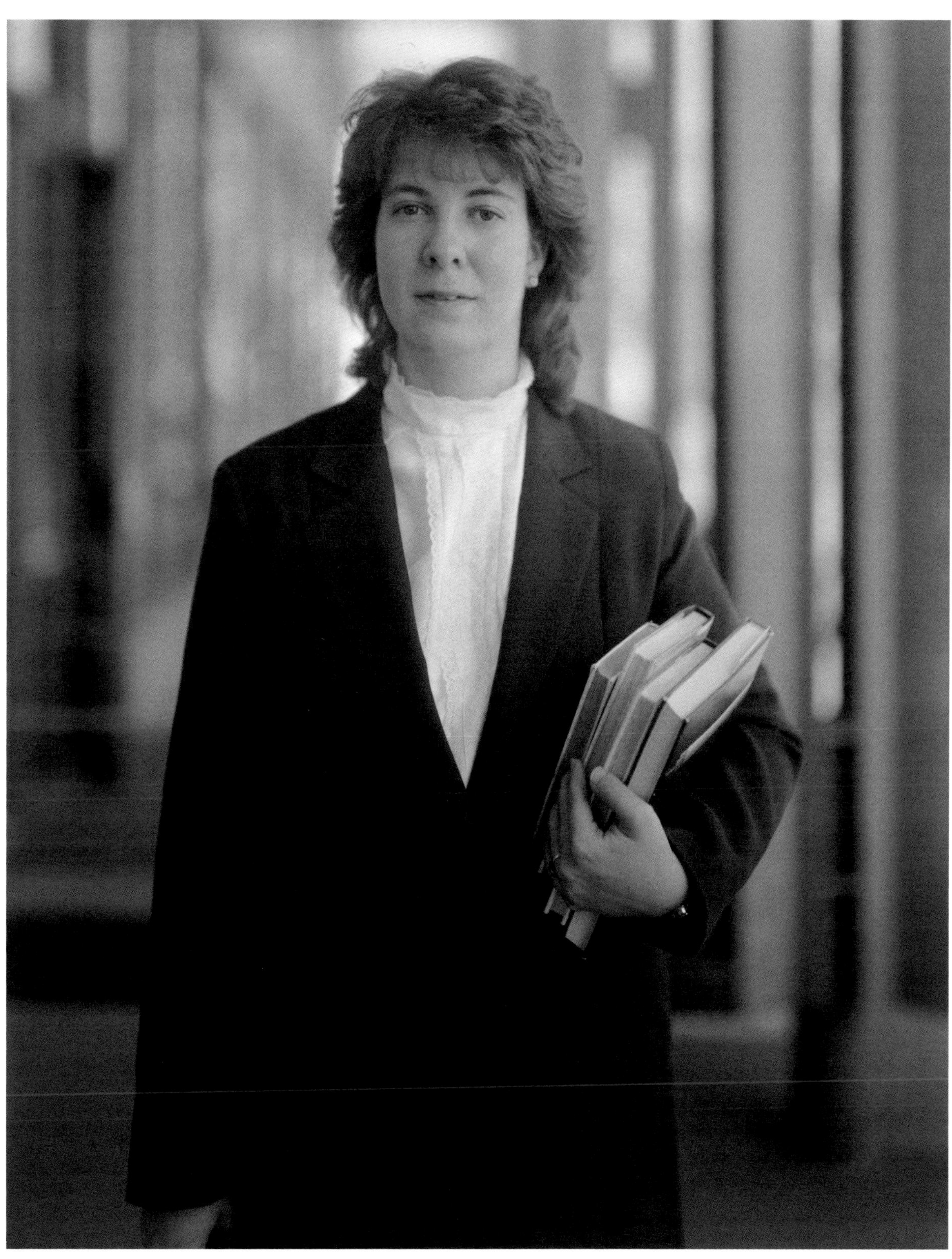

Ohne Titel | Untitled

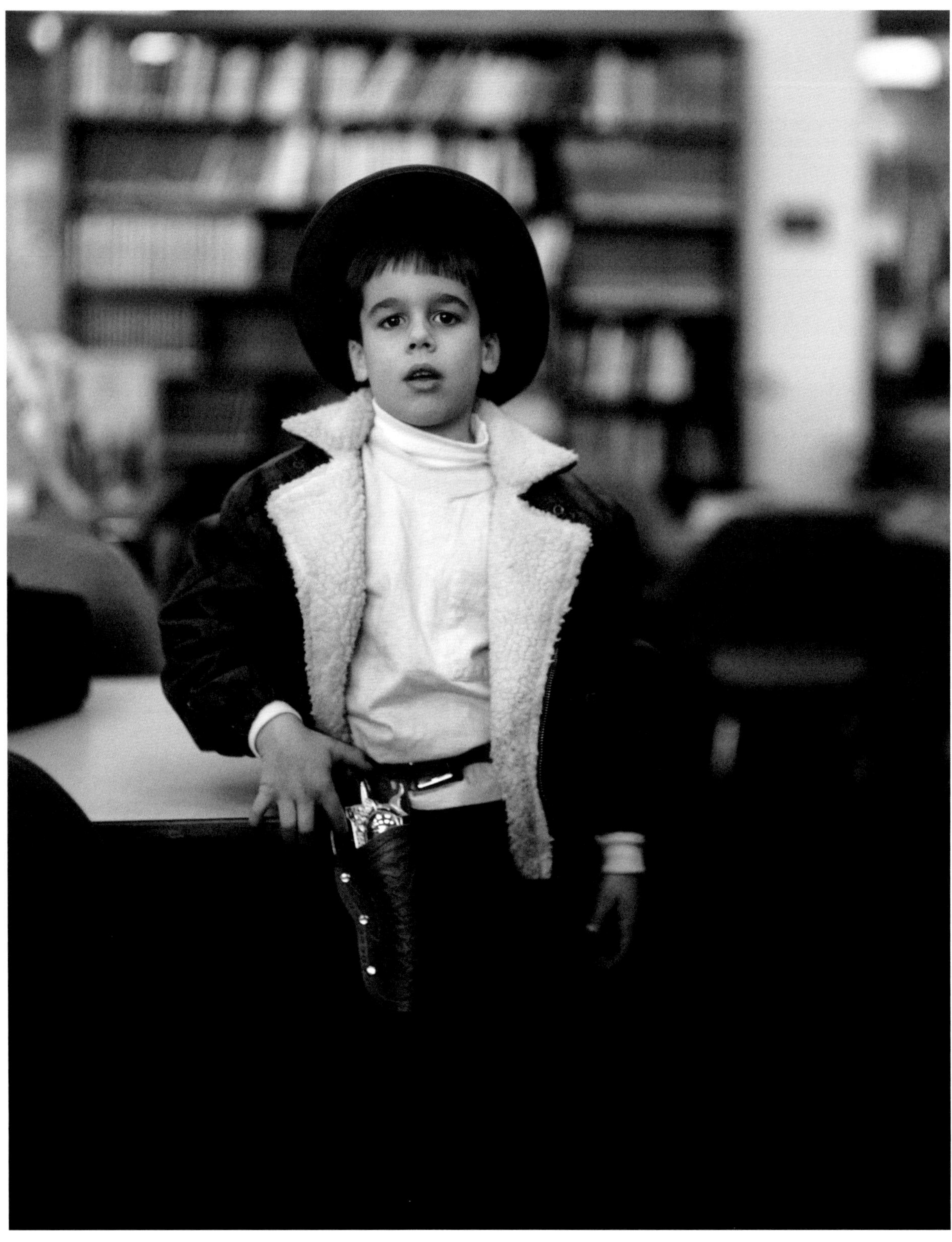

Ohne Titel | Untitled

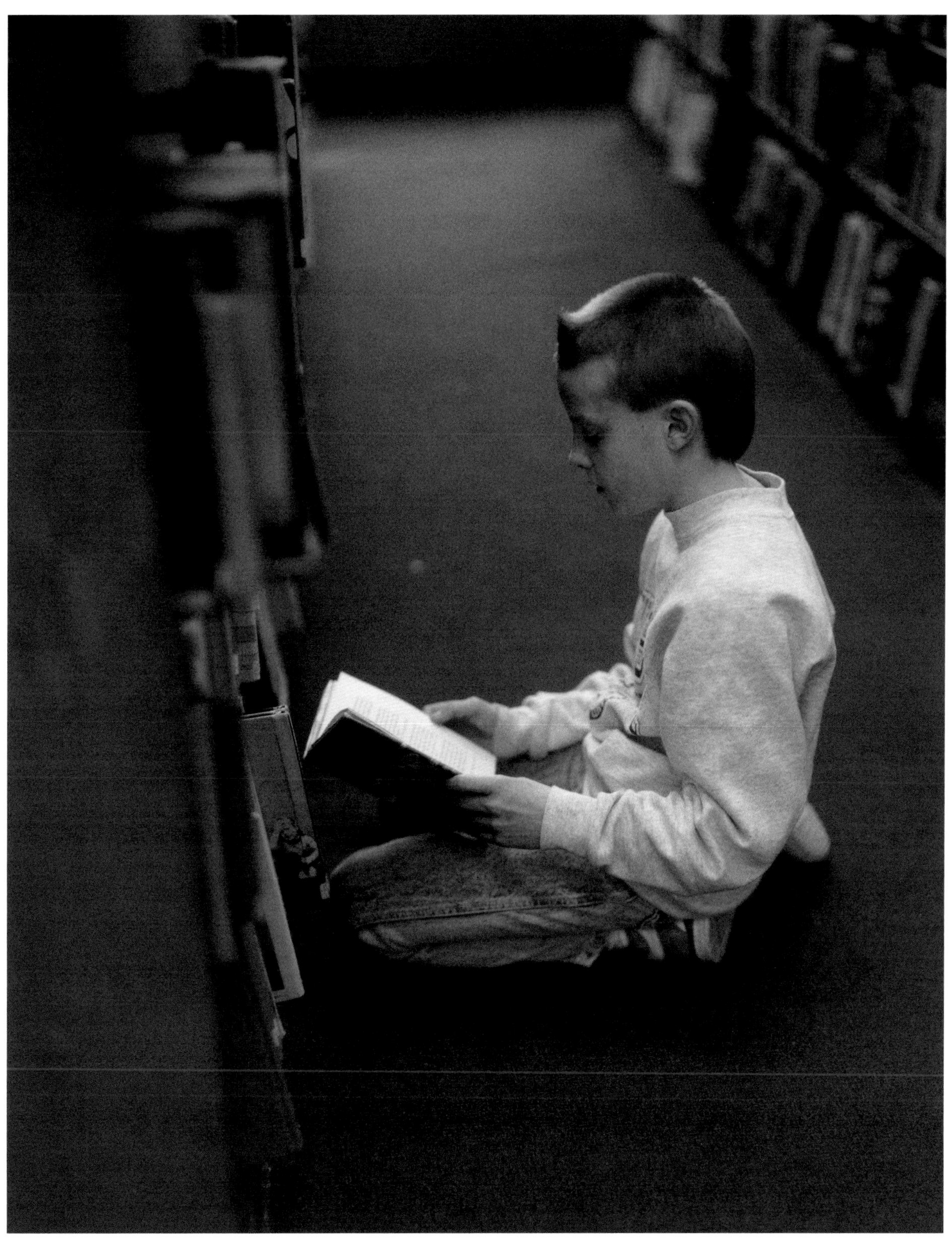

Ohne Titel | Untitled

Paris, 2003–2006

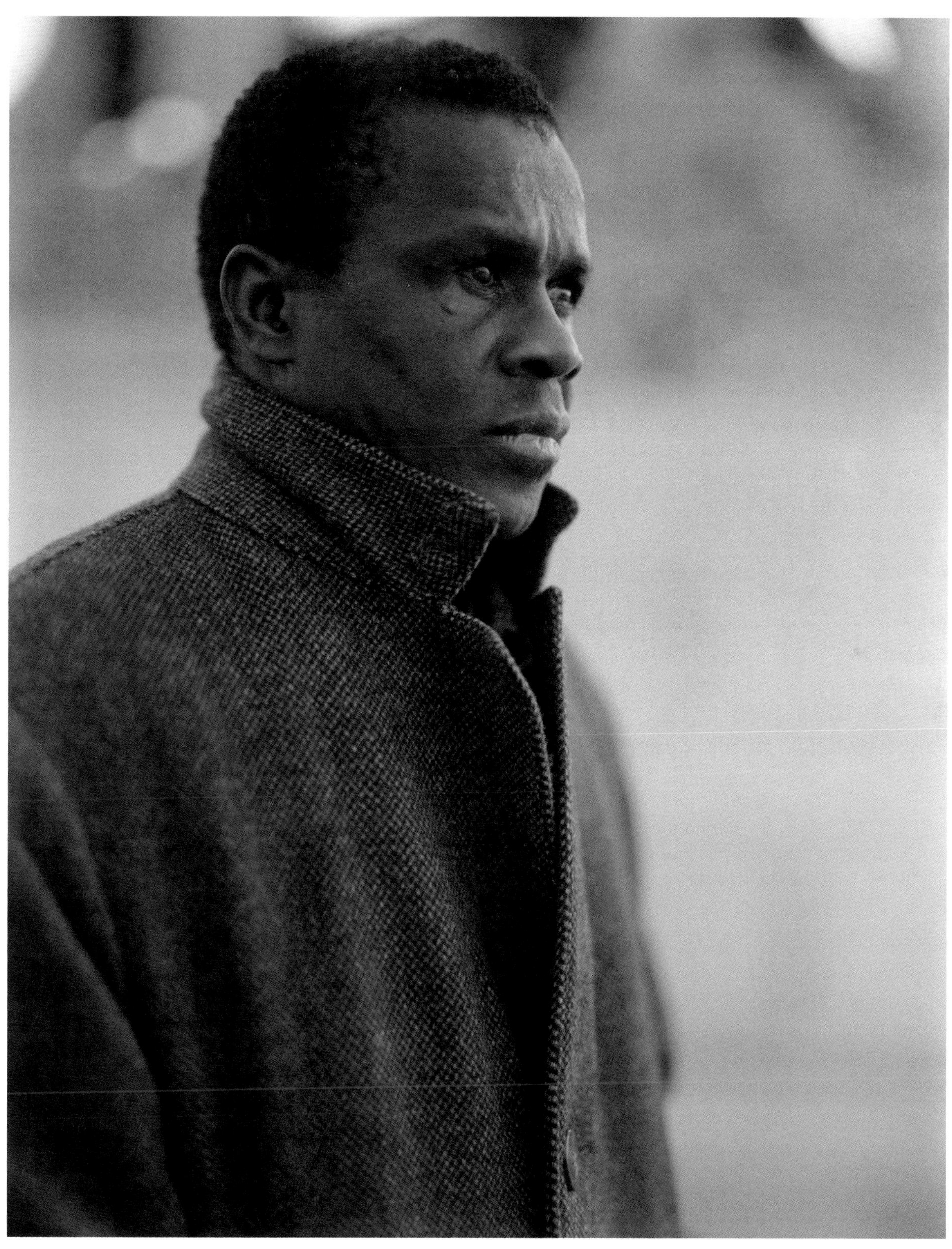

Seydou Camera, Place de la Concorde, 2006

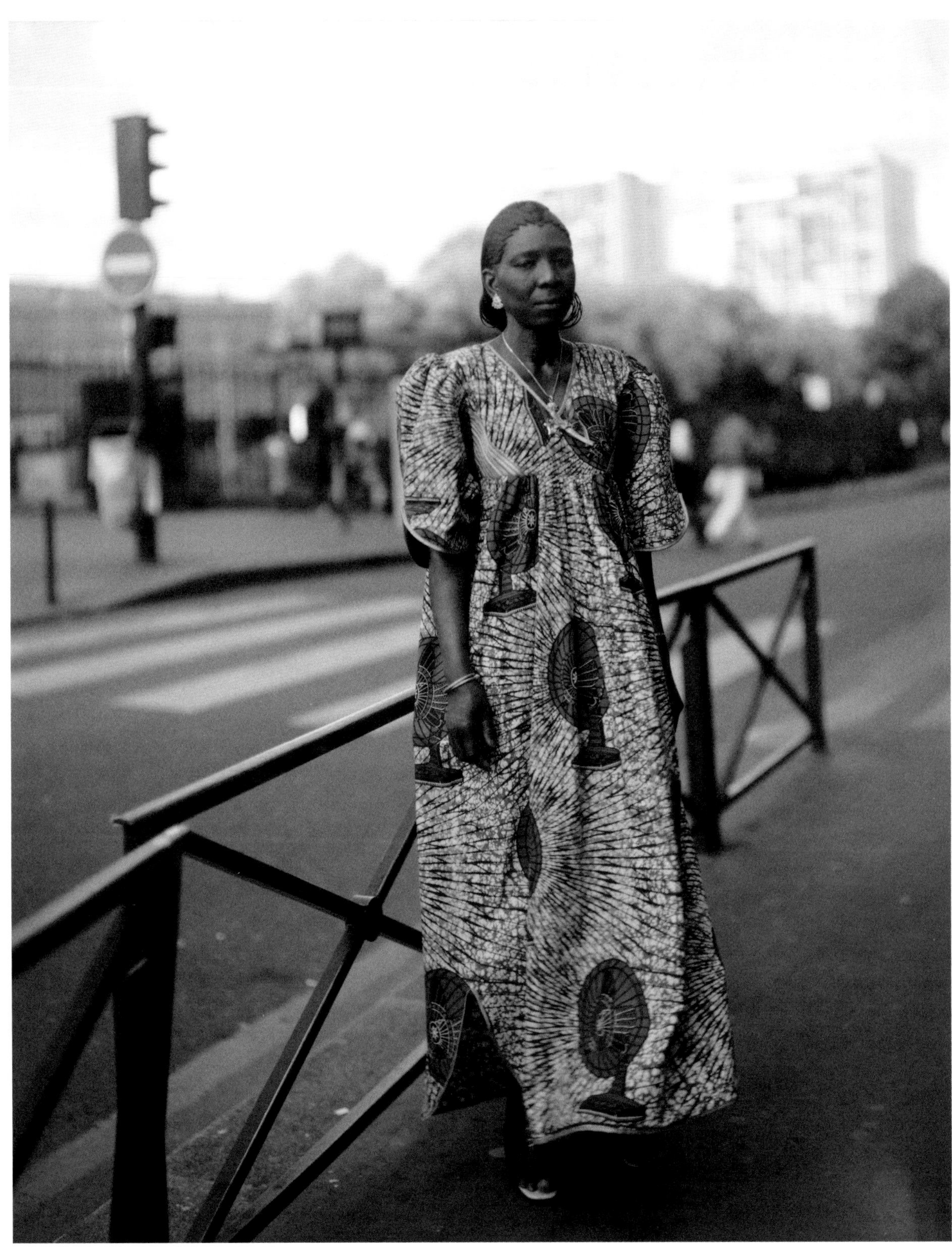

Madame Magassouba, Porte de Clignancourt, 2003

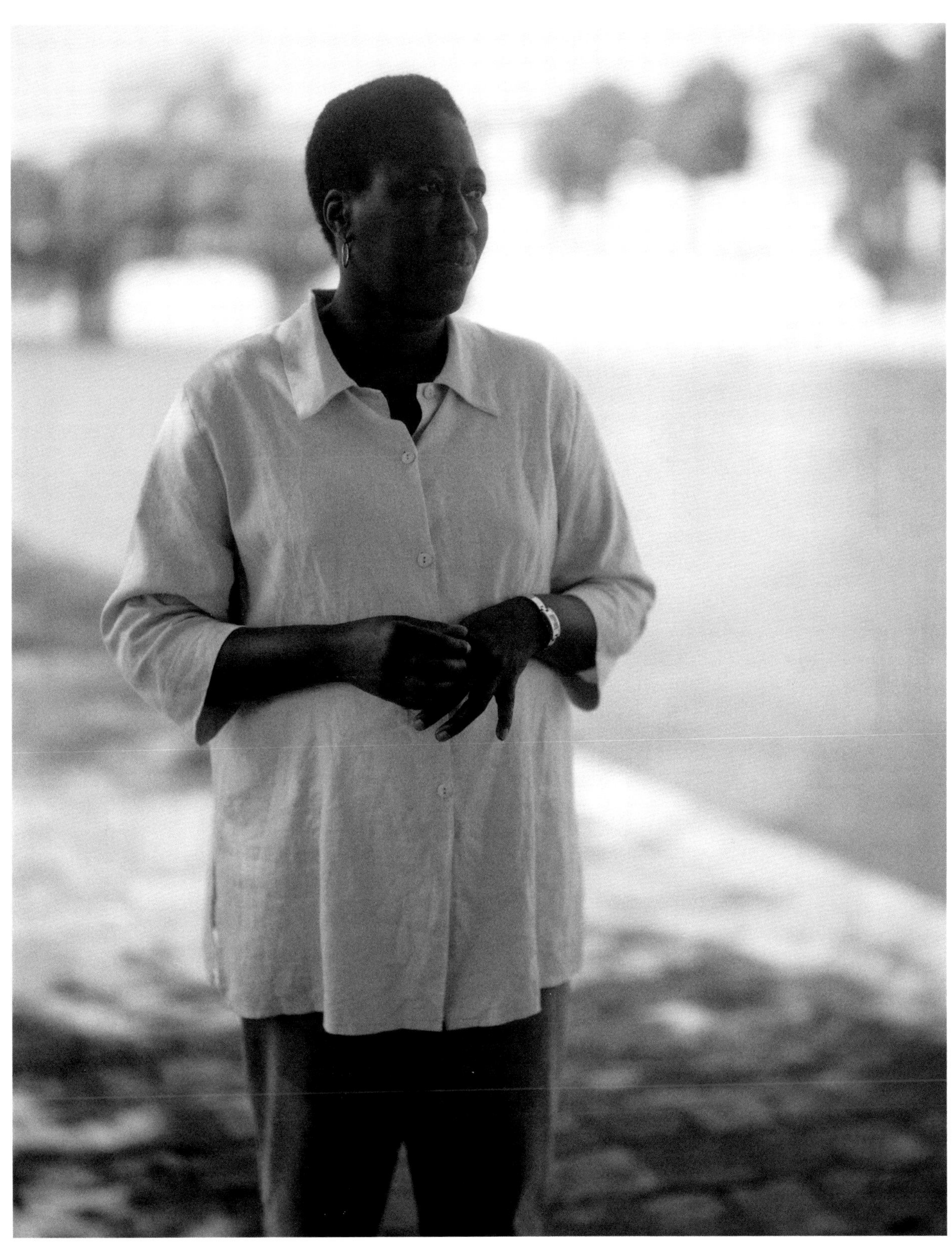

Laura Mandala, Square du Vert-Galant, 2003

After Church, 2005–2009

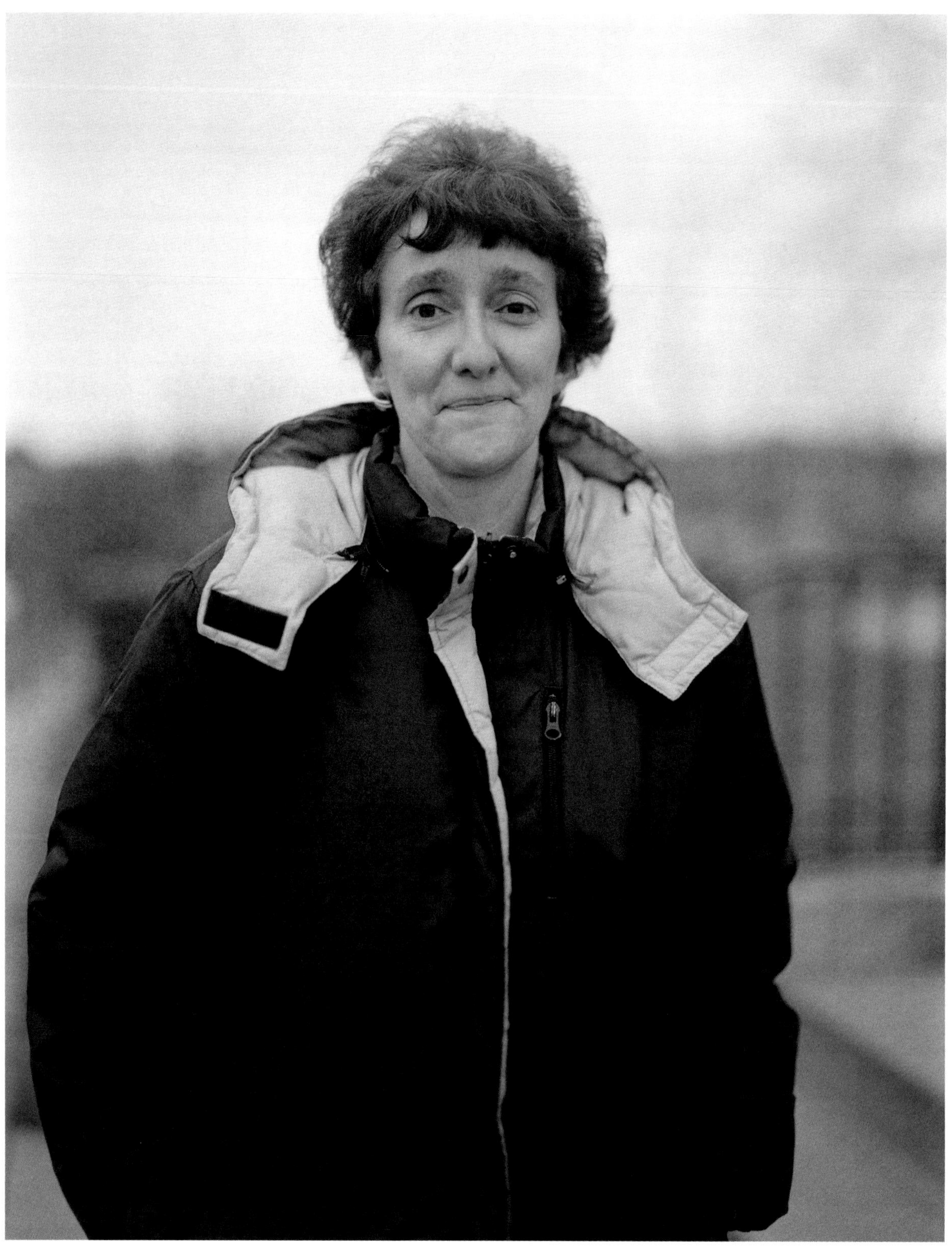

Ohne Titel | Untitled, Sellersville, Pennsylvania, 2005

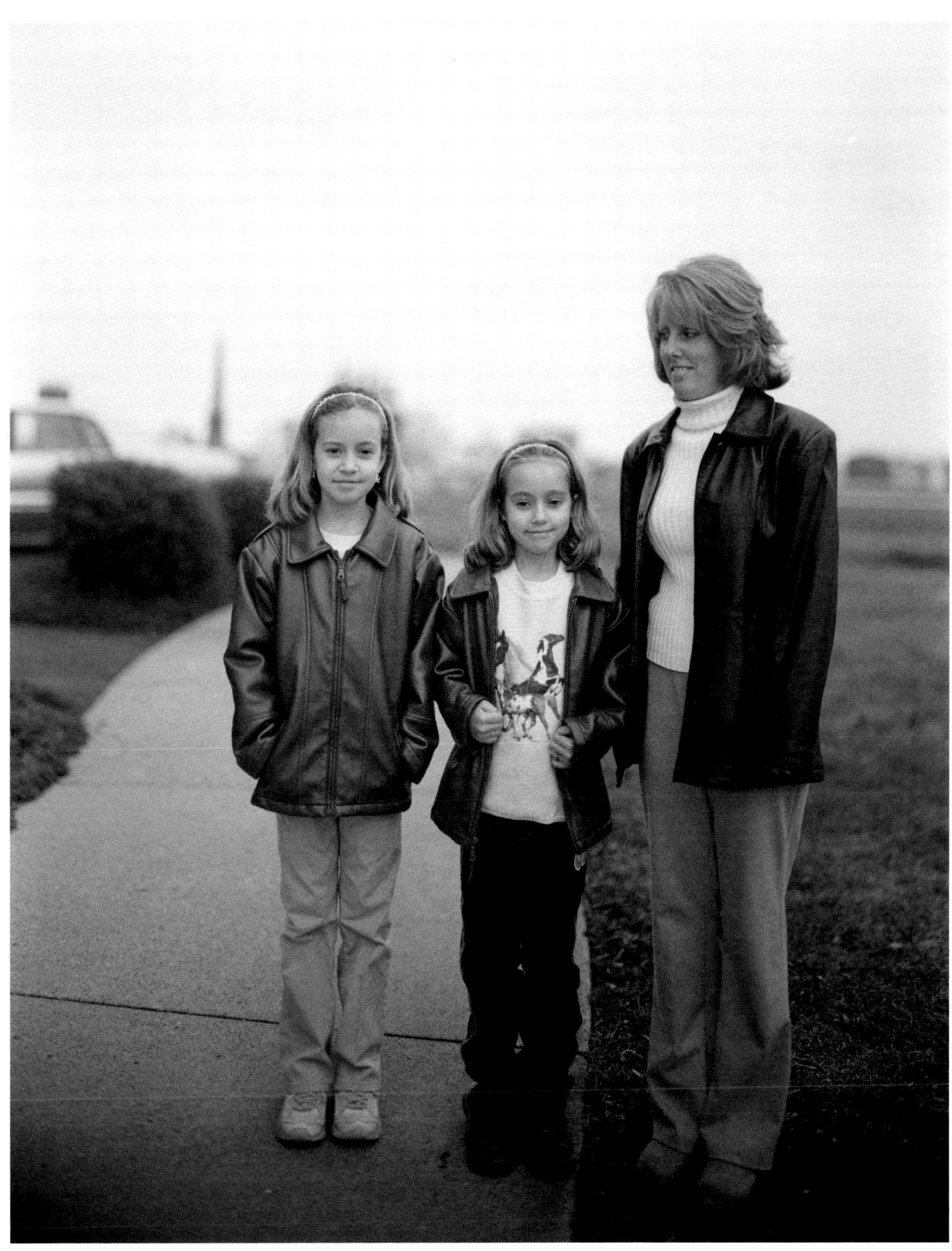

Ohne Titel | Untitled, Sellersville, Pennsylvania, 2005

Portraits of the Hazleton Public Schools, 1992–1994

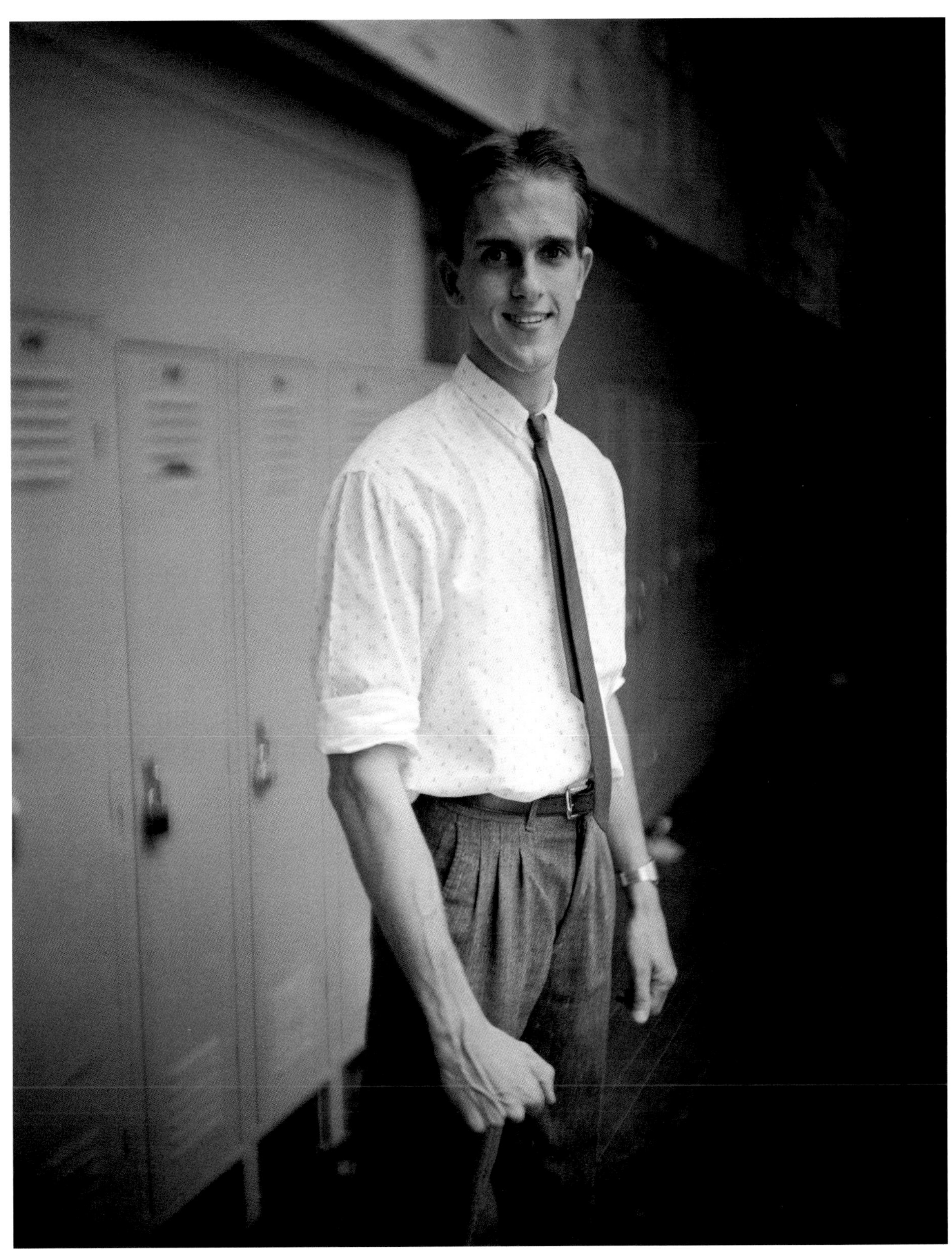

Junglehrer | First-Year Teacher,
H. F. Grebey Junior High School, 1992

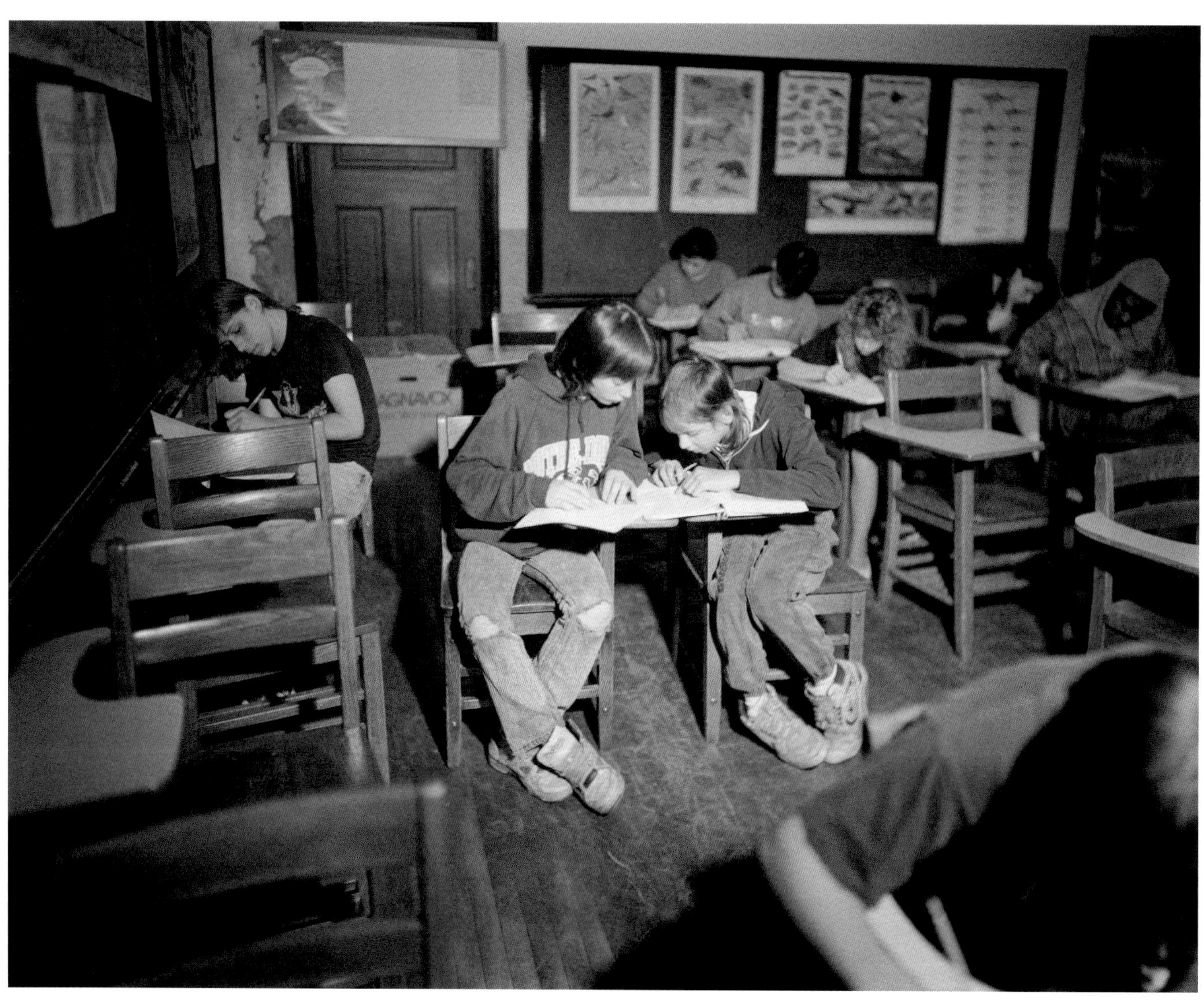

Schulfreunde | Study Buddies,
H. F. Grebey Junior High School, 1992

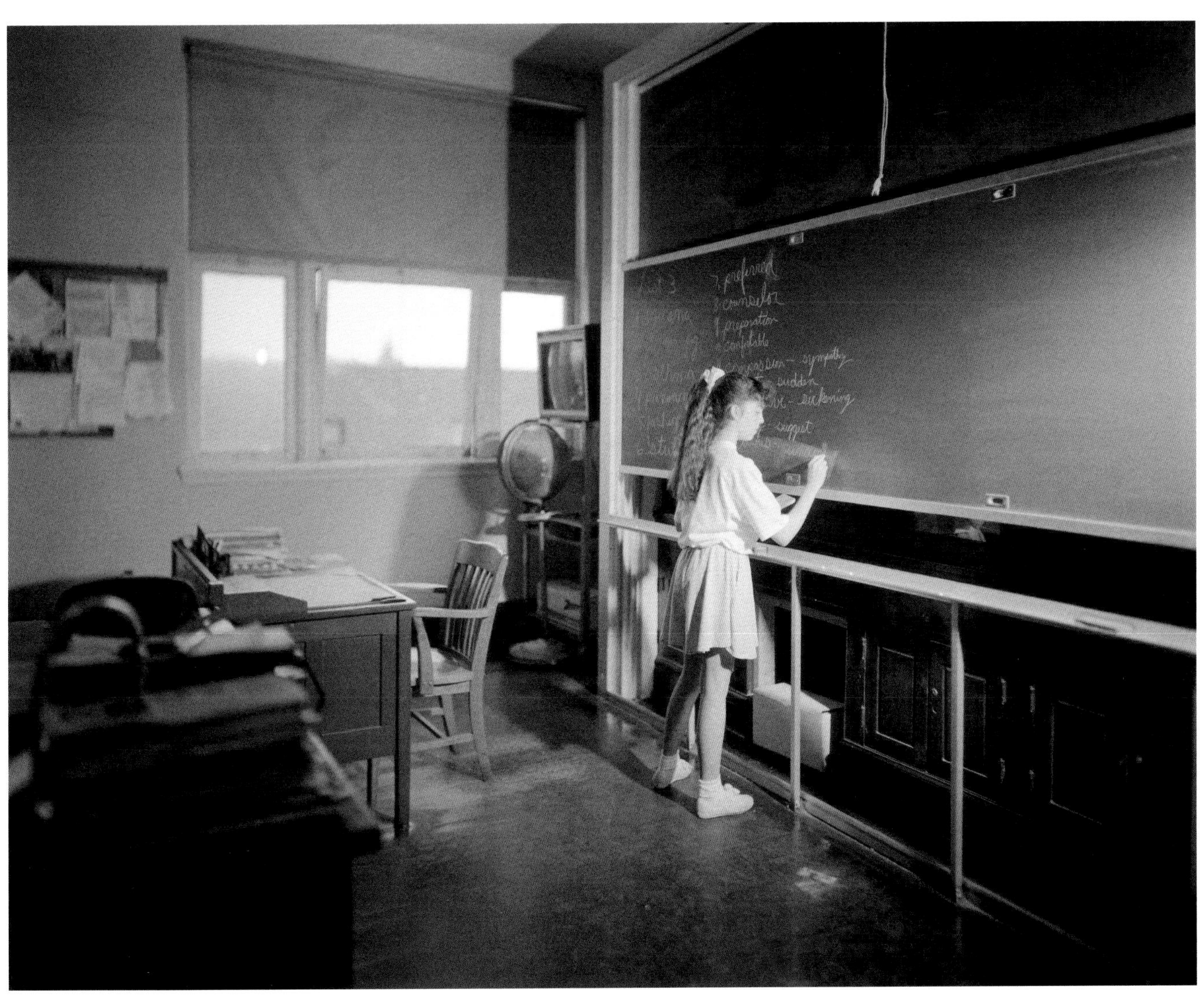

Unterricht in Rechtschreibung, 7. Klasse | 7th Grade
Spelling Lesson, H. F. Grebey Junior High School, 1992

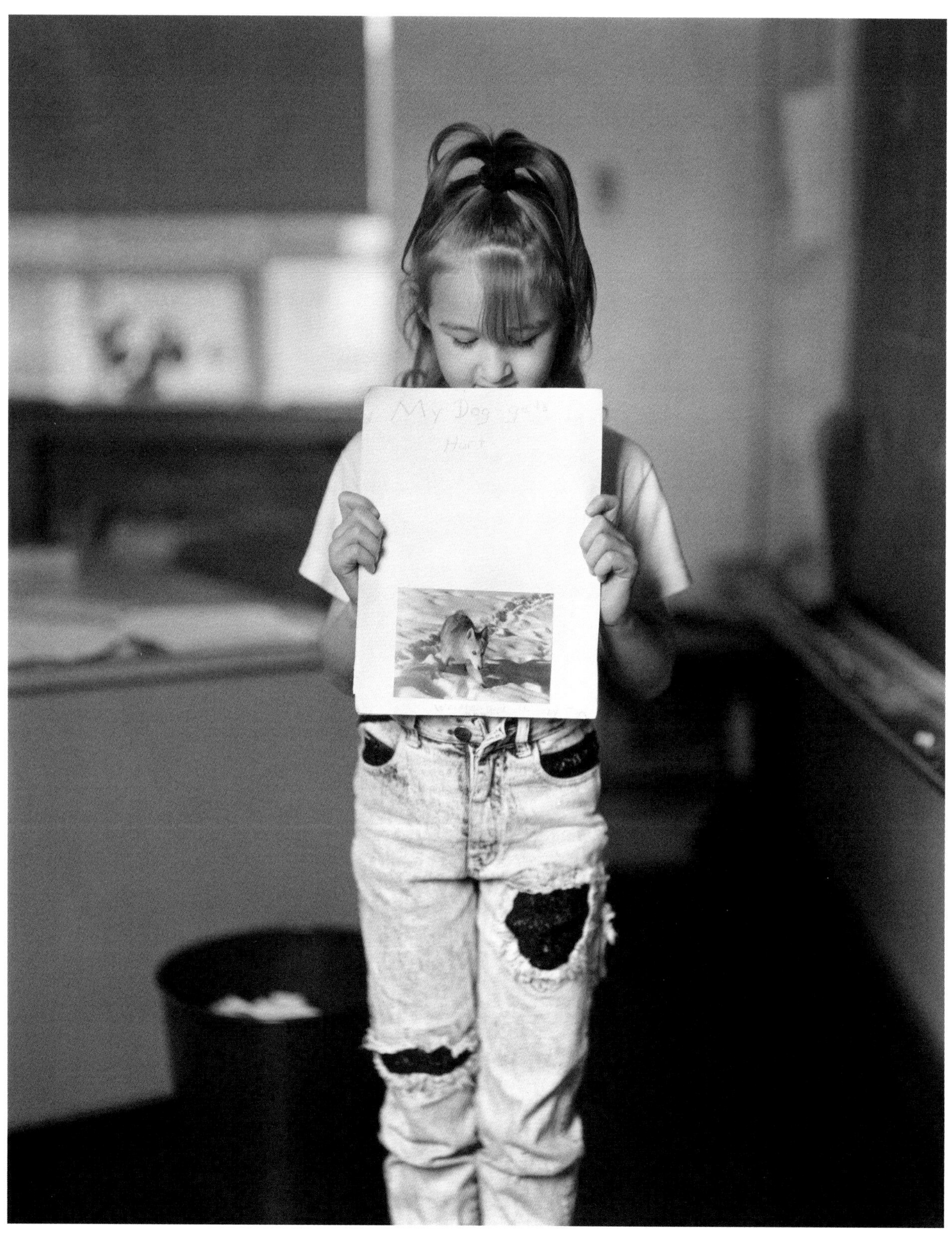

Tara Schwenks Buch *Als mein Hund verletzt wurde* | Tara Schwenk's Book Report *My Dog Gets Hurt,* A. D. Thomas Elementary School, 1992

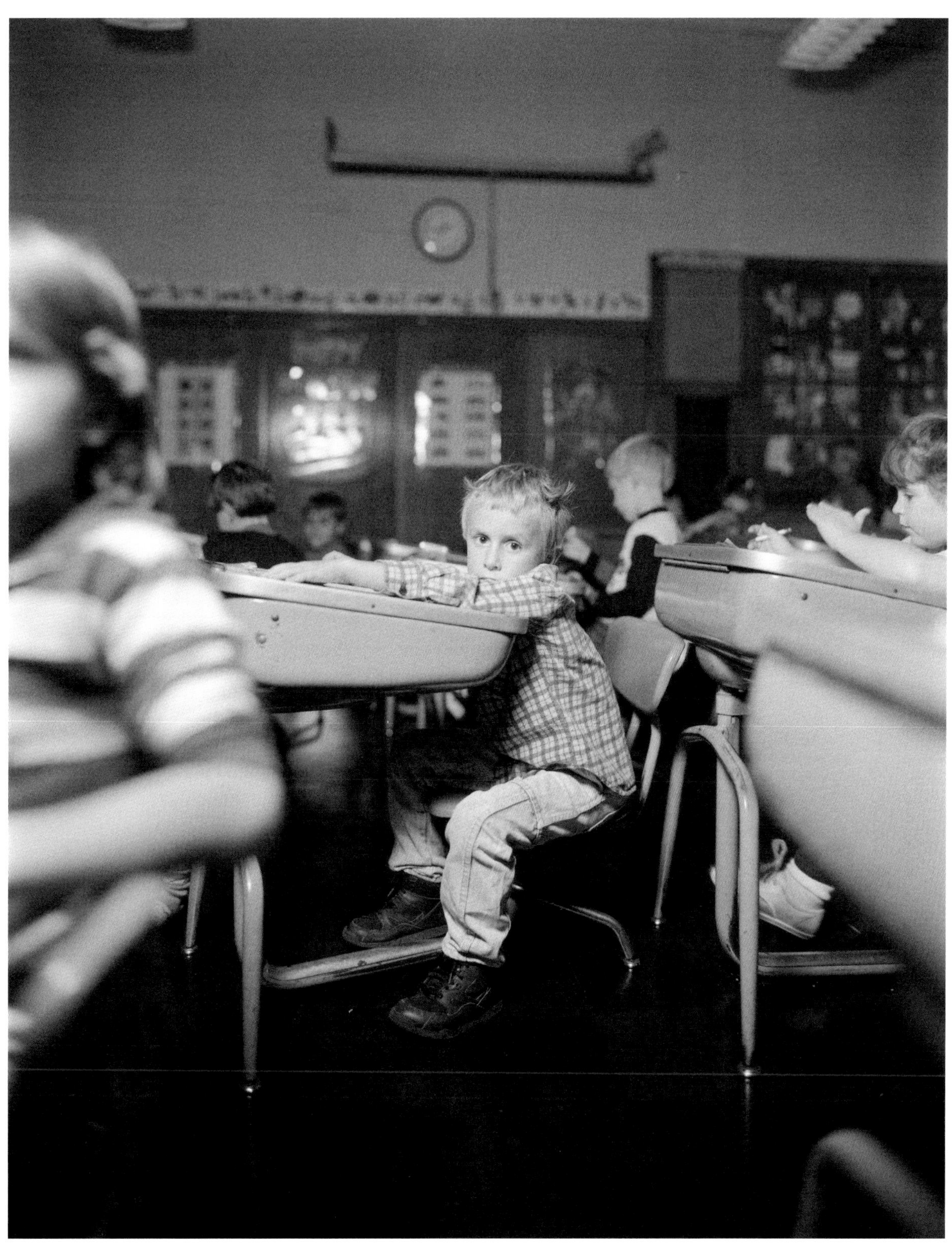

Randy Sartori, Frau Starkeys 1. Klasse | Randy Sartori, 1st Grade, Mrs. Starkey's Class, A. D. Thomas Elementary School, 1992

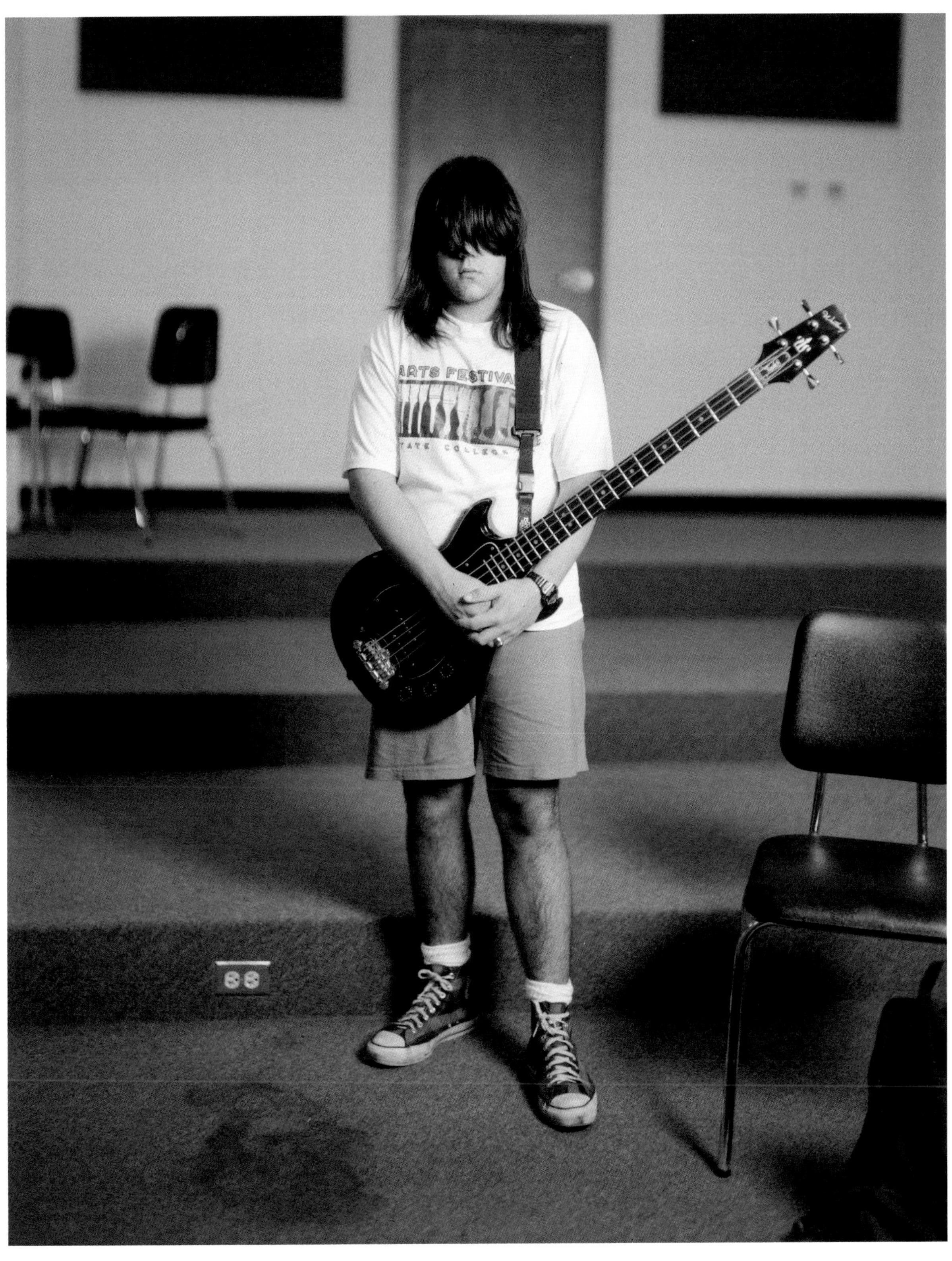

John Lonczynski aus Herrn Rosatos Musikklasse | John Lonczynski in Mr. Rosato's Band Class, Hazleton Area High School, 1994

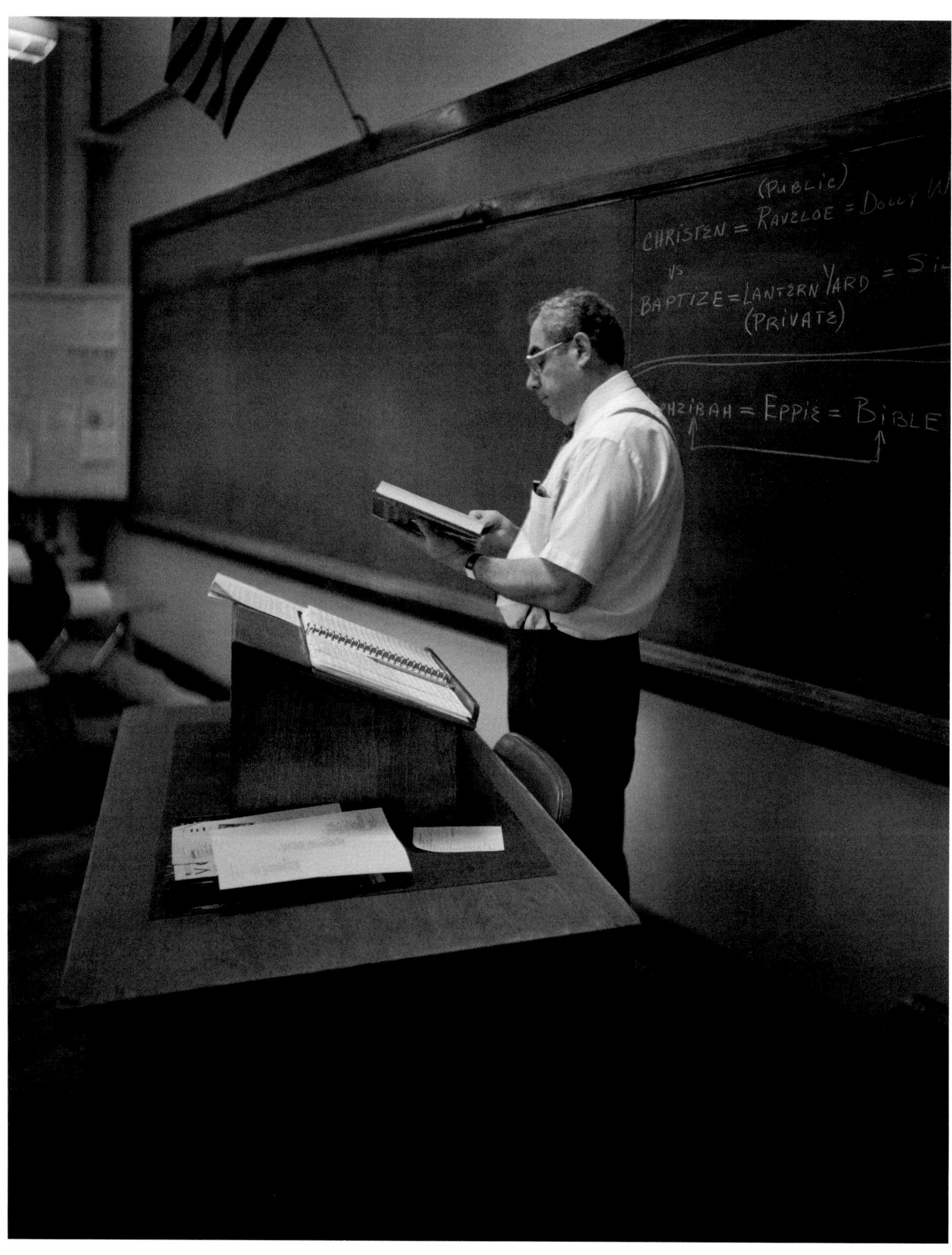

Mr. Robert Gaudio, Englischlehrer für die 10. Klasse |
10th Grade English Teacher, Hazleton High School, 1992

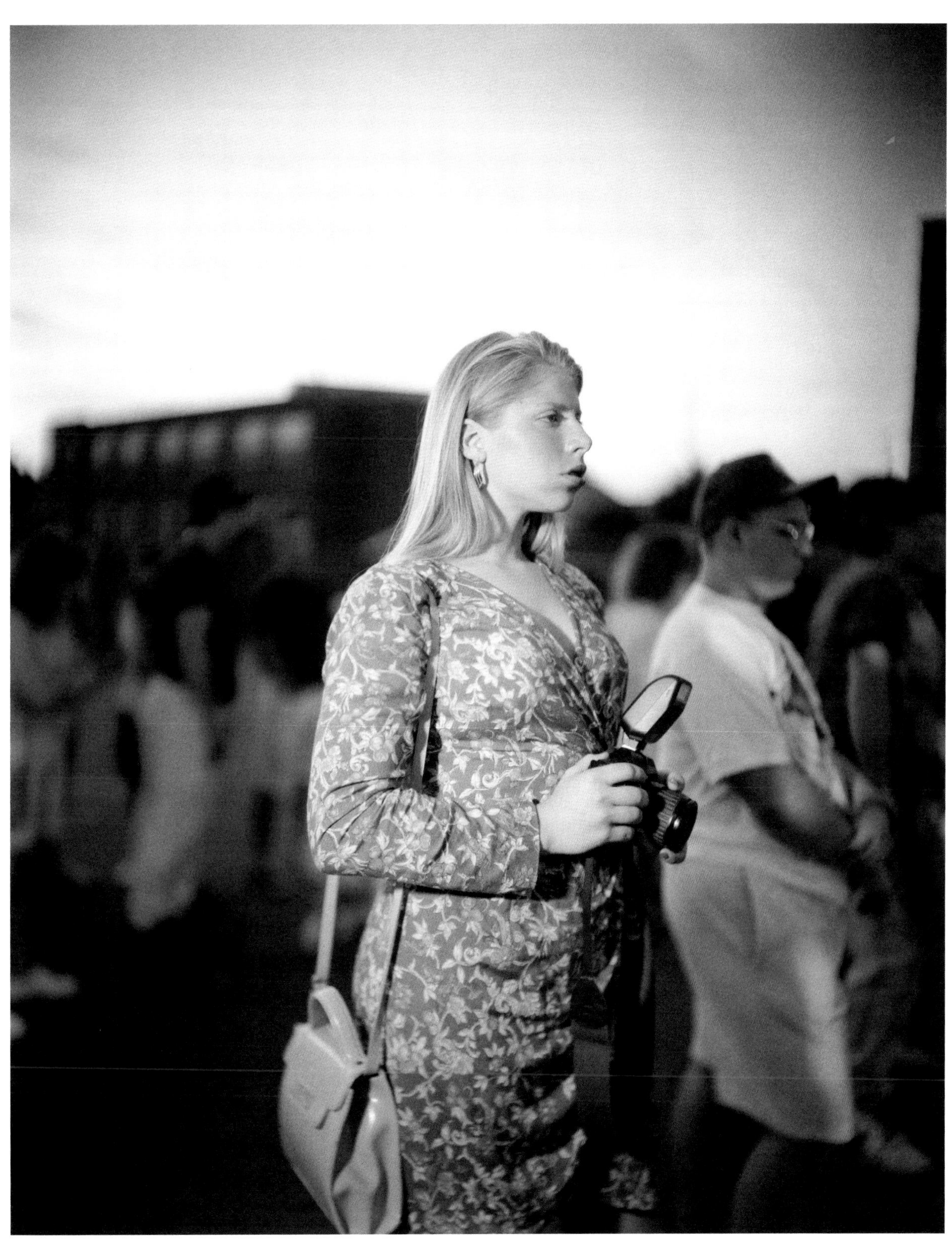

Abschlussfeier | Graduation,
Hazleton High School, 1992

Gallagher Junior High School, Cleveland, 1993

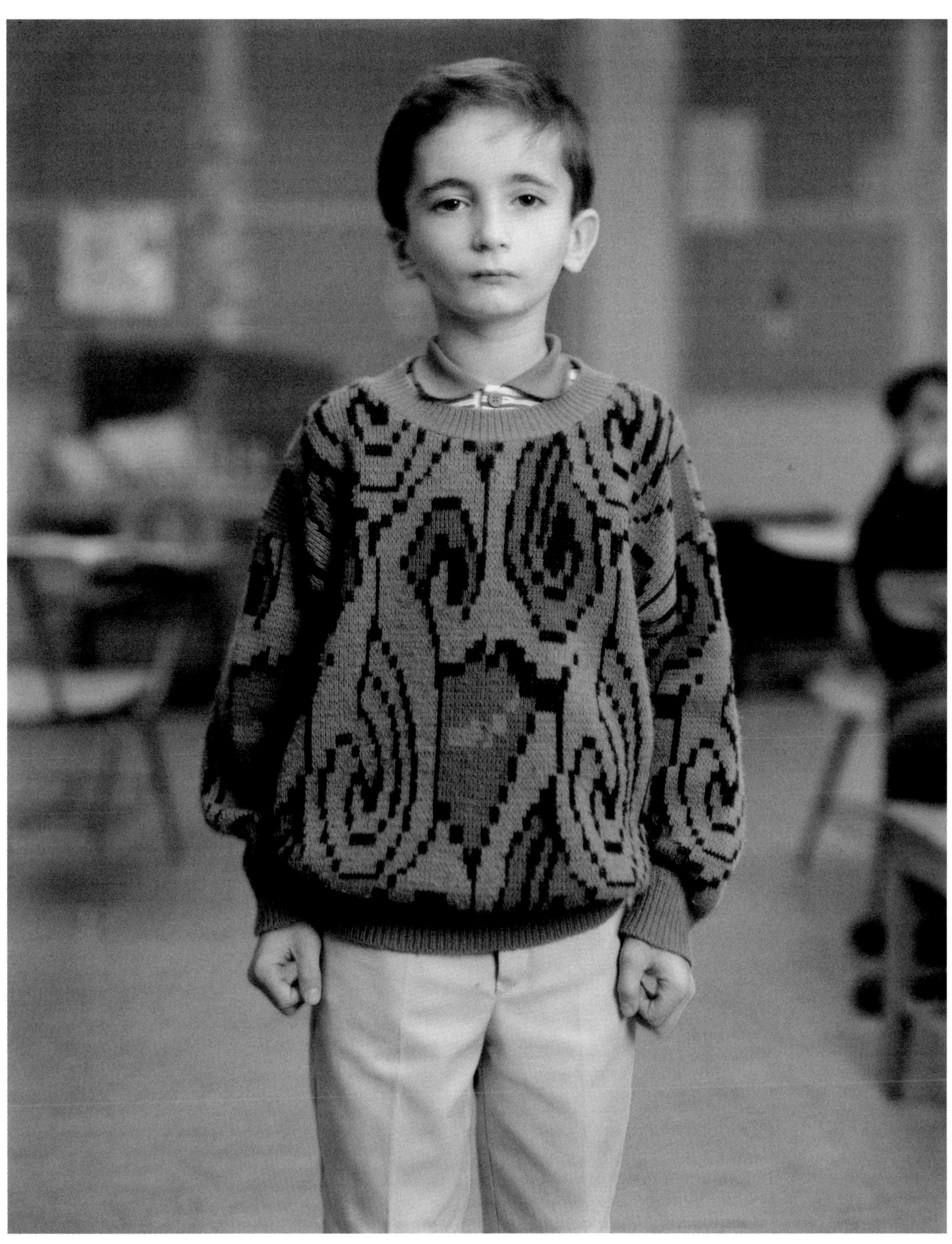

Svyatoslav Gera

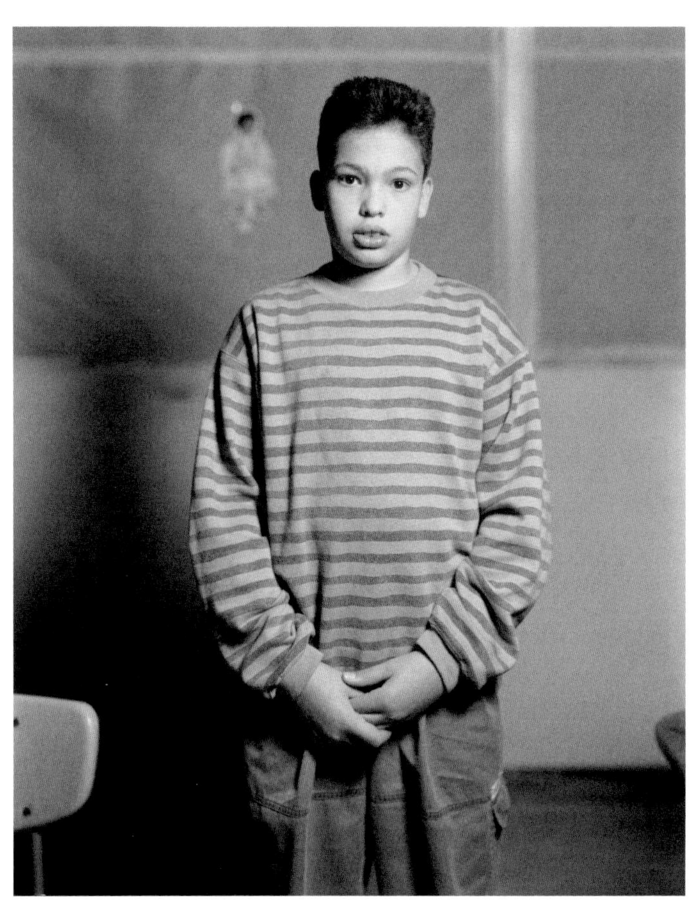

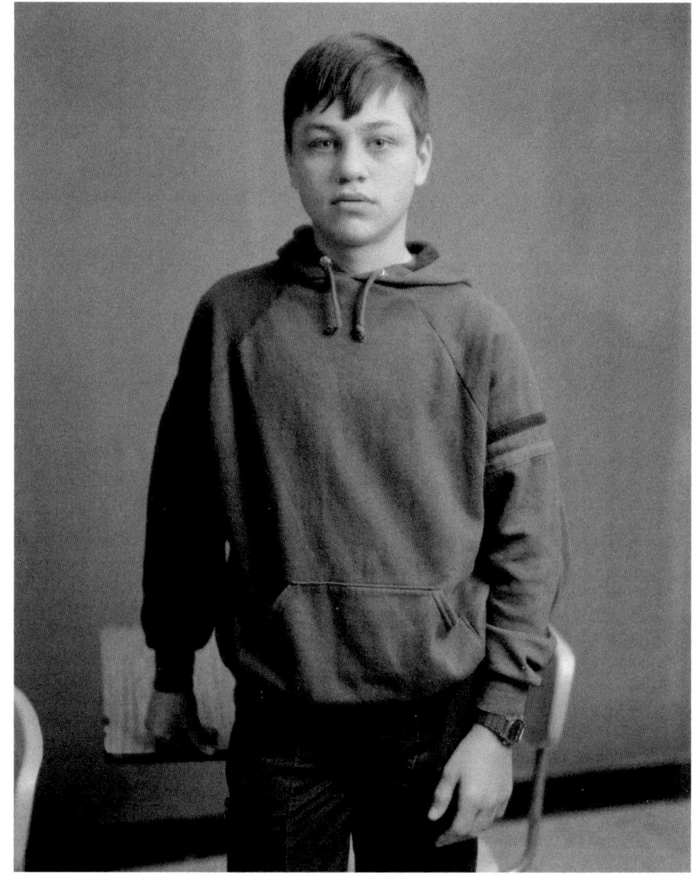

Juan Correa

Vladimir Kustnir

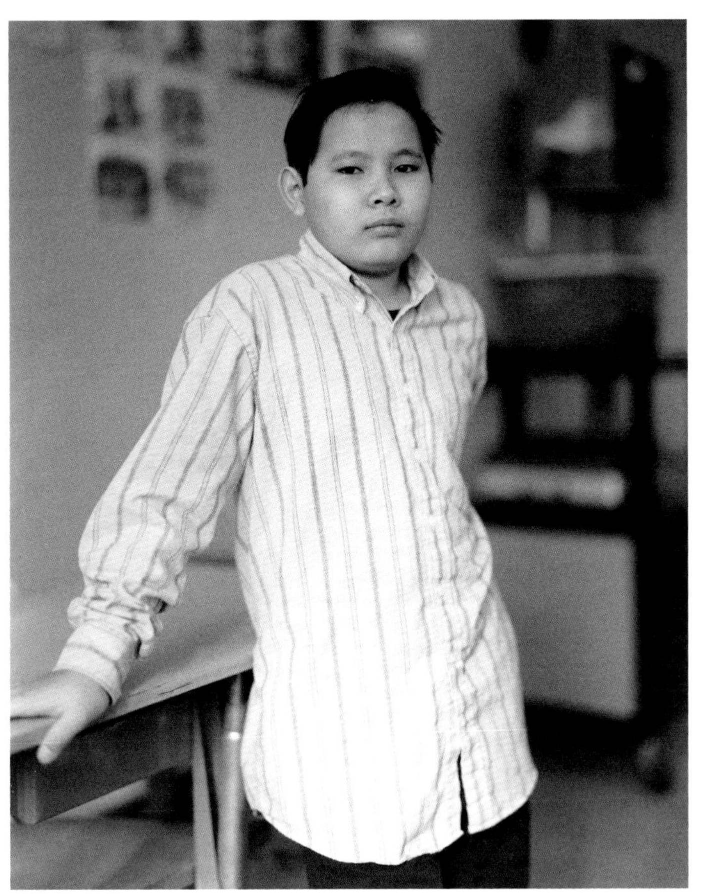

Ky Vuong

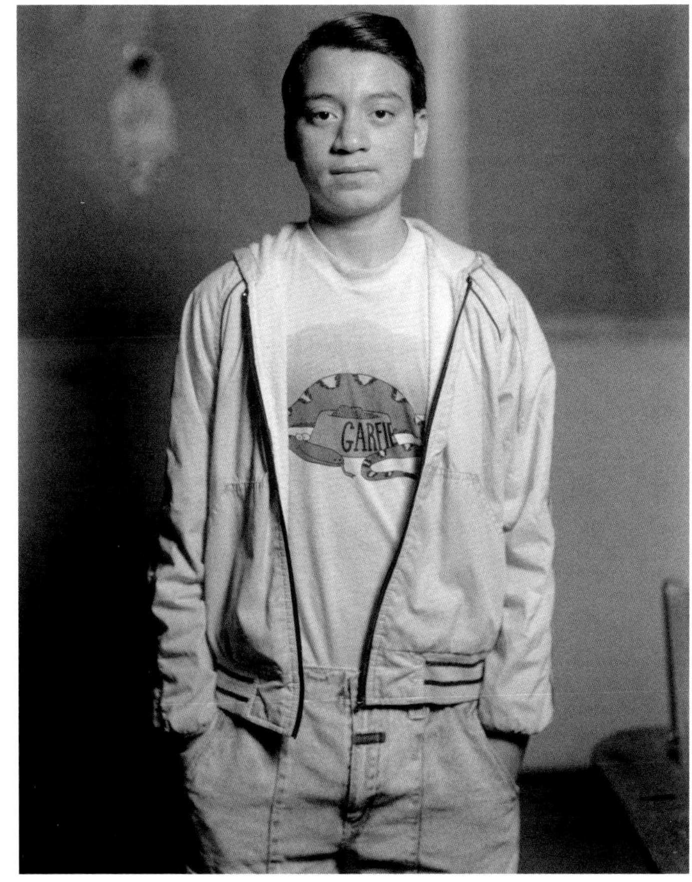

Leonico Cardona

Freeland, Pennsylvania, 2004

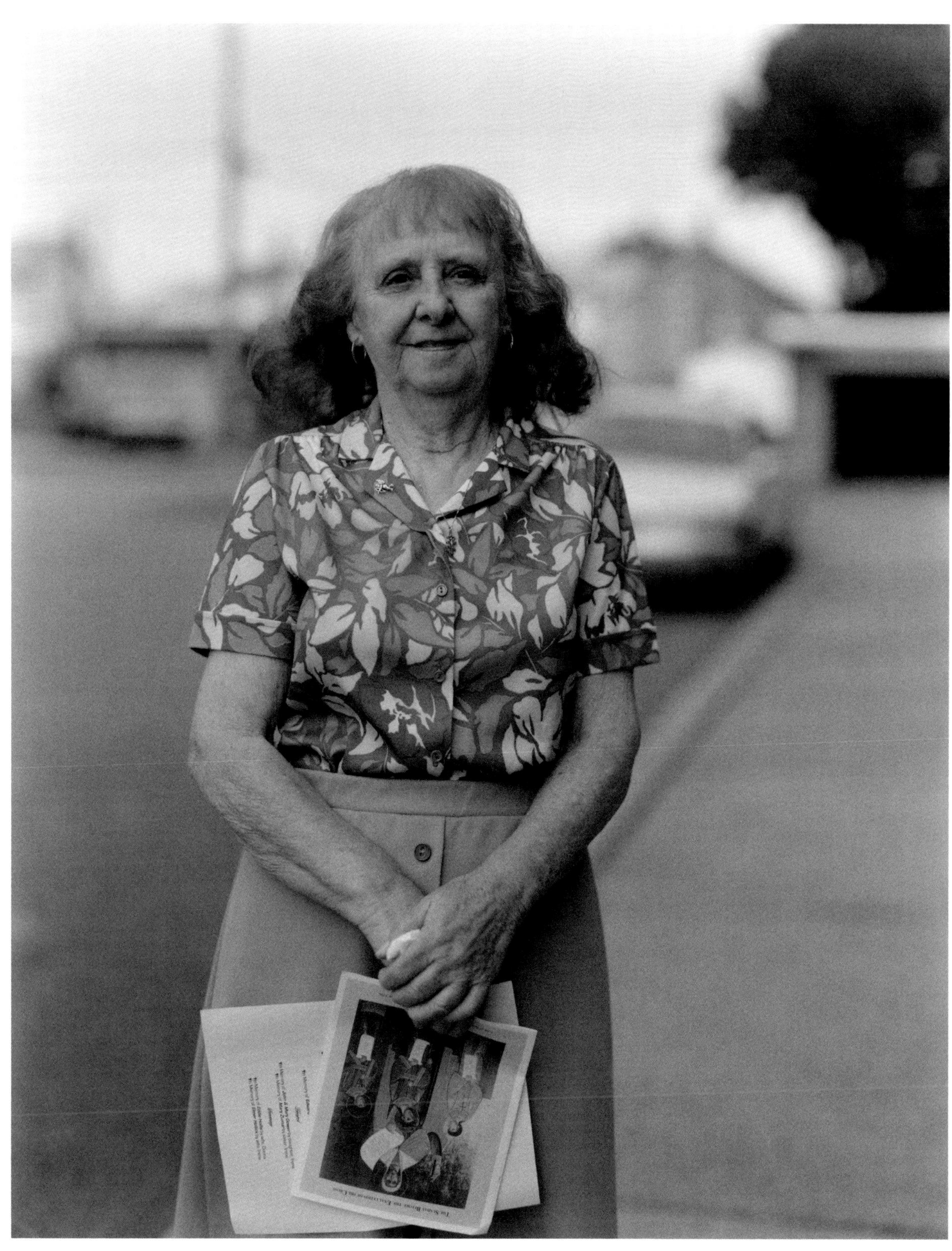

Kirchgängerin nach der Messe | Woman coming from Church

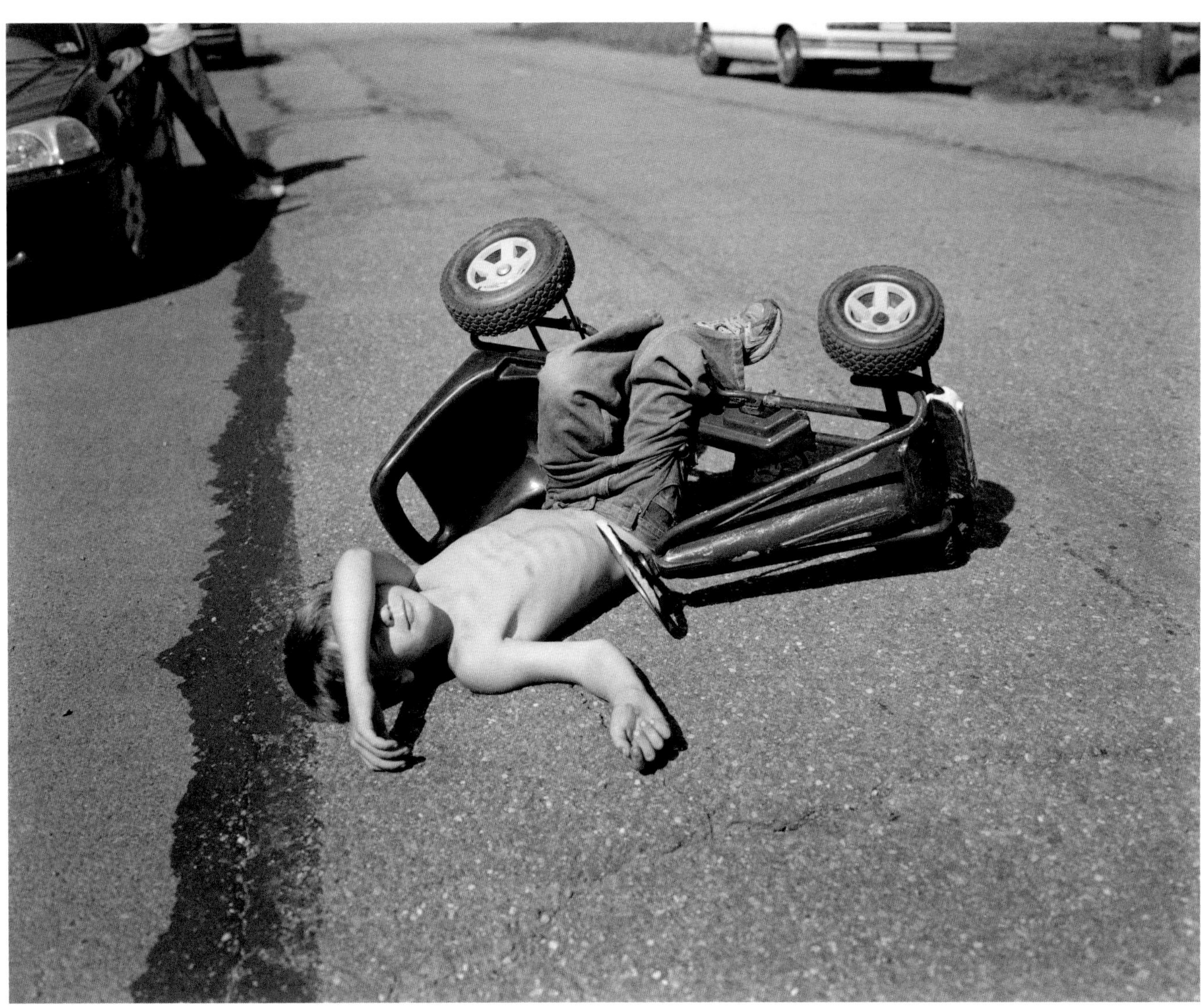

Tylers Unfall | Tyler's Crash

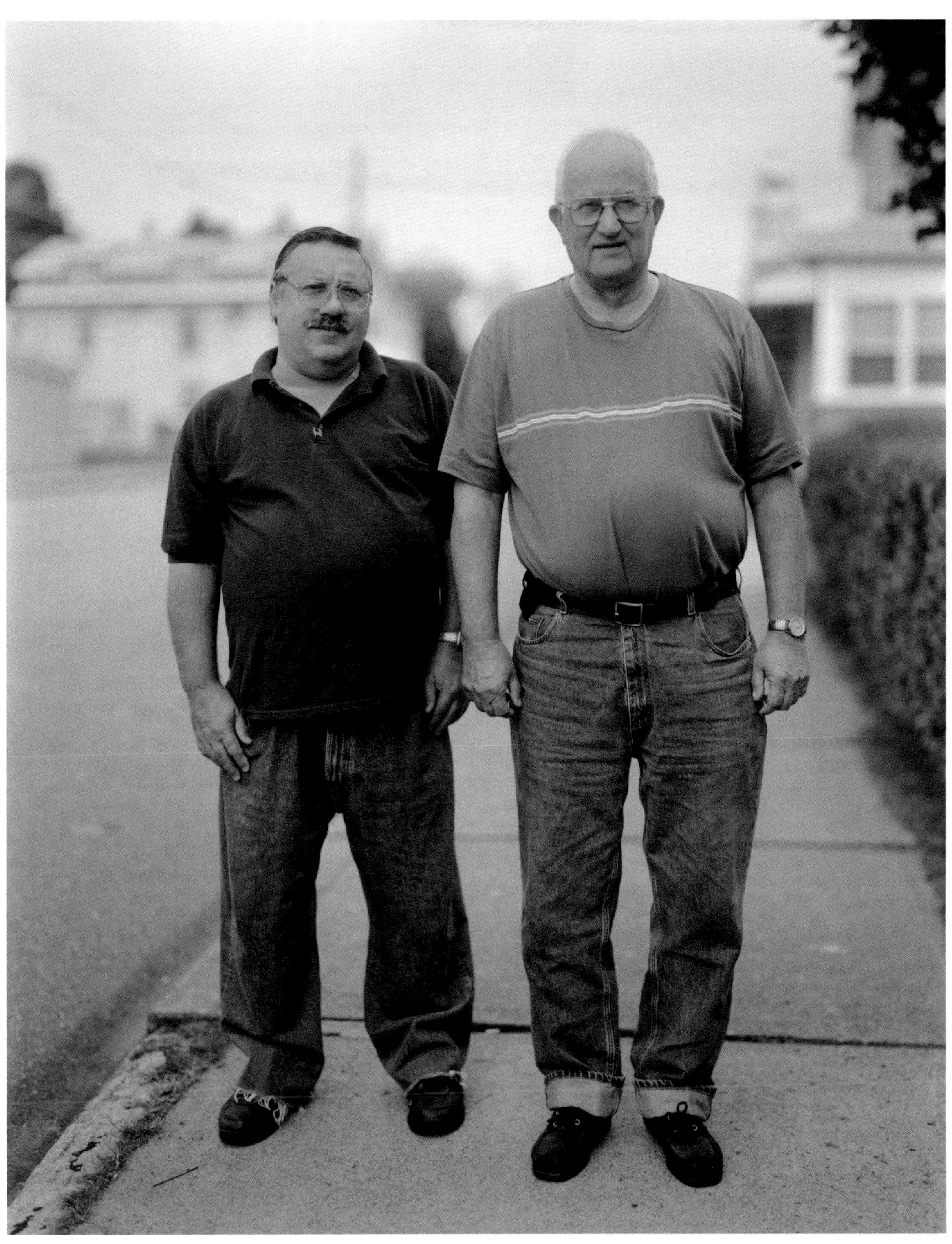

Frank Mancini, Joe Wessel

2046, 1996

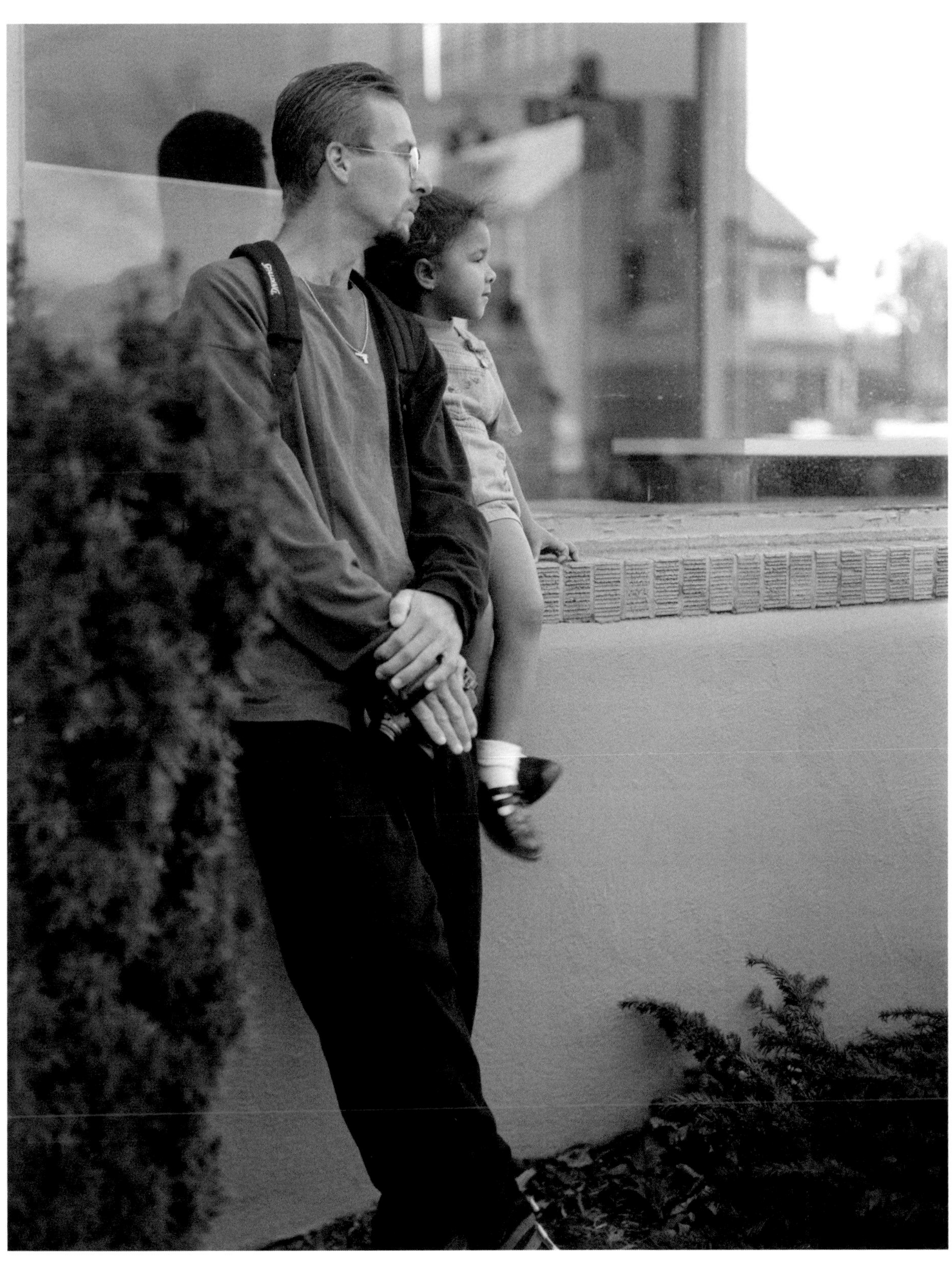

Ohne Titel | Untitled, Bethlehem, Pennsylvania

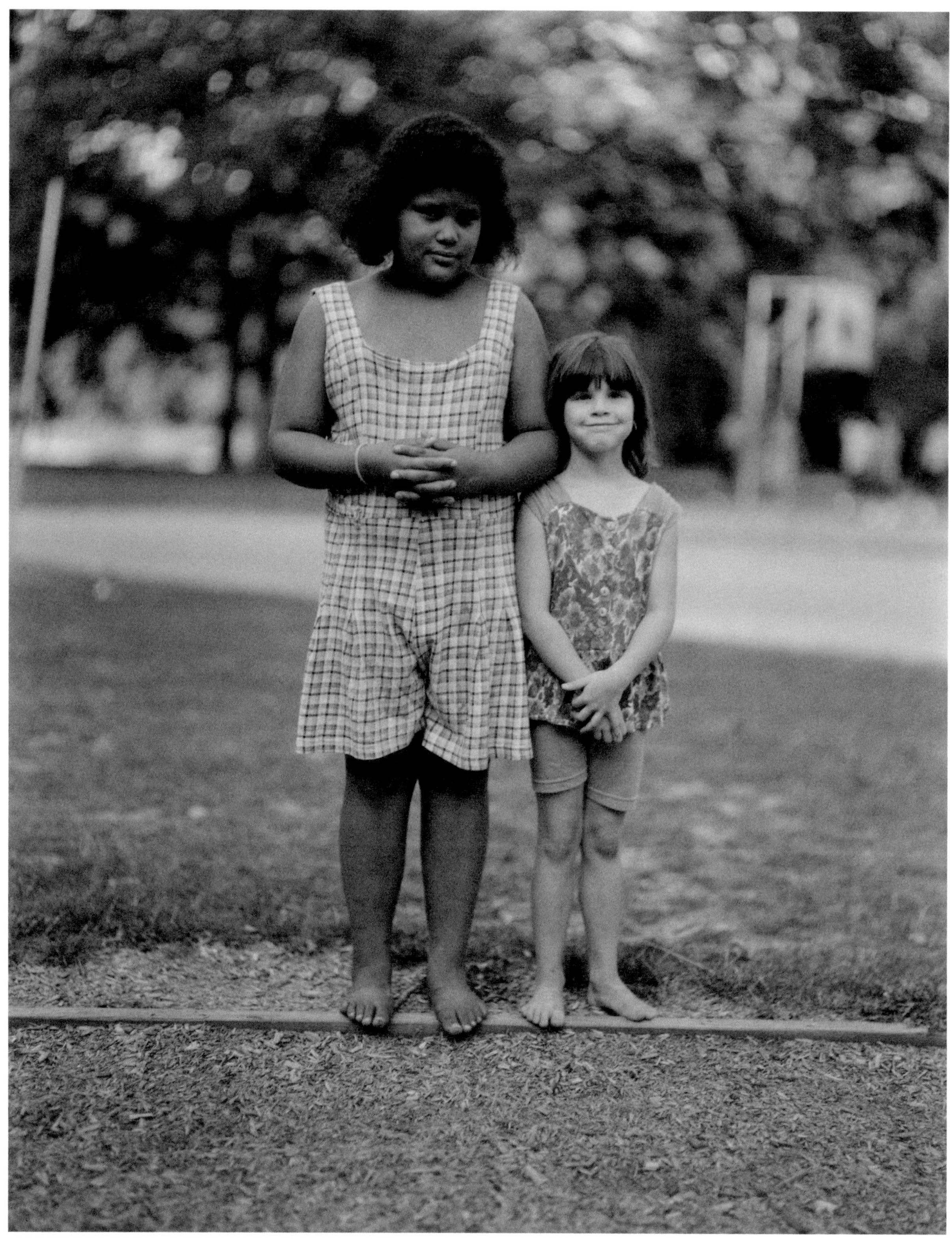

Ohne Titel | Untitled, Allentown, Pennsylvania

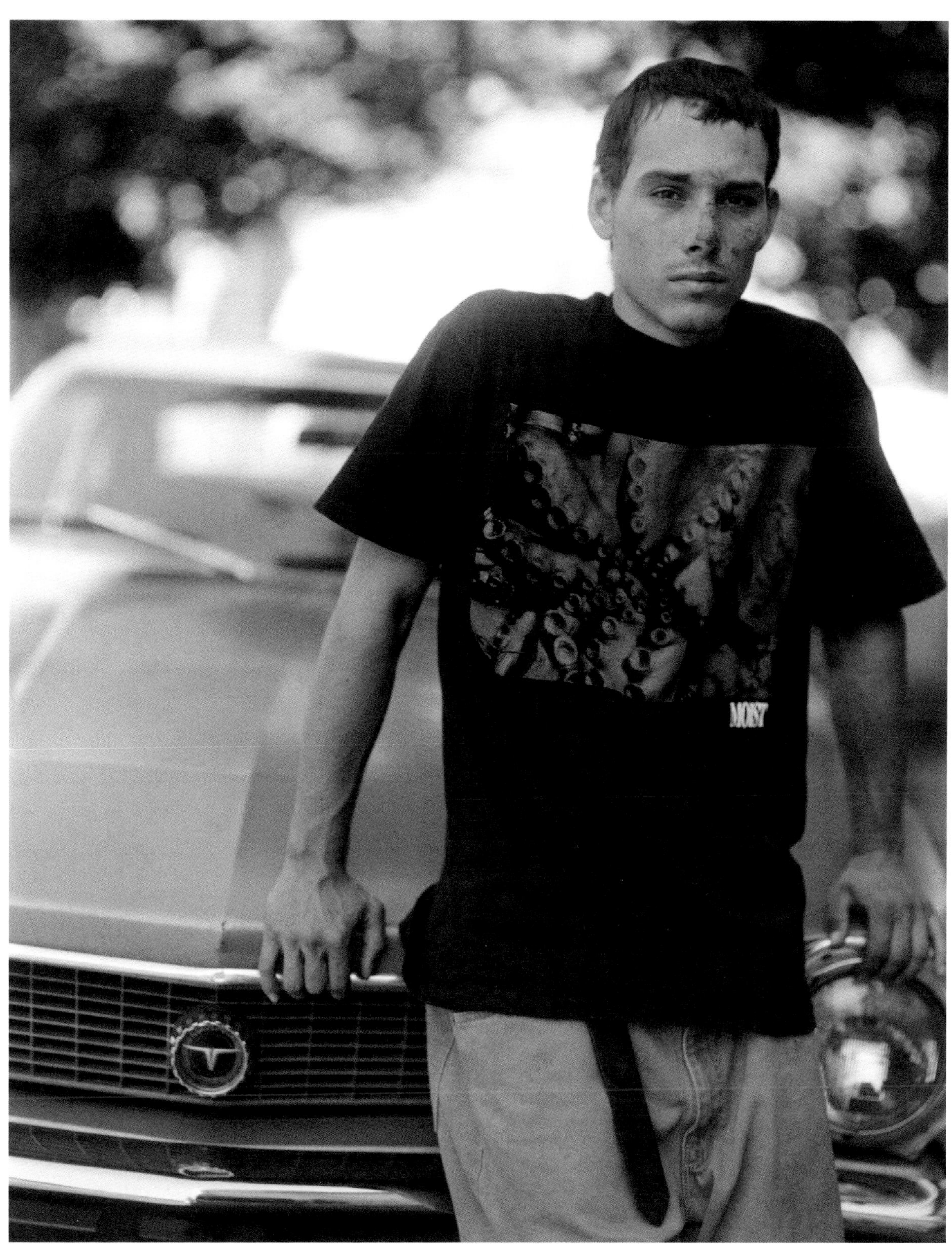

Ohne Titel | Untitled, Bethlehem, Pennsylvania

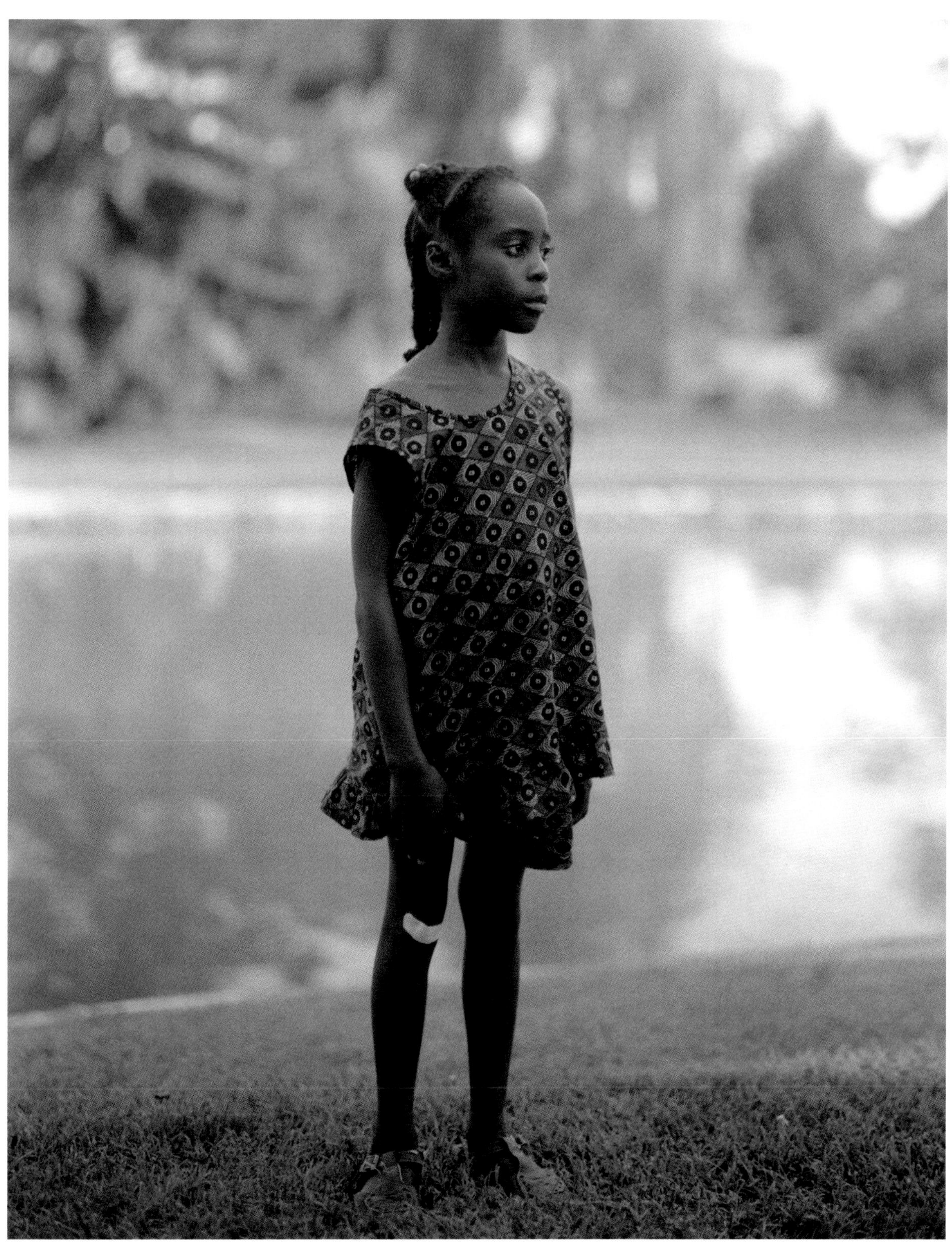

Ohne Titel | Untitled, Allentown, Pennsylvania

Elections, 1990–2008

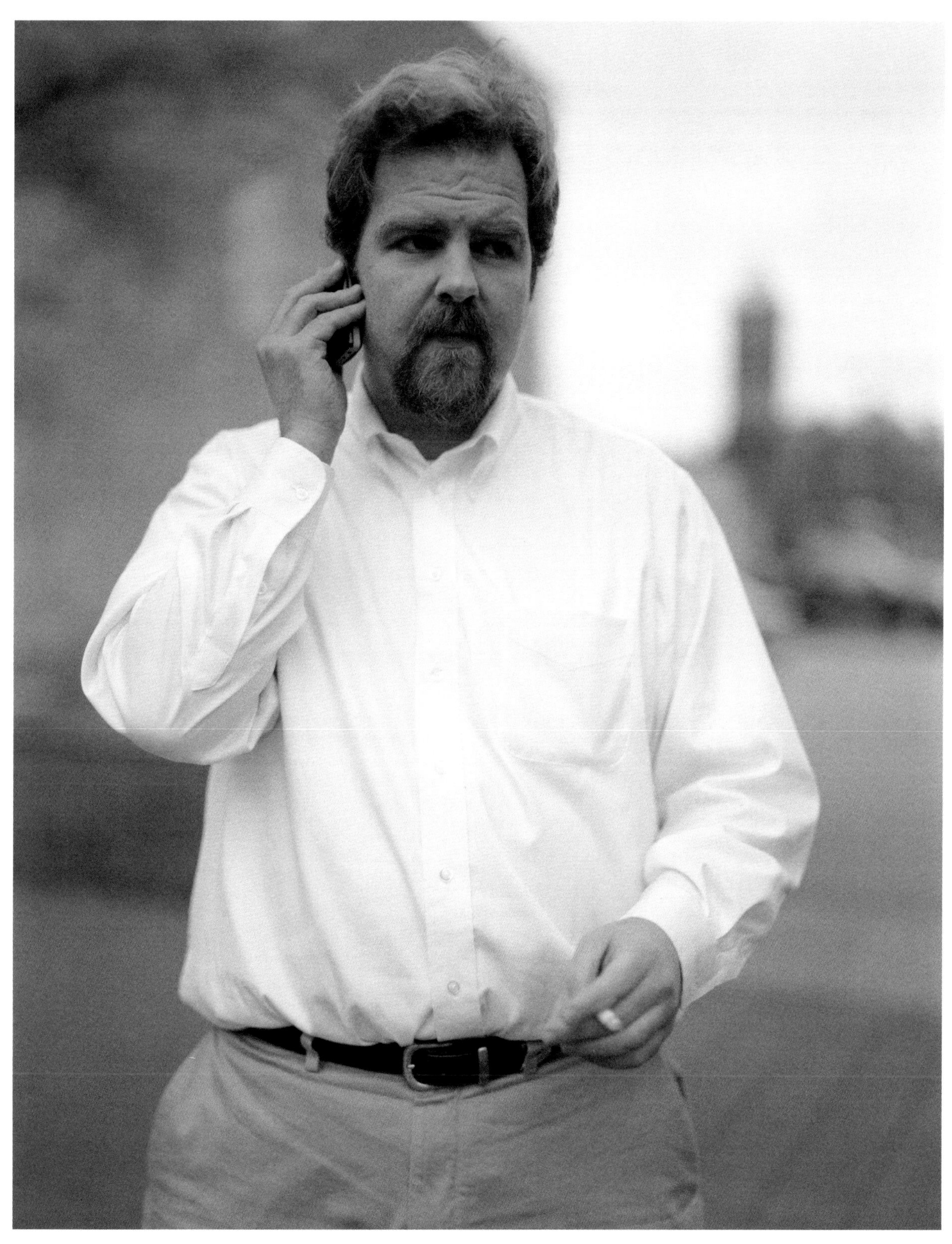

John Borongo, Organisator „Kerry for President", Hauptquartier der Demokraten, Wilkes-Barre, Pennsylvania | Field Organizer "Kerry for President", Democratic Headquarters, Wilkes-Barre, Pennsylvania, 2004

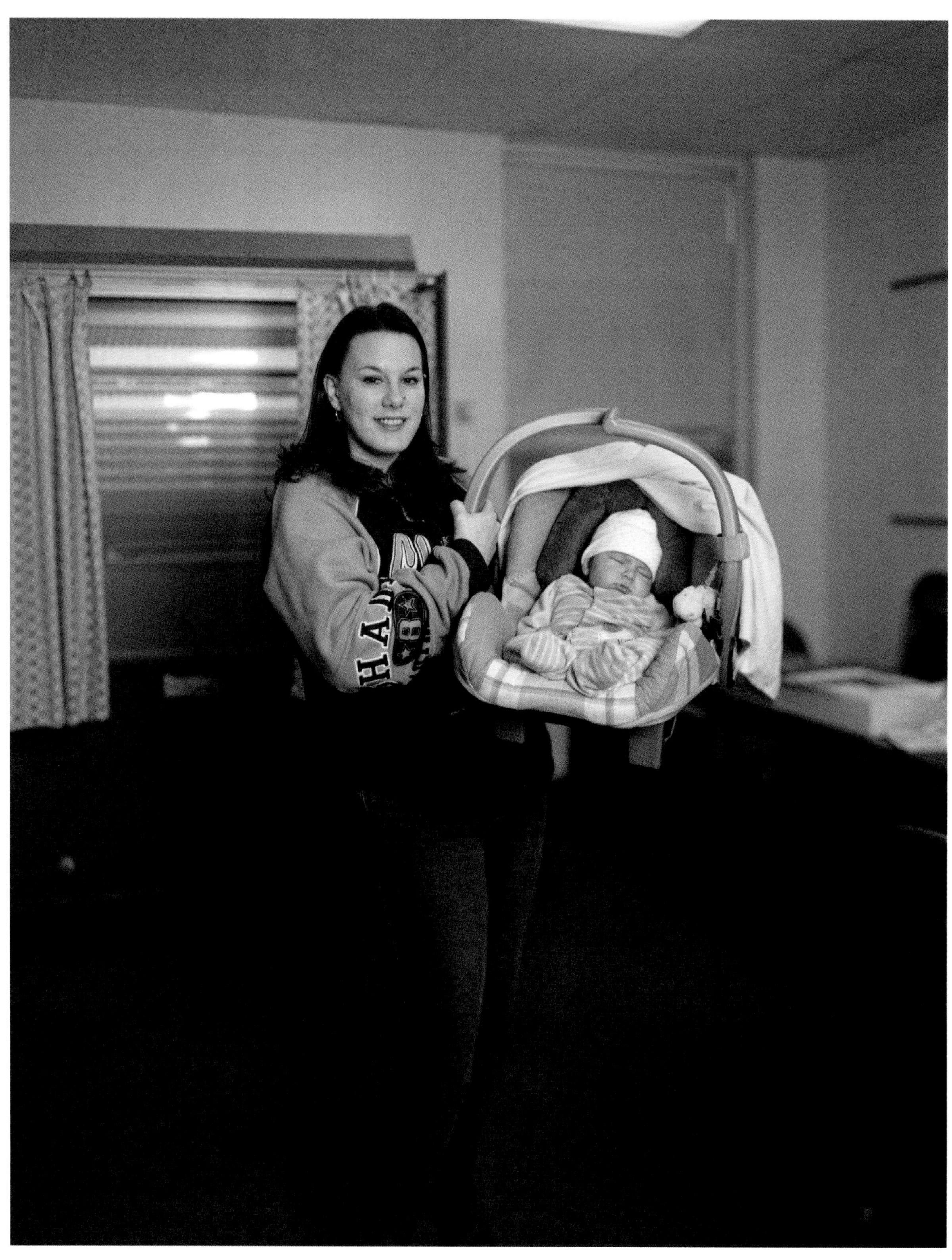

Wählerin | Voter, 10th Ward Polling Station,
Bethlehem, Pennsylvania, 2004

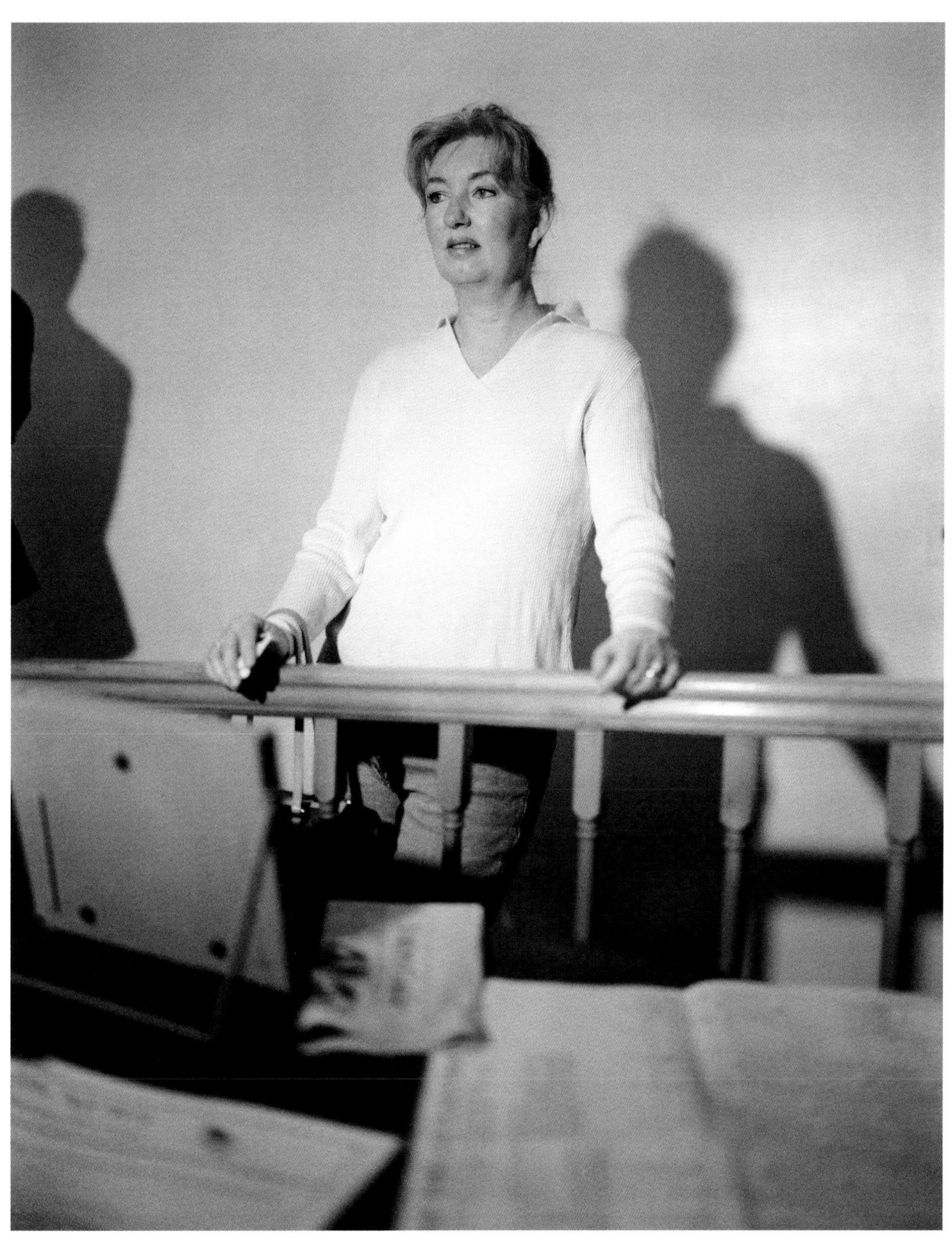

Wartende Wählerin | Woman waiting
to vote, Bethlehem, Pennsylvania, 2004

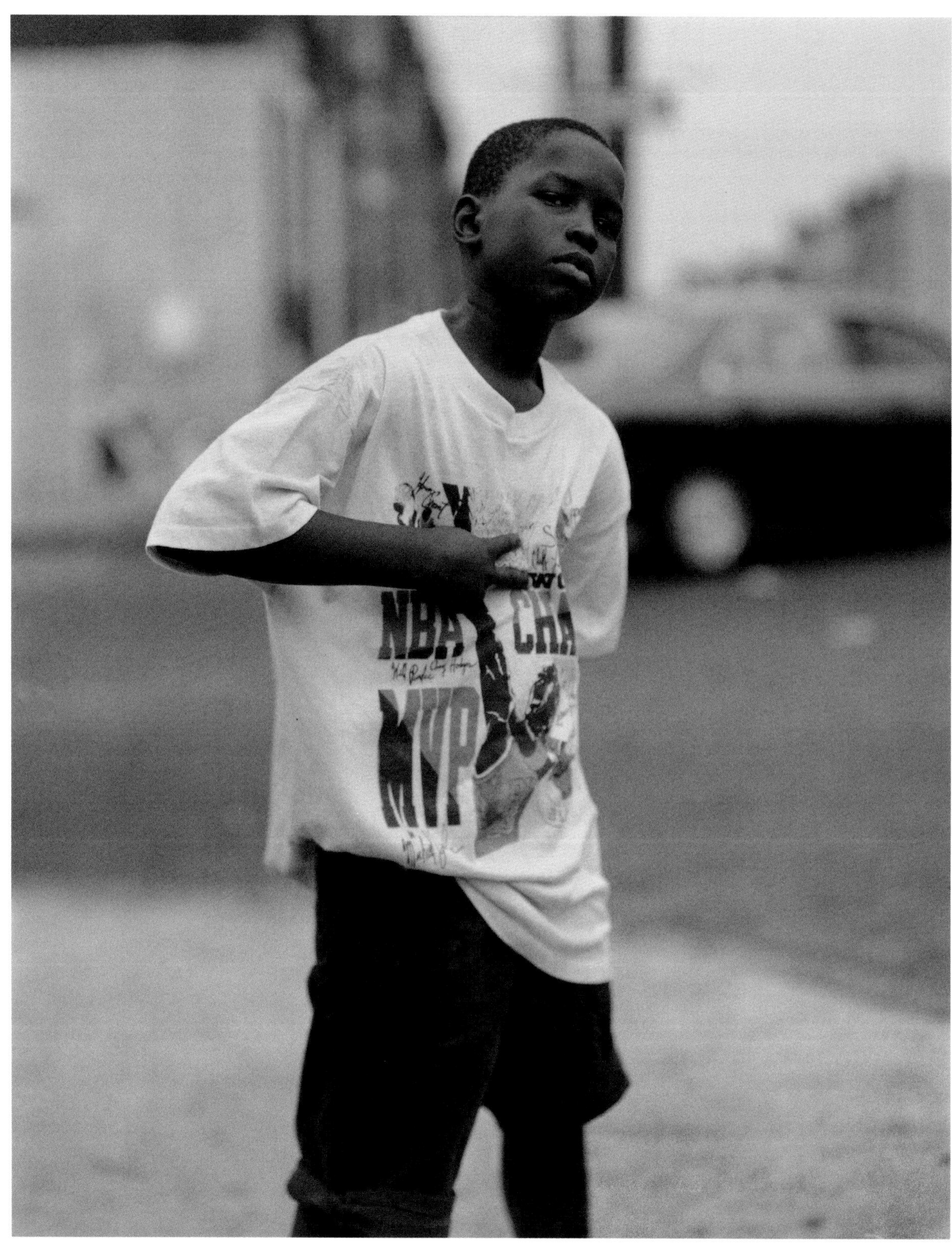

Ohne Titel | Untitled

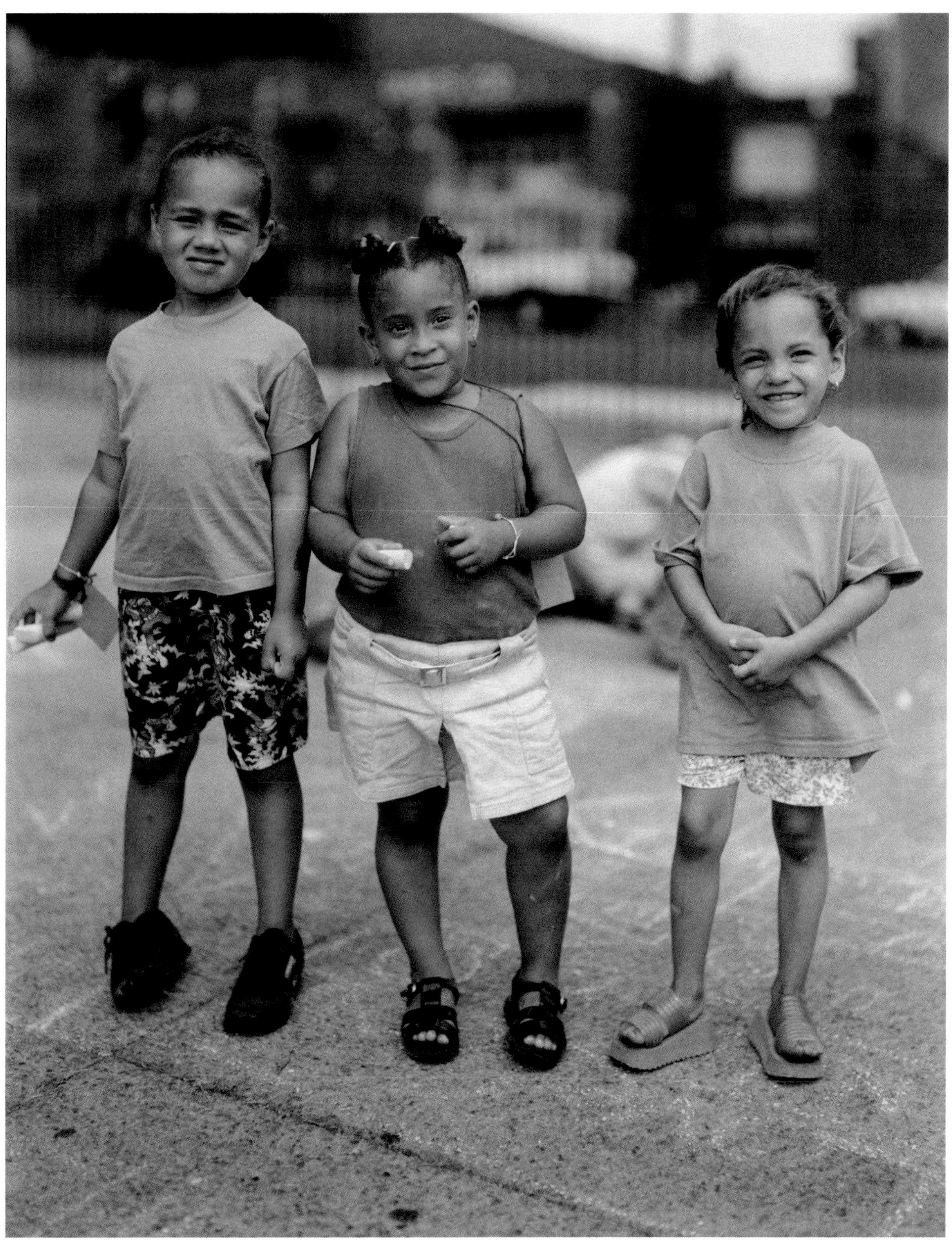

Ohne Titel | Untitled

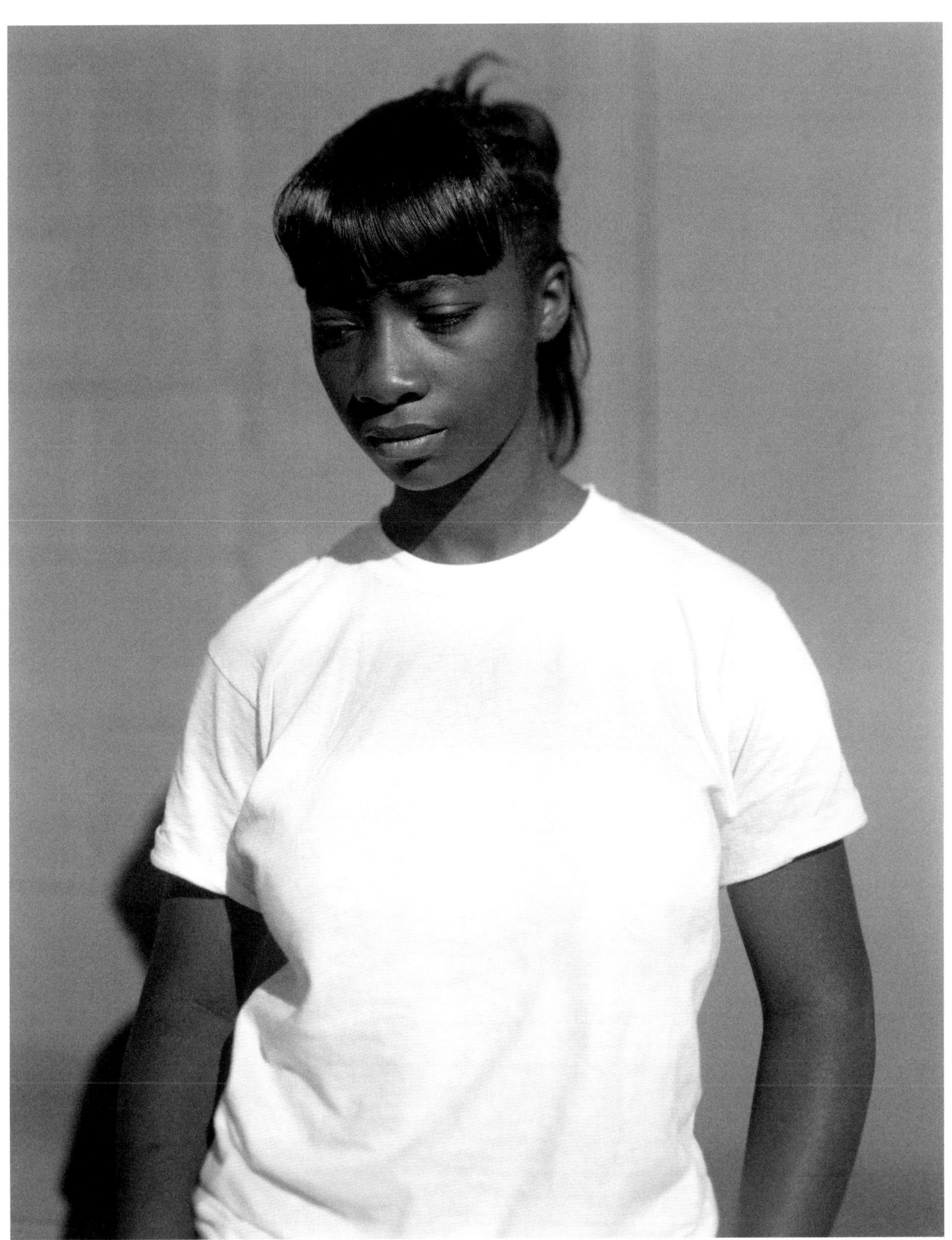

Ohne Titel | Untitled

Washington Square Park, New York, 2001

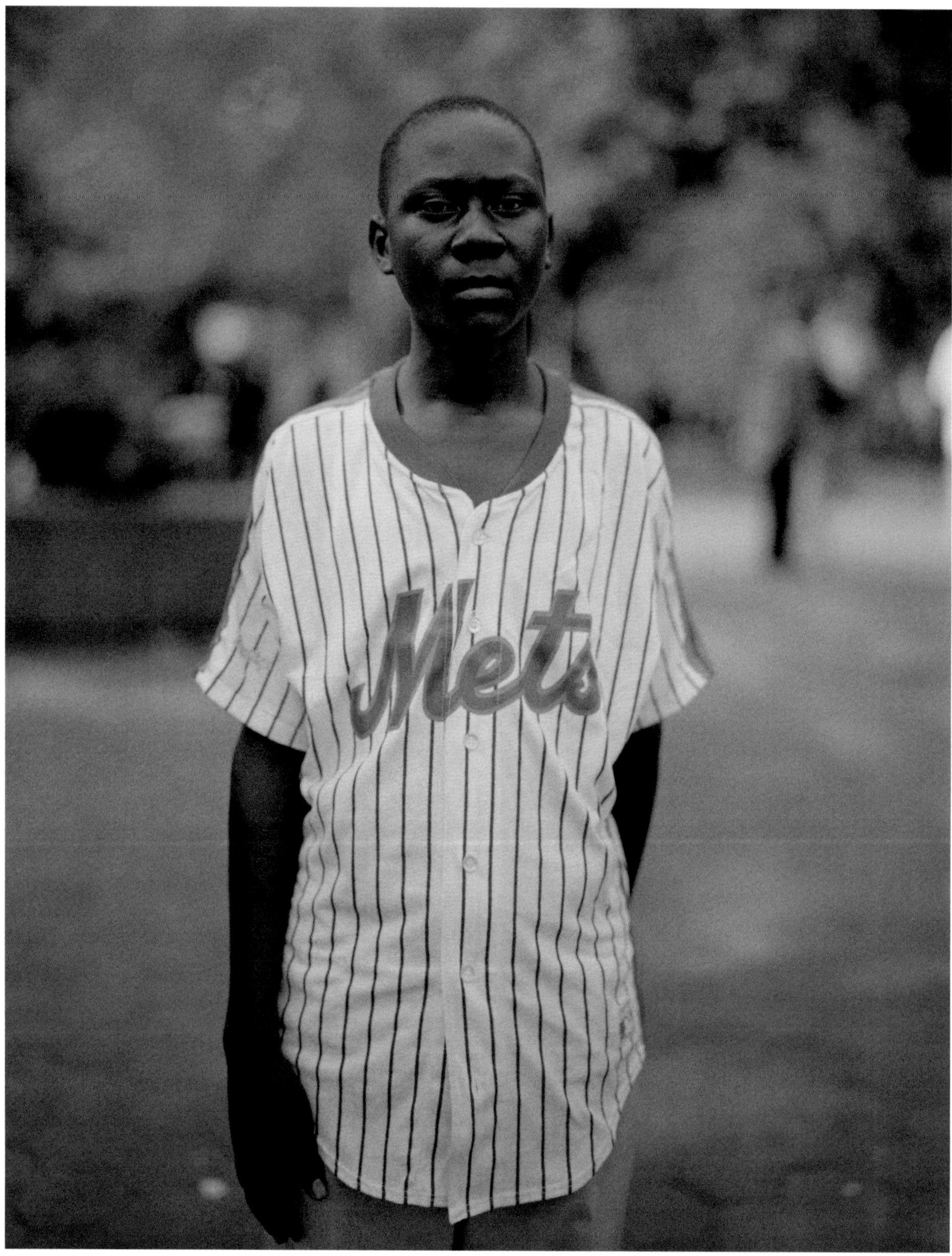

Otema Alimadi Samuel, 15, ehemaliger
Kindersoldat | former Child Soldier, 21. September

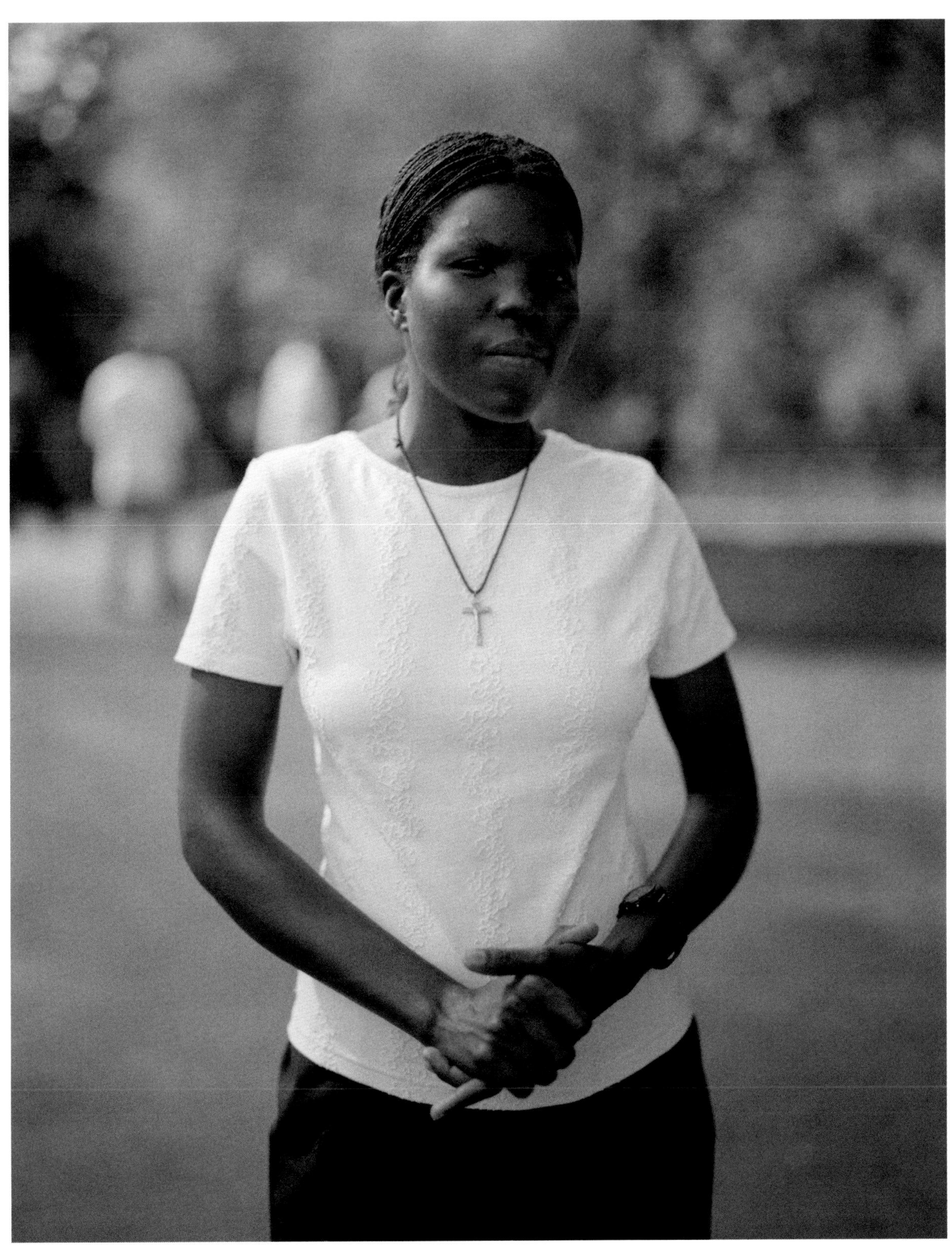

Akello Betty Openy, 17, vertriebene Uganderin | internally displaced Ugandan, 21. September

Protest the War, 2006–2007

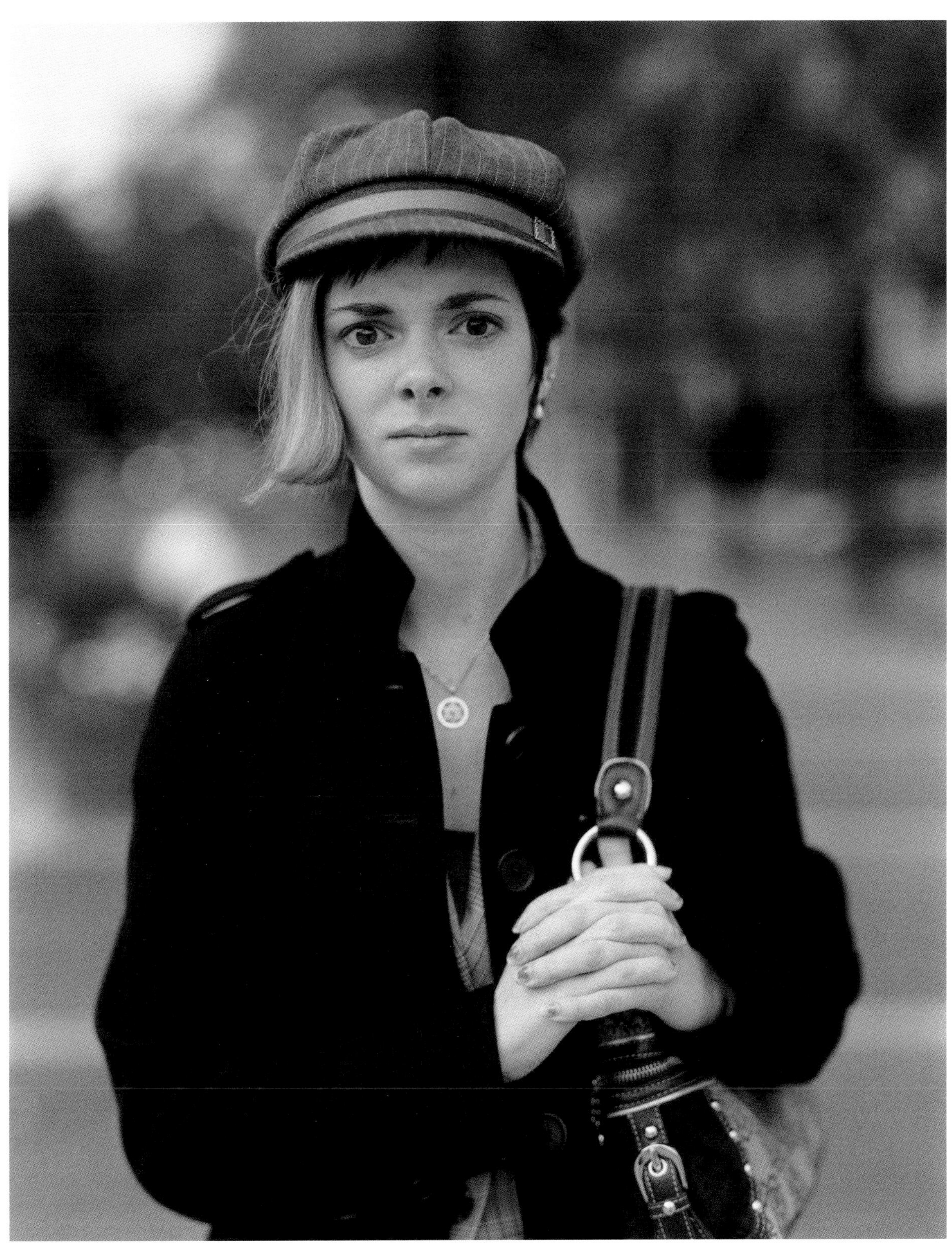

Michelle Fraser, Bethlehem, Pennsylvania, 2006

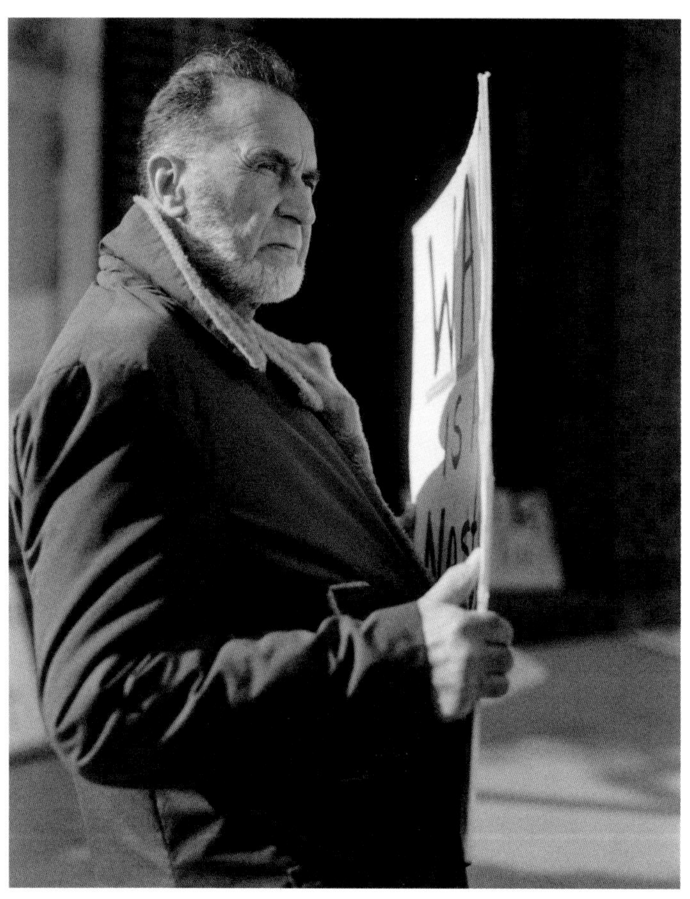

Art Landis, Sellersville, Pennsylvania, 2006

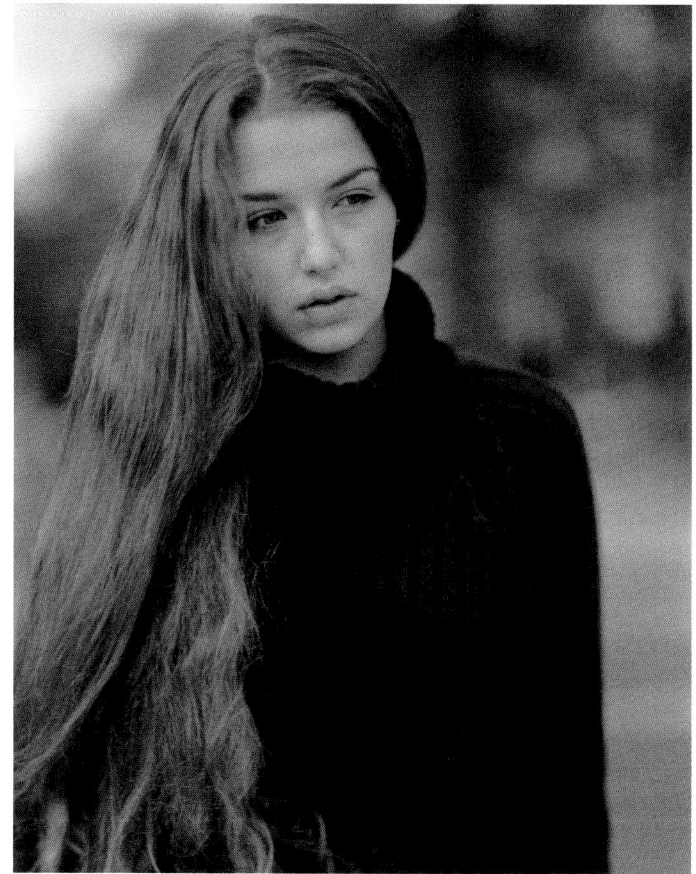

Layne Cole, Bethlehem, Pennsylvania, 2006

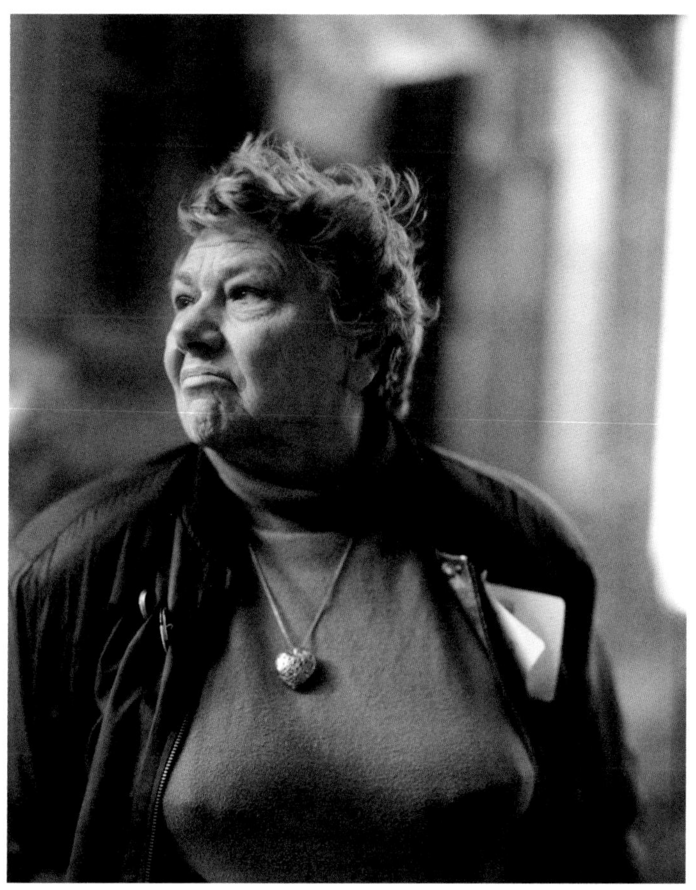

Marie Bond, Reading, Pennsylvania, 2006

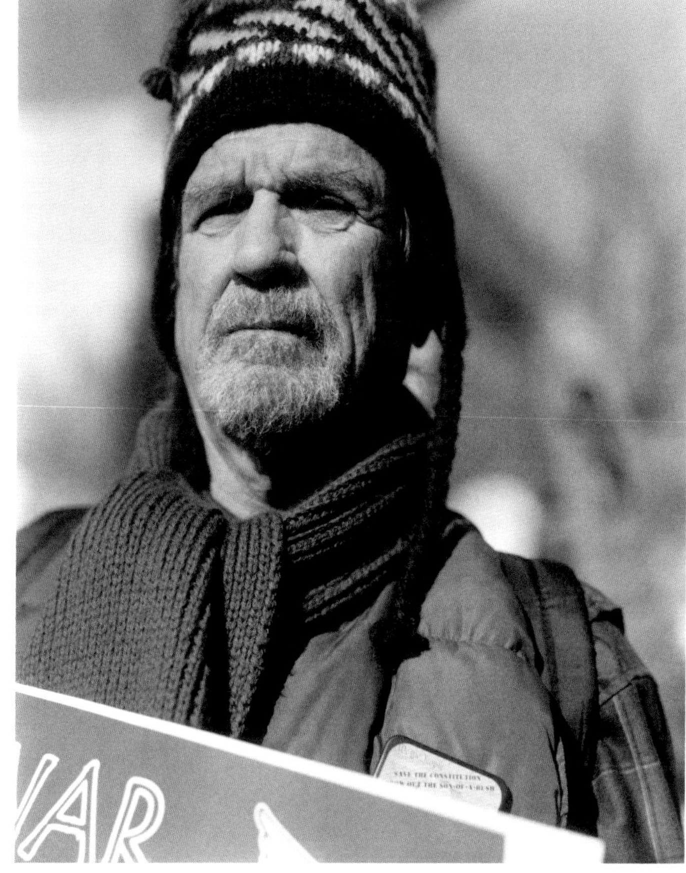

Bill Gorman, Marsch nach Washington | March on Washington, 2007

People/Animals, 2005–2011

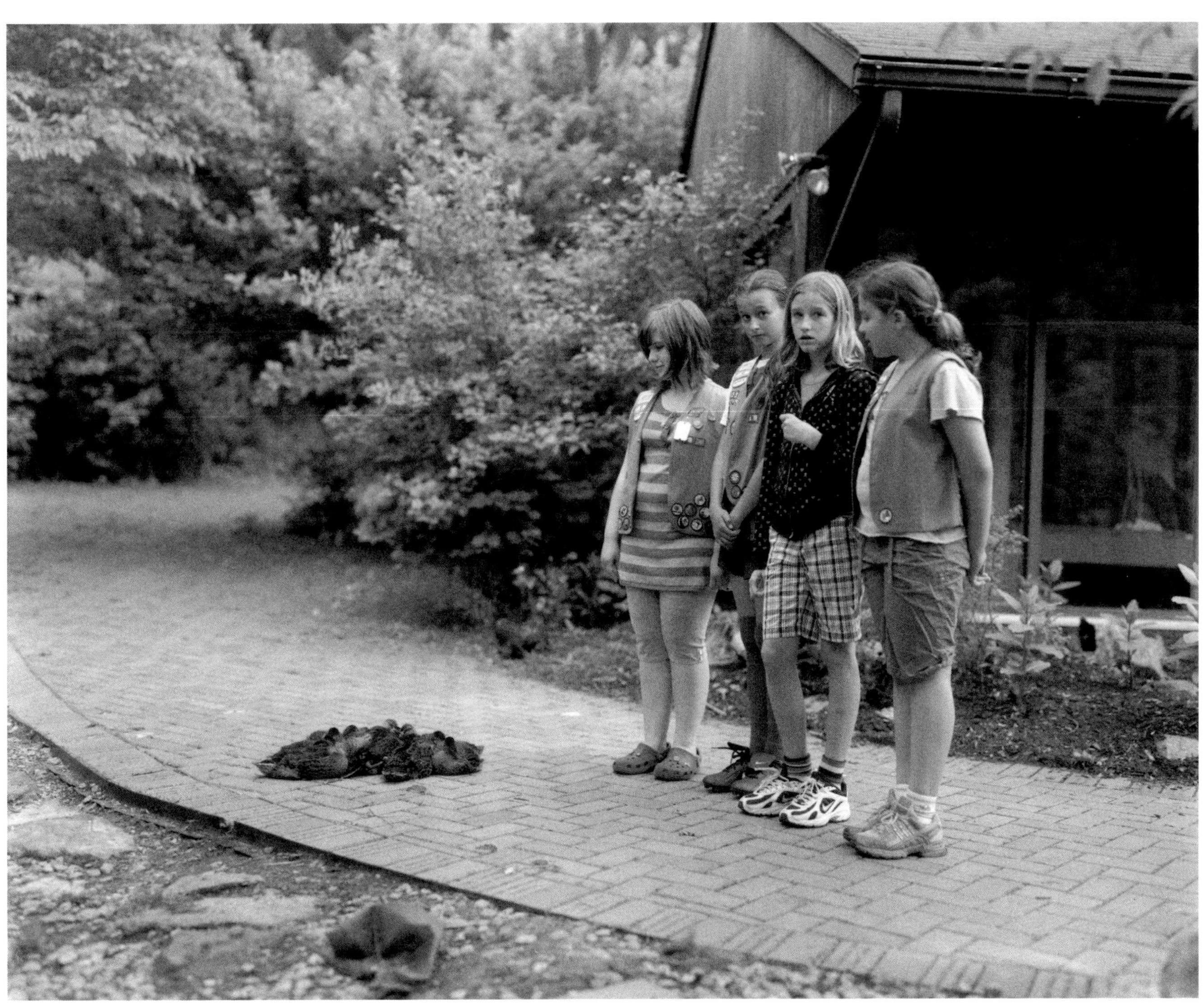

Pfadfinderinnen und Enten | Girl Scouts with ducks, 2009

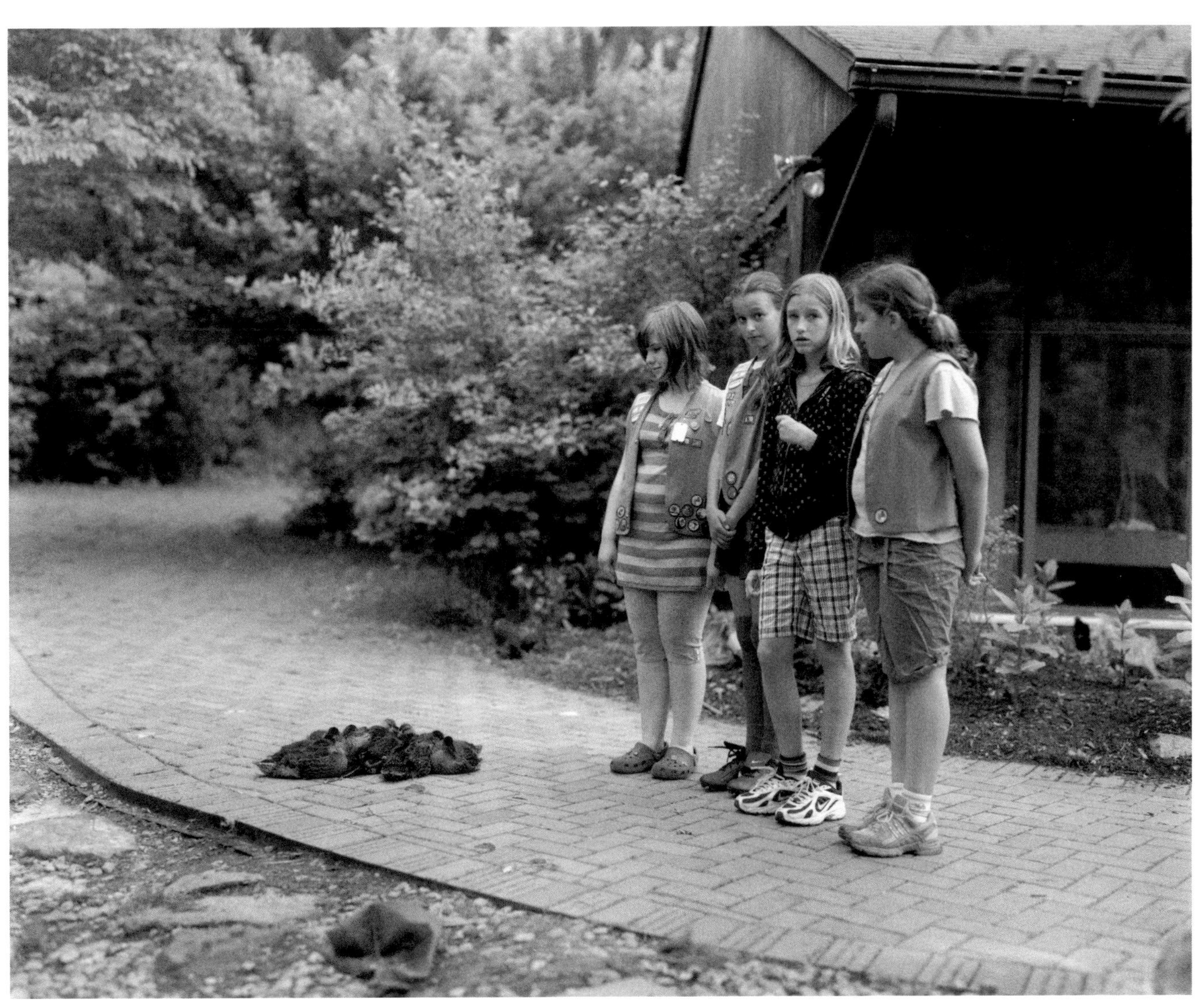

Pfadfinderinnen und Enten | Girl Scouts with ducks, 2009

Biographie | Biography

1946
geboren in | born in Hazleton, Pennsylvania

1964
Moore College of Art, Philadelphia, Pennsylvania

1968
Institute of Design, Illinois Institute of Technology, Chicago, Illinois

1985
John Simon Guggenheim Memorial Foundation Fellowship

1986
Artist Fellowship, National Endowment for the Arts

1988
City of Easton / Pennsylvania Council on the Arts Grant

1992
Charles Pratt Memorial Award
The George Gund Foundation

1993
Pennsylvania Council on the Arts Grant

1998
Andrea Frank Foundation Award

2000
Anonymous Was A Woman Award

Judith Joy Ross lebt und arbeitet in Bethlehem, Pennsylvania | lives and works in Bethlehem, Pennsylvania

Ausstellungen | Exhibitions
(Auswahl | Selection)

Einzelausstellungen | Solo exhibitions

1985
Photographs by Judith Joy Ross: Eurana Park Series, Allentown Art Museum, Allentown, Pennsylvania

1987
Portraits of the United States Congress, Pennsylvania Academy of the Fine Arts, Philadelphia (weitere Station | further venue: Lehigh University Art Galleries, Bethlehem, Pennsylvania, 1989)

1988
Easton Portraits, Young Women's Christian Association, Easton, Pennsylvania

1990
Eurana Park, Weatherly, Pennsylvania, Laurence Miller Gallery, New York

1991
Judith Joy Ross/A Survey, James Danziger Gallery, New York

1993
New Work: Photographs by Judith Joy Ross, San Francisco Museum of Modern Art, San Francisco, Kalifornien | California
Portraits at the Vietnam Veterans Memorial, Washington, D.C., 1983–84, James Danziger Gallery, New York

1996
Judith Joy Ross. Portraits, Sprengel Museum Hannover | Hanover
Portraits from the Hazleton Public Schools, 1992–1994, James Danziger Gallery, New York (weitere Station | further venue: Addison Gallery of American Art, Andover, Massachusetts)

1997
Judith Joy Ross: Retrospective, Allentown Art Museum, Allentown, Pennsylvania

1999
PaceWildenstein Gallery, New York

2001
Sabine Schmidt Galerie, Köln | Cologne

2002
Judith Joy Ross, Die Photographische Sammlung/SK Stiftung Kultur, Köln | Cologne
Portraits. Judith Joy Ross, Pace/MacGill Gallery, New York

2003
Judith Joy Ross. Portraits in America, Josef Albers Museum Quadrat, Bottrop

2004
Vietnam War Memorial. Judith Joy Ross, Jan Mot, Brüssel | Brussels

2005
Judith Joy Ross, Sabine Schmidt Galerie, Köln | Cologne

2006
Judith Joy Ross. Stories, Pace/MacGill Gallery, New York

2007
Judith Joy Ross, Sabine Schmidt Galerie, Köln | Cologne

2008
Eyes wide open. Judith Joy Ross, Sabine Schmidt Galerie, Köln | Cologne
Judith Joy Ross. Living with War. Portraits, Josef Albers Museum Quadrat, Bottrop (weitere Stationen | further venues: Galerie der Hochschule für Grafik und Buchkunst, Leipzig, 2008; C/O Berlin, 2008; Museum für Photographie, Braunschweig, Martin Art Gallery, Muhlenberg College, Allentown, Pennsylvania, 2009)
Protest the War. Judith Joy Ross, Pace/MacGill Gallery, New York (zeitgleich mit | at the same time *Josef Koudelka Invasion 68 Prague*)
Robert C. May Photography Endowment Lecture Series. Judith Joy Ross, University of Kentucky Art Museum, Lexington, Kentucky

2009
Judith Joy Ross. Photographs, Davison Art Center, Wesleyan University, Middleton, Connecticut

Gruppenausstellungen | Group exhibitions

1979
Intentions & Techniques 1979, Photographs from the Lehigh University Collection, Lehigh University Art Galleries, Bethlehem, Pennsylvania

1981
Pennsylvania Photographers II, Allentown Art Museum, Allentown, Pennsylvania

1983
Pennsylvania Photographers III, Allentown Art Museum, Allentown, Pennsylvania

1985
Intentions & Techniques 1985, An Exhibition of Photographs from the Lehigh University Collection and Nineteenth Century Pennsylvania Photography as a Folk Art from the Williams C. Darrah Collection, Lehigh University Art Galleries, Bethlehem, Pennsylvania
New Photography. Zeke Berman, Tony Mendoza, Judith Joy Ross, Michael Spano, The Museum of Modern Art, New York
Swimmers, Pace/MacGill Gallery, New York
The Sensuous Image, Paul Cava Gallery, Philadelphia, Pennsylvania

1987
Intentions & Techniques 1987: A Celebration, Lehigh University Art Galleries, Bethlehem, Pennsylvania
Pennsylvania Photographers V, Allentown Art Museum, Allentown, Pennsylvania
Recent Acquisitions: Photography, The Museum of Modern Art, New York
Twelve Photographers Look at US, Philadelphia Museum of Art, Philadelphia, Pennsylvania

1988
Real Faces, Whitney Museum of American Art at Philip Morris, New York
Rethinking American Myths, Laurence Miller Gallery, New York

1989
Intentions & Techniques 1989: Selected Photographs and Recent Acquisitions from the Lehigh University Art Galleries, Lehigh University Art Galleries, Bethlehem, Pennsylvania
Pennsylvania Photographers VI, Allentown Art Museum, Allentown, Pennsylvania
Photography Until Now, The Museum of Modern Art, New York (weitere Station | further venue: Cleveland Museum of Art, Cleveland, Ohio, 1990)

1990
The Indomitable Spirit, The International Center of Photography, Midtown, New York (weitere Station | further venue: Los Angeles Municipal Art Gallery, Los Angeles, 1990)

1991
Pennsylvania Photographers VII, Allentown Art Museum, Allentown, Pennsylvania

1992
Intentions & Techniques 1992: Photographs from the Lehigh University Collection, Lehigh University Art Galleries, Bethlehem, Pennsylvania
More Than One Photography: Works since 1980 from the Collection, The Museum of Modern Art, New York
Representatives: Women Photographers from the Permanent Collection, Center for Creative Photography, Tucson, Arizona
The Charles Pratt Memorial Award Exhibition, Center for Creative Photography, Tucson, Arizona

1993
Magicians of Light: Photographs from the Collection of the National Gallery of Canada, National Gallery of Canada, Ottawa
Observing Traditions: Contemporary Photographs 1975–1993, National Gallery of Canada, Ottawa
Pennsylvania Photographers 8, Allentown Art Museum, Allentown, Pennsylvania
Photographs from the Collection of Carlton Willers, University of Iowa Museum of Art, Iowa City, Iowa
Photographs from the Real World, Lillehammer Art Museum, Lillehammer
The Body in Nature, James Danziger Gallery, New York

1994
American Politicians: Photographs from 1843 to 1993, The Museum of Modern Art, New York (weitere Stationen | further venues: San Francisco Museum of Modern Art, San Francisco; Corcoran Gallery of Art, Washington, D.C.)
The American Portrait, The Art Complex Museum, Duxbury, Massachusetts

1995
Close to Life: 3. Internationale Foto-Triennale Esslingen, Villa Merkel, Bahnwärterhaus, Galerien der Stadt Esslingen am Neckar
Foto – en tekenwerk / Drawings and Photographs, Galerie Paul Andriesse, Amsterdam
Pennsylvania Photographers 9, Allentown Art Museum, Allentown, Pennsylvania
Warworks: Women, Photography and the Art of War, Victoria and Albert Museum, London

1997
Adolescents, Julie Saul Gallery, New York
The Photography Collection in Review, Allentown Art Museum, Allentown, Pennsylvania

1998
Women, Klemens Gasser und Tanja Grunert GmbH, Köln | Cologne

1999
Female, Wessel & O'Connor, New York

2000

How you look at it. Fotografien des 20. Jahrhunderts, Sprengel Museum Hannover | Hanover (weitere Station | further venue: Städelsches Kunstinstitut, Frankfurt/M.)

Innocence and Experience, The Museum of Modern Art, New York

Mining the Store: A 60th Anniversary Celebration of the Museum Collection, Allentown Art Museum, Allentown, Pennsylvania

Modern Starts: War, The Museum of Modern Art, New York

The Persistence of Photography in American Portraiture, Yale University Art Gallery, New Haven, Connecticut

Walker Evans & Company, The Museum of Modern Art, New York

2002

Erwerbungen seit 1995, Museum Folkwang, Essen

Menschenbilder, Galerie Monika Reitz, Frankfurt/M.

2003

A City Seen: Photographs from The George Gund Foundation Collection, Cleveland Museum of Art, Cleveland, Ohio

Cara a Cara, Fundação Caixa Geral de Depósitos – Culturgest, Lissabon | Lisbon

Einblicke in Privatsammlungen, Museum Folkwang, Essen

Making Faces: The Death of the Portrait, Musée de l'Elysée, Lausanne (weitere Station | further venue: Hayward Gallery, London)

2004

44 in 10 – Ausstellungen 1994–2004, Sabine Schmidt Galerie, Köln | Cologne

About Face, Denise Bibro Fine Art, Inc., New York

Best of. Blick in die Sammlung, Die Photographische Sammlung/SK Stiftung Kultur, Köln | Cologne

Behind Faces. Jeanne Faust, Gregor Neuerer, Judith Joy Ross, Sharon Yaari, Galerie Martin Janda, Wien | Vienna

2005

Bilanz in zwei Akten. Sammlung Niedersächsische Sparkassenstiftung, Akt 1 und Akt 2, Kunstverein Hannover | Hanover

Child's Play: Children from the Addison Collection, Addison Gallery of American Art, Andover, Massachusetts

Porträt // Fotografie. Sammlung Niedersächsische Sparkassenstiftung, Landesvertretung Niedersachsen, Berlin

2006

Click Doubleclick. Das dokumentarische Moment, Haus der Kunst, München | Munich (weitere Station | further venue: Palais des Beaux-Arts, Brüssel | Brussels)

Fragile Treasure: Works on Paper from the Collection, Allentown Art Museum, Allentown, Pennsylvania

In Focus: 75 Years of Collecting American Photography, Addison Gallery of American Art, Andover, Massachusetts

Portrait und Menschenbild, Sonderschau der Photographischen Sammlung/SK Stiftung Kultur anlässlich der Art Cologne, Köln | Cologne

2007

Girls on the Verge: Portraits of Adolescence, The Art Institute of Chicago, Chicago, Illinois

Second View. Amerikanische Fotografie aus der Sammlung der Niedersächsischen Sparkassenstiftung Hannover, Kunstmuseum Kloster Unser Lieben Frauen, Magdeburg

2008

Everyday Ideologies. Standort Alltag, Kunstmuseum Kloster Unser Lieben Frauen, Magdeburg

2009

Das Porträt. Fotografie als Bühne. Von Mapplethorpe bis Nan Goldin, Kunsthalle Wien | Vienna

day by day. Amerikanische Fotografie aus der Sammlung Niedersächsische Sparkassenstiftung, Kunstmuseum Dieselkraftwerk, Cottbus

Face of Our Time: Four shows – Yto Barrada, Guy Tillim, Judith Joy Ross, Leo Rubinfien, San Francisco Museum of Modern Art, San Francisco, Kalifornien | California

Süßer Vogel Jugend. Kindheit und Jugend in der zeitgenössischen Fotografie. Arbeiten aus den Beständen der Sammlung Moderne Kunst sowie Neuerwerbungen, Pinakothek der Moderne, München | Munich

2010

American Documents, FotoMuseum Provincie Antwerpen | Antwerp

Inside, Outside, Upstairs, Downstairs: the Addison Anew, Addison Gallery of American Art, Andover, Massachusetts

Pictures by Women: A History of Modern Photography, The Museum of Modern Art, New York

2011

Portraits in Serie. Fotografien eines Jahrhunderts, Museum für Kunst und Gewerbe, Hamburg

Bibliographie | Bibliography
(Auswahl | Selection)

Publikationen zu Einzelausstellungen | Publications for solo exhibitions

1991
Vicki Goldberg: *Judith Joy Ross*, New York: James Danziger Gallery (Ausstellungsbroschüre | exhibition brochure)

1992
Judith Joy Ross, Jahresbericht | Annual Report The George Gund Foundation, Cleveland, Ohio

1993
Sandra S. Phillips: *New Work: Photographs by Judith Joy Ross*, San Francisco: San Francisco Museum of Modern Art (Ausstellungsbroschüre | exhibition brochure)

1995
Judith Joy Ross, The Museum of Modern Art, New York, Essay: Susan Kismaric, New York: Harry N. Abrams, Inc. [Contemporaries: A Photography Series]

1996
Judith Joy Ross. Portraits, Sprengel Museum Hannover, Text: Thomas Weski, Hannover | Hanover

2006
Judith Joy Ross. Portraits of the Hazleton Public Schools. Hazleton, Pennsylvania 1992–1994, Yale University Art Gallery, Text: Jock Reynolds, New Haven & London: Yale University Press

2007
Judith Joy Ross. Protest the War, Text: Andrew Szegedy-Maszak, Göttingen: Steidl, Pace/MacGill

2008
Judith Joy Ross. Living with War – Portraits, Hrsg. | ed.: Heinz Liesbrock für das | for the Josef Albers Museum Quadrat, Bottrop, Text: Heinz Liesbrock, Göttingen: Steidl

2009
Clare Rogan: *Judith Joy Ross. Photographs*, Middleton: Davison Art Center, Wesleyan University (Ausstellungsbroschüre | exhibition brochure)

Publikationen zu Gruppenausstellungen und weitere Veröffentlichungen | Publications for group exhibitions and further volumes

1987
„Twelve Photographers Look at US“, *Philadelphia Museum of Art Bulletin*, Text: Martha Chahroudi, Bd. | vol. 83, Nr. | no. 354/355, Frühling | spring

1988
Max Kozloff: *Real Faces*, New York: Whitney Museum of Art at Philip Morris (Ausstellungsbroschüre | exhibition brochure)
Searching Out the Best: Ten Years of the Morris Gallery of the Pennsylvania Academy of the Fine Arts, Hrsg. | ed.: Jacolyn A. Mott, Philadelphia: Pennsylvania Academy of the Fine Arts

1989
John Szarkowski: *Photography Until Now*, The Museum of Modern Art, New York, Boston, Toronto: Bulfinch Press, Little, Brown and Company

1990
The Indomitable Spirit, Hrsg. | eds.: Andy Grundberg, Marvin Heiferman, New York: Harry N. Abrams, Inc.
Constance Sullivan: *Women Photographers*, New York: Harry N. Abrams, Inc.

1993
James Borcoman: *Magicians of Light: Photographs from the Collection of the National Gallery of Canada*, Ottawa: National Gallery of Canada
Jo-Ann Conklin: *Photographs from the Collection of Carlton Willers*, Iowa City: University of Iowa Museum of Art

1994
Robert Adams: *Why People Photograph*, New York: Aperture
American Politicians: Photographs from 1843 to 1993, The Museum of Modern Art, New York, Text: Susan Kismaric, New York: Harry N. Abrams, Inc.
Photographs from the Real World, Hrsg. | ed.: Dag Alveng, Oslo: De Norske Bokklubbene [The Cultural Program of the XVII Winter Olympic Games at Lillehammer]
Val Williams: *Warworks: Women, Photography and the Iconography of War*, London: Virago Press

1995
3. Internationale Foto-Triennale Esslingen. Dicht am Leben – Close to Life, Hrsg. | ed.: Renate Damsch-Wiehager, Texte | texts: Renate Damsch-Wiehager, Ulrich Bischoff, Thomas Weski, Ostfildern: Cantz-Verlag

1999

Martha Kreisel: *American Women Photographers: A Selected and Annotated Bibliography*, Westport, Connecticut, London: Greenwood Press

2000

How you look at it. Fotografien des 20. Jahrhunderts, Hrsg. | eds.: Heinz Liesbrock, Thomas Weski, Texte | texts: Gerry Badger, Heinz Liesbrock, Thomas Wagner, Peter Waterhouse, Thomas Weski, Köln | Cologne: Oktagon

2005

Bilanz in zwei Akten. Sammlung Niedersächsische Sparkassenstiftung, Hrsg. | ed.: Sabine Schormann für die | for the Niedersächsische Sparkassenstiftung, Texte | texts: Stephan Berg, Thomas Deecke, Monika Hallbaum, Heinz Liesbrock, Thomas Mang, Ulrike Schneider, Dieter Schwarz, Thomas Weski, Ludwig Zerull, Düsseldorf: Richter Verlag

Agnes Matthias: *Die Kunst, den Krieg zu fotografieren. Krieg in der künstlerischen Fotografie der Gegenwart*, Marburg: Jonas Verlag

2006

Click Doubleclick. Das dokumentarische Moment, Hrsg. | ed.: Thomas Weski, Texte | texts: Jean-François Chevrier, Johan de Vos, Thomas Weski, Köln | Cologne: Verlag der Buchhandlung Walther König

2010

Everyday Ideologies. Standort Alltag, Hrsg. | eds.: Annegret Laabs, Uwe Gellner, Nürnberg | Nuremberg: Verlag für moderne Kunst

Modern Women: Women Artists at the Museum of Modern Art, Hrsg. | eds.: Cornelia Butler, Alexandra Schwartz, New York: The Museum of Modern Art

2011

Portraits in Serie. Fotografien eines Jahrhunderts, Hrsg. | ed. Museum für Kunst und Gewerbe Hamburg, Texte | texts: Gabriele Betancourt Nuñez, Ulrike Schneider, Berlin, Leipzig: Christof Kerber Verlag

Artikel in Zeitungen und Zeitschriften | Articles in newspapers and magazines

1984

N.N. | author unknown: „City native's photos in Allentown exhibit", in: *Hazleton Standard-Speaker*, Hazleton, Pennsylvania, 29. Nov., S. | p. 29

Albert Hofammann: „Allentown Art Museum Marking Dual Milestones", in: *The Sunday Call-Chronicle*, Allentown, Pennsylvania, 2. Dez. | Dec., S. | pp. F1, F8

1985

Stephen Perloff: „Eurana Park, Judith Joy Ross", in: *The Photo Review*, Langhorne, Pennsylvania, Bd. | vol. 8, Nr. | no. 2, Frühling | spring, S. | pp. 2–3

Betty Harlor: „Hazleton native exhibits at Museum of Modern Art", in: *Hazleton Standard-Speaker*, Hazleton, Pennsylvania, 21. Aug., S. | p. 35

Peter Kerr: „The Ghosts of War", in: *The New York Times*, 23. Aug., S. | p. C1

Guy Trebay: „An Opinionated Survey of the Week's Events: New Photography", in: *The Village Voice*, New York, Bd. | vol. 30, Nr. | no. 35, 27. Aug., S. | pp. 64–65

Jane Maulfair: „Art Develops", in: *The Morning Call*, Allentown, Pennsylvania, 1. Sept., S. | pp. F1–2

Adrienne Redd: „LV professor seeks out truth with a camera", in: *The Sunday Globe*, Bethlehem, Pennsylvania, 1. Sept., S. | pp. F1, F3

Andy Grundberg: „Photography View; The Modern Focuses on Contemporary Visions", in: *The New York Times,* 15. Sept., Sektion | section 2, S. | p. 29

E. Sheila Cerulli: „In Search of Meaning: Photographer Judith Joy Ross pursues truth", in: *The Express*, Easton, Pennsylvania, 20. Dez. | Dec., S. | pp. D1, D10–11

1987

Sandy Sorlien: „Snap Judgments", in: *Philadelphia Daily News*, 10. Apr., S. | p. 72

Edward J. Sozanski: „An Unsentimental Focus on America", in: *The Philadelphia Inquirer*, 26. Apr., S. | pp. H1, H16

Eric Levin: „Twelve Photographers Look at U.S.", in: *People Magazine*, New York, Bd. | vol. 27, Nr. | no. 20, 18. Mai | May, S. | pp. 28–29

Kathryn Livingston: „We The People. In Philadelphia a well-constituted national portrait", in: *American Photographer*, Bd. | vol. 19, Nr. | no. 1, Juli | July, S. | pp. 30, 32

N.N. | author unknown: „Faces of Power", in: *The Philadelphia Inquirer*, 23. Juli | July, S. | pp. D1, D5

Brian Peterson: „Born in the U.S.A.", in: *Afterimage*, Rochester, New York, Bd. | vol. 15, Nr. | no. 3, Okt. | Oct., S. | pp. 19–20

1988

N.N. | author unknown: „Choices", in: *The Village Voice*, New York, Bd. | vol. 33, Nr. | no. 24, 14. Juni | June, S. | p. 53

Andy Grundberg: „Portraits Return in a New Perspective", in: *The New York Times*, 26. Juni | June, Sektion | section 2, S. | p. 31

N.N. | author unknown: „Choices", in: *The Village Voice*, New York, Bd. | vol. 33, Nr. | no. 33, 16. Aug., S. | p. 41

John Gross: „About the Arts: New York; How different are the Famous from the Faces in the Crowd?", in: *The New York Times*, 18. Sept., S. | pp. 2/39

Robert Raczka: „Judith Joy Ross", in: *New Art Examiner*, Chicago, Bd. | vol. 15, Nr. | no. 6, S. | p. 62
Raphael Meyer Rubinstein: „Real Faces: Struggling for the Soul of Photography", in: *Arts Magazine*, Bd. | vol. 63, Nr. | no. 3, Nov., S. | pp. 72–75

1989
N.N. | author unknown: „Self and Shadow", in: *Aperture*, New York, Nr. | no. 114, Frühling | spring, S. | pp. 20–21
N.N. | author unknown: „Photos capture reality of kids: They're 'OK'", in: *The Express,* Easton, Pennsylvania, 10. Apr., S. | p. A7

1990
Alan G. Artner: „The New View", in: *Chicago Tribune*, Sektion | section 13, 25. Feb., S. | pp. 14–15
Edward J. Sozanski: „Developments in Photography", in: *The Philadelphia Inquirer*, 25. Feb., S. | pp. J1, J6
Ralph Novak: „The Indomitable Spirit, by Photographers and Friends United Against AIDS", in: *People Magazine*, New York, Bd. | vol. 33. Nr. | no. 13, 2. Apr., S. | p. 29
Janie Welker: „Photography Until Now", in: *The Express*, Easton, Pennsylvania, 13. Apr., S. | p. D10
Philip Gefter: „Interview with John Szarkowski", in: *Photo Metro*, Bd. | vol. 8, Nr. | no. 78, S. | p. 20
Belinda Rathbone: „The Backyard (& Other Scenes of Virtuous Materialism)", in: *The Print Collector's Newsletter*, New York, Bd. | vol. 21, Nov., Dez. | Dec., S. | pp. 178–179

1991
Vince Aletti: „Ties that Bind: Judith Joy Ross Redefines Family", in: *The Village Voice*, New York, Bd. | vol. 36, Nr. | no. 5, 29. Jan., S. | p. 79
Charles Hagen: „Reviews, New York: Judith Joy Ross, James Danziger Gallery", in: *Artforum*, New York, Bd. | vol. 29, Nr. | no. 8, Apr., S. | p. 123
Ingrid Sischy: „Goings on about Town: Photography", in: *The New Yorker*, Bd. | vol. 66, Nr. | no. 50, S. | p. 12

1992
Charles Hagen: „Review/Photography; 2 Goals in One Show: Diversity and Unity", in: *The New York Times*, 29. Mai | May, S. | p. C28

1993
Charles Hagen: „Art in Review: The Body in Nature", in: *The New York Times*, 9. Juli | July, S. | p. C26
Charles Hagen: „Art in Review: Judith Joy Ross, James Danziger Gallery", in: *The New York Times*, 1. Okt. | Oct., S. | p. C23
Vicki Goldberg: „Photography View: Is it the Year of the Women, or of Making Amends?", in: *The New York Times*, 10. Okt. | Oct., S. | pp. 2/37

1995
Sue Hubbard: „Kensington Gore", in: *New Statesman & Society*, London, 13. Jan., S. | p. 33
Amanda Hopkinson: „Pieces of war", in: *The British Journal of Photography*, London, 18. Jan., S. | p. 24
John Kelleher: „Women and the Dogs of War", in: *The Times Educational Supplement*, London, 27. Jan., Teil | part 2, S. | p. 22
Pietje Tegenbosch: „Zwart-wit dwarsverbanden", in: *Het Parool*, Amsterdam, 10. Nov., S. | p. 11
N.N. | author unknown: „Judith Joy Ross", in: *NRC Handelsblad*, Cultureel Supplement, Rotterdam, 17. Nov., S. | p. 4
Kathryn McAuley Richards: „Photographer's monograph reflects inner glow of the ordinary", in: *The Morning Call*, Allentown, 10. Dez. | Dec., S. | p. F3
Val Williams: „Women at War: New Tales from the War Zone", in: *Creative Camera*, Nr. | no. 331, Dez. | Dec. | Jan., S. | pp. 24–29

1996
Richard B. Woodward: „Double Exposure", in: *The New York Times*, 7. Jan., S. | pp. 7/22
cz: „Fotografien von Judith Joy Ross", in: *Cellesche Zeitung*, 2. Feb.
Henning Queren: „Judith Joy Ross im Sprengel-Museum. Wuchtige Plattenkamera für Porträts der Mächtigen und des Volkes", in: *Neue Presse*, Hannover | Hanover, 14. Feb., S. | p. 14
lni: „Fotografien von Ross im Sprengel-Museum", in: *Oldenburgische Volkszeitung*, 15. Feb.
N.N. | author unknown: „Ross: Momente der Betroffenheit", in: *Deister- und Weserzeitung*, Hameln, 15. Feb.
N.N. | author unknown: „Fotografien von Ross im Sprengel Museum", in: *Münsterländische Tageszeitung*, Cloppenburg, 15. Feb.
N.N. | author unknown: „Ross: Momente der Betroffenheit", in: *Schaumburger Zeitung*, Rinteln, 15. Feb.
Jochen Stöckmann: „Risse in der Fassade. Die Fotoporträts von Judith Joy Ross im Sprengel Museum", in: *Hannoversche Allgemeine Zeitung*, 19. Feb.
Charles Hagen: „Art in Review. Judith Joy Ross, James Danziger Gallery", in: *The New York Times*, 29. März | March, S. | p. C25
N.N. | author unknown: „Judith Joy Ross", in: *Nobilis*, Hannover | Hanover, Nr. | no. 4, S. | p. 54
bno: „Die Porträts von Judith Joy Ross", in: *Süddeutsche Zeitung*, München | Munich, 25. Apr., S. | p. 15
N.N. | author unknown: „100 Years of Pictures: Who's Who", in: *The New York Times*, 9. Juni | June, S. | pp. 6/74
Hans-Jörg Loskill: „Besondere Momente im Leben von Menschen. Bottrop zeigt Fotografien von J.J. Ross", in: *Westdeutsche Allgemeine Zeitung*, Ausgabe | issue Dortmund, 26. Juni | June

1997
Edward J. Sozanski: „Looking at the plain, simple truth straight on", in: *The Philadelphia Inquirer*, 9. Mai | May, S. | p. 44
Holland Cotter: „Art in Review. Adolescents. Julie Saul Gallery", in: *The New York Times*, 1. Aug., S. | p. C25

1999
Johnson: „Art Guide. Judith Joy Ross", in: *The New York Times*, 16. Juli | July, S. | p. E38

2000
Vince Aletti: „Finding the Modern Tradition's Common Denominator", in: *The Village Voice*, New York, 21. März | March
N.N. | author unknown: „Ex Libris. Photographers Adam Bartos and Judith Joy Ross celebrate public libraries | The Bethlehem, Pennsylvania, Public Library by Judith Joy Ross", in: *Double Take*, Boulder, 6:2, Frühling | spring, S. | pp. 87–91
Deborah Rieders: „An Open Book. The photographer Judith Joy Ross capture the intimate moments shared by young people in libraries", in: *School Library Journal*, New York, Nov., S. | pp. 46–49

2002
Jo Thomas: „Arts in America; A City's Many Faces Reflect Photographers' Visions", in: *The New York Times*, 25. Dez. | Dec., S. | p. E2

2006
Mia Fineman: „The Portraits of Judith Joy Ross: Not just Faces in the Crowd", in: *The New York Times*, 2. Apr.
R.C. Baker: „Ids of Clay (Judith Joy Ross, Pace/MacGill)", in: *The Village Voice*, New York, 18. Apr.
Heinz Schütz: „click doubleclick, das dokumentarische Moment'", in: *Kunstforum International*, Ruppichteroth, Bd. | vol. 180, Mai | May – Juni | June, S. | pp. 354–357

2008
HJL: „Wie Identität verloren geht", in: *Westdeutsche Allgemeine Zeitung*, Essen, 8. März | March
Volker Engel: „Stille Wut auf den Krieg im Irak. Ausstellung: Fotos von J.J. Ross in Bottrop", in: *Ruhr Nachrichten*, Dortmund, 25. März | March
Hans-Jörg Loskill: „Besondere Momente im Leben der Menschen", in: *Westdeutsche Allgemeine Zeitung*, Essen, 16. Juni | June
N.N. | author unknown: „Kunst – Judith Joy Ross", in *Kreuzer*, Leipzig, Nr. | no. 6
N.N. | author unknown: „Leben mit dem Krieg", in: *Frizz*, Leipzig, Nr. | no. 6, S. | p. 38
Markus Weckesser: „Judith Joy Ross. Living with war. Portraits 1983–2007", in: *Photonews. Zeitung für Fotografie*, Hamburg, Nr. | no. 6, S. | p. 5
N.N. | author unknown: „Judith Joy Ross. Living with war", in: *Schwarzweiß*, Nr. |no. 64, Juni | Juli | June | July
Robert Schimke: „Krieg ohne Pathos", in: *taz*, Berlin, 16. Juni | June, S. | p. 14
sti: „Menschenbilder", in: *Westfälischer Anzeiger*, Hamm, 1. Juli | July
Lucia Tirado: „Zorn und Trauer im Blick", in: *Neues Deutschland*, Berlin, 25. Juli | July
Imke Schridde: „C/O Berlin: ‚Living with War', Fotografien von Judith Joy Ross", in: *Kulturradio am Morgen*, 31. Juli | July
Uli Eberhardt: „Judith Joy Ross. Leben mit dem Krieg", in: *http://fokussiert.com/2008/08/14/judith-joy-ross-leben-mit-dem-krieg/*, 14. Aug. (Stand | status: Feb. 2011)
ksk: „Konzentration und Stille", in: *Neue Zürcher Zeitung*, 23./24. Aug.
Thomas W. Kuhn: „Judith Joy Ross – Living with War. Mit Kriegen leben", in: *Kunstforum International*, Ruppichteroth, Bd. | vol. 193, Sept.–Okt. | Oct., S. | p. 289
N.N. | author unknown: „Gesichter des Krieges", in: *Der Spiegel*, Hamburg, Nr. | no. 37, 8. Sept., S. | p. 59
James Danziger: „Judith Joy Ross", in: *The Year in Pictures*, *http://pictureyear.blogspot.com/2008/09/judith-joy-ross.html*, 25. Sept. (Stand | status: Feb. 2011)
Björn Trauwein: „Gesichter des Krieges", in: *JS Magazin. Die evangelische Zeitung für junge Soldaten*, Frankfurt/M., Okt. | Oct., S. | pp. 26–27
Boris Snauwaert: „Unarmed Protest in Pictures. Josef Koudelka *Invasion 68* and Judith Joy Ross *Protest the War*", in: *Extra. A biannual magazine on photography*, Hrsg. | ed.: Fotomuseum Provincie Antwerpen, Winter, S. | pp. 19–25
Bettina Lockemann: „Judith Joy Ross: Living with War", in: *http://www.booksports.de/Inhalt.htm* (Stand | status: Apr. 2011)

2009
Kenneth Baker: „SECA Art Award show, as usual, disappoints", in: *San Francisco Chronicle*, 7. März | March, S. | p. E–10

2010
Holland Cotter: „A Gathering of Women with Cameras", in: *The New York Times,* 28. Mai | May, S. |. p. C 27
Vince Aletti: „Critic's Notebook: XX Factor", in: *The New Yorker*, 7. Juni | June, S. | p. 17

Arbeiten von Judith Joy Ross in öffentlichen und privaten Sammlungen | Works by Judith Joy Ross in public and private collections

Addison Gallery of American Art, Andover, Massachusetts

Allentown Art Museum, Allentown, Pennsylvania

Sammlung Paul Andriesse, Amsterdam

Lehigh University Art Galleries, Bethlehem, Pennsylvania

Metropolitan Museum of Art, New York

Museum of Fine Arts, Boston, Massachusetts

Museum of Fine Arts, Houston, Texas

Museum Folkwang, Essen

Museum Ludwig, Köln | Cologne

The Museum of Modern Art, New York

National Gallery of Canada, Ottawa

Niedersächsische Sparkassenstiftung, Hannover | Hanover

Die Photographische Sammlung/SK Stiftung Kultur, Köln | Cologne

San Francisco Museum of Modern Art, San Francisco

Sprengel Museum Hannover | Hanover

Astrid Ullens, Brüssel | Brussels

Victoria and Albert Museum, London

Yale University Art Gallery, New Haven, Connecticut